& Co.

Deck

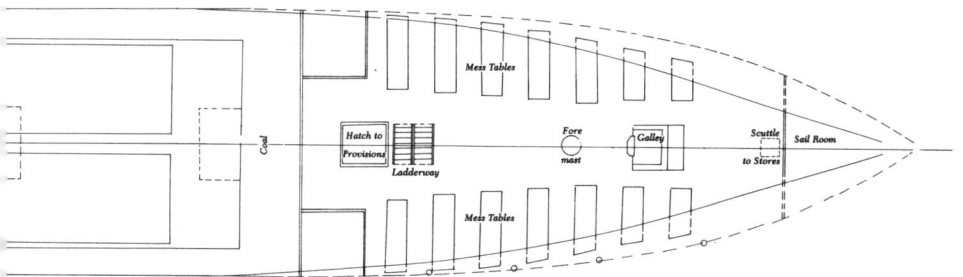

Mess Tables

Coal | Hatch to Provisions | Ladderway | Fore mast | Galley | Scuttle to Stores | Sail Room

Mess Tables

Works

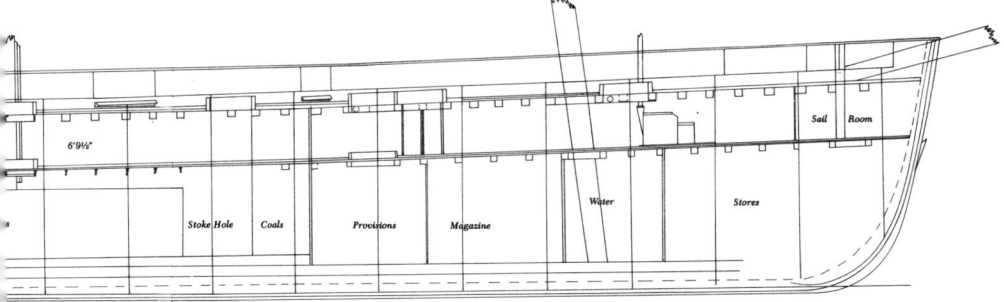

6'9½"

Stoke Hole | Coals | Provisions | Magazine | Water | Stores | Sail Room

BENEATH THE

STAINLESS

BANNER

John McIntosh Kell, CSN

With selections from his *Recollections of a Naval Life*

Edited by R. Thomas Campbell

 BURD STREET PRESS

This Burd Street Press publication
was printed by
Beidel Printing House, Inc.
63 West Burd Street
Shippensburg, PA 17257-0152 USA

In respect for the scholarship contained herein, the acid-free paper used in this book meets the guidelines for permanence and durability of the Committee on Production Guidelines for Book Longevity of the Council on Library Resources.

For a complete list of available publications
please write
Burd Street Press
Division of White Mane Publishing Company, Inc.
P.O. Box 152
Shippensburg, PA 17257-0152 USA

Library of Congress Cataloging-in-Publication Data

Kell, John McIntosh, 1823-1900.
    [Recollections of a naval life. Selections]
    Beneath the stainless banner : with selections from his
Recollections of a naval life / John McIntosh Kell : edited by R.
Thomas Campbell.
       p.   cm.
    Contains some selections from part one and an edited version of
part two of Kell's Recollections of a naval life, published in 1900.
    Includes bibliographical references and index.
    ISBN 1-57249-147-7 (acid-free paper)
    1. Kell, John McIntosh, 1823-1900. 2. Confederate States of
America. Navy--Biography. 3. United States--History--Civil War,
1861-1865--Naval operations. 4. United States--History--Civil War,
1861-1865--Personal narratives, Confederate. 5. Alabama (Ship)
6. Sumter (Confederate cruiser) 7. Sailors--Confederate States of
America--Biography. I. Campbell, R. Thomas, 1937-   . II. Title.
E596.K4472   1999
973.7'13'092--dc21
[B]   98-46744
                                                 CIP

To the officers and men who donned the navy gray and struggled against insurmountable odds for their country's freedom, I dedicate these few pages. John Kell would have liked that.

Contents

Channel; arrival at Cape Town; depressing news from home; arrival at Cherbourg, France.

Illustrations

*A*uthor's *N*ote
Origin of the "Stainless Banner"

On May 1, 1863, Representative Peter W. Gray of Houston, Texas, submitted a final amendment to Senate Bill No. 132 which read as follows:

> AN ACT to establish the flag of the Confederate States.
>
> *The Congress of the Confederate States of* America do enact, That the flag of the Confederate States shall be as follows: The field to be white, the length double the width of the flag, with the union (now used as the battle flag) to be a square of two-thirds the width of the flag, having the ground red; thereon a broad saltier of blue, bordered with white, and emblazoned with white mullets or five-pointed stars, corresponding in number to that of the Confederate States.

In this form Senate Bill No. 132 passed the House of Representatives and was returned to the Senate for acceptance of the amendment. With little or no debate, the Senate approved and later that afternoon, after President Davis had affixed his signature, the Confederate States of America had a new national flag.

This second national flag, which took the place of the "Stars and Bars," was referred to as the "Stainless Banner" because of its pure white field, which to many symbolized the purity of the Cause which it represented. Unfortunately, one of the first official uses of the "Stainless

xi

Banner" was to drape the coffin of General Thomas J. "Stonewall" Jackson. On the evening of May 2, 1863, General Jackson was mistakenly fired upon by some of his own troops at the Battle of Chancellorsville. His left arm was amputated, and his health seemed to improve until May 7, by which time he had developed pneumonia. On May 10, the immortal "Stonewall" was dead, and on May 12, his body lay in state in the chamber of the Confederate House of Representatives. By order of the president, his coffin was draped with the very first of the new national flags to be manufactured.

On May 26, 1863, the Confederate Navy adopted the national flag for its naval ensign. The only modification was to shorten the flag by specifying that the width of the ensign be two-thirds its length. This flag was normally flown from the stern of the vessel and was the flag under which John McIntosh Kell served while on board the CSS *Alabama*, including the duel with the USS *Kearsarge* off Cherbourg, France, in June of 1864. After returning home, Kell served beneath the "Stainless Banner" in the James River Squadron until the end of the war.

The flag was changed again on March 4, 1865, adding a red stripe at the tip of the fly, but there is no evidence that the navy, given the chaotic conditions prevailing at this late stage of the war, adopted the third national flag as it ensign.

Preface

John McIntosh Kell was the inconspicuous hero of the famous Confederate raider, the CSS *Alabama*. Most students of the War Between the States are familiar with the exploits of the Southern cruiser and her celebrated captain, Raphael Semmes. By the time of her climatic battle with the USS *Kearsarge* off the coast of France in June of 1864, the *Alabama* and her flamboyant commander had practically swept the seas of Northern merchant vessels, destroying more United States shipping than any other Confederate warship. But the individual who oversaw the day-to-day operation of the ship, the man who ran the cruise of the *Alabama* at the direction of his commander, was the ship's executive officer — First Lieutenant John McIntosh Kell. Working together, in the long-standing tradition of all nineteenth-century navies where the commander ran his ship through his executive officer, Semmes and Kell, during their three years together, became an extremely efficient — and deadly — team.

Semmes, writing in his *Memoirs of Service Afloat*, gave Kell his highest praise when he stated:

> [He is] a tall, well-proportioned gentleman, of middle age, with brown, wavy hair, and a magnificent beard, inclining to red. See how scrupulously neat he is dressed, and how suave, and how affable he is with his associates.

His eye is now beaming gentleness and kindness. You will scarcely recognize him as the same man when you see him again on deck, arraigning some culprit, "at the mast," for a breach of discipline.

Many years after the war, John Kell was still an impressive figure. A visitor to his home in Sunnyside, Georgia, in 1883, observed that he looked much younger than his sixty years:

> Captain Kell is of tall and commanding appearance; his face is deeply bronzed; his eyes twinkle with good humor; his hair is dark and curly; his mustache is heavy, and his beard is long and pointed. In manner he is somewhat nervous. His voice, clear and ringing, indicating that he was born to command, can express in his very tones the utmost kindness and the most genial hospitality. Although most of his life has been spent upon the sea, where self-assertion is absolutely a necessary qualification to success, Captain Kell is a very modest man, and shrinks from the public gaze. He is about sixty years of age, and yet he is as strong and as energetic as if he were but forty. A native of Georgia, hailing from "The State of Liberty," he is the peer of any other man ever produced by the Commonwealth.

In 1898, after incessant requests from his family and friends, Semmes' one-time executive officer finally finished writing his own memoirs. Entitled *Recollections of a Naval Life Including the Cruises of the Sumter and Alabama*, Kell's book was published in 1900 by the Neale Company of Washington, D.C. The book as originally published is divided into two fairly equal but distinctly different parts. "Part One" deals exclusively with Kell's early life and his career in the United States Navy, including his involvement in the Mexican War and his participation in Perry's historic expedition to Japan. He writes little, however, of a fateful and defining moment in his life when he was court-martialed and dismissed from the U.S. Navy. Important not for the details of his case, (for he was later re-instated) but prophetic in that his defense counsel was a young Alabama attorney by the name of Raphael Semmes.

Part One of *Recollections* and additional aspects of Kell's early life will be covered briefly in this work, and will serve as an introduction to "Part Two." The second half of his book covers the period that encompasses the War Between the States, and is reproduced here, in its entirety. Footnotes have been inserted in Kell's work at various points which, hopefully, will help to clarify and enlighten the original text. In addition, at the end of each of Kell's chapters, I have taken the liberty of inserting a selection of photographs which I trust will be of interest.

If the reader is interested in a more comprehensive study of Kell's life, a full and extremely readable biography of him exists in Norman C. Delaney's, *John McIntosh Kell of the Raider Alabama*, published by the University of Alabama Press in 1973. The reader is directed to this work for additional information on the life and times of Semmes' first lieutenant.

Kell, by his own admission, was not a prolific writer, and because his book appeared after the publication of Semmes' work, he felt there was little he could add that his one-time commander had not already stated. He was mistaken, however, for his *Recollections* offer a fascinating glimpse into the activities of the Confederate Navy, and in particular the day-to-day operations of the cruisers *Sumter* and *Alabama*.

Kell's additional motives for putting his *Recollections* on paper are best expressed at the end of his own preface where he wrote:

> My regrets are that many who were with us when I began to write will never con these simple pages, for many, indeed most, of the friends of my youth have passed before me "on that road from which no traveler e'er returns."
>
> To their children (then), and my own posterity I leave in these pages the truth of history and hope they will not be without interest to the young. To my brothers, the "United Confederate Veterans," I give the narrative of our times, the "times that tried men's souls," that left us naught save honor, a love of country, the sacred memory of valiant lives and deeds, and a hope in God!
>
> JNO. MCINTOSH KELL.

Sunnyside, Georgia, May 3, 1898

R. Thomas Campbell
September 1998

$\mathcal{A}$cknowledgments

It has been a richly rewarding experience in getting to know John Kell. After reading his book, *Recollections of a Naval Life*, several times, and Norman C. Delaney's excellent biography, *John McIntosh Kell of the Raider Alabama*, I have come to know, understand, and appreciate Commander Kell as a devoted naval officer, who loved his country, his family and his God. It is with esteemed pleasure, therefore, that I reproduce the second part of his book which deals with the War Between the States.

I wish to thank the administrators of the Civil War Library and Museum in Philadelphia, Pennsylvania, and the Tennessee State Library and Archives in Nashville, Tennessee, for their kind assistance in researching Kell's life. In addition, I am most grateful to Ms. Eileen A. Ielmini of the Georgia Historical Society in Savannah, Georgia, for her in-depth information pertaining to Kell's family. Lastly, I wish to acknowledge the encouragement and assistance of my wife Carole. Without her support and editing expertise, Kell's "Recollections" might never have been brought to light again.

PART ONE

The Formative Years

John McIntosh Kell was born at Laurel Grove near Darien, Georgia, in McIntosh County on January 23, 1823. The son of John Kell, (b. November 3, 1784, d. November 10, 1827), and Margery S. Baillie (b. 1794, d. 1870), young John was named after his Kell and McIntosh ancestors (Margery's mother was a McIntosh). "Donny," as he was called by his family, shared the family estate with three older sisters, Mary, Evelyn, and Hester.[1] A younger brother was born five years after Donny's arrival. Kell wrote briefly of his early childhood:

> When I was four years old my father died, leaving to my mother's care five little children. My childhood was spent upon our plantation, "Laurel Grove," McIntosh County, often varied by visits to Sapelo Island, the residence of my mother's first cousin, Hon. Thomas Spalding, whose son Randolph, a few months my senior, grew up with me in the intimacy of brothers. Our grandmothers were sisters, Marjory and Hester McIntosh. Marjory married James Spalding and Hester (my grandmother) married Alexander Baillie, and died leaving an infant, my mother, who was reared by her aunt, Mrs. Marjory Spalding, for whom she was named.
>
> My boyhood was passed as the Southern boy of that day, in the healthful, manly sports of hunting, riding, boating, and fishing, varied by school attendance in Darien, the county seat of McIntosh County, which was settled by my ancestors, Clan McIntosh, and first named "New Inverness," for their distant home in Scotland. My first teacher was Mr. Bradwell, who was famous in the seaboard counties as a teacher of great merit and ability. Shortly after, Dr. James Troup, the friend and physician of our family, was elected to the Legislature, and going up in his carriage to Milledgeville (for it was before the days of railroad travel), stopped at "Perry Mills" during the examination of a school kept by one Musgrove, a Scotchman. Being pleased with his mode of teaching, especially mathematics and English grammar, on his return to Darien, Dr. Troup persuaded my mother to allow him to take me with his son and daughter and place us there at school. This school, however, was of short duration. The poor old Scotchman got on a big "spree," and remaining so for some time, we were sent home. My next teacher was Mr. Pincheon, who conducted a large and prosperous school in Darien till he was called to take charge of the Chatham Academy, in Savannah. To this school I was sent in company with my cousin, Henry K. Rees, now Episcopal Evangelist of the State of Georgia, an earnest worker in his Master's vineyard, honored and beloved in his profession. From this school I returned home and remained a year.[2]

At age sixteen the young Kell had completed his formal education. During the winter of 1839–1840, he worked in Savannah as an apprentice at the accounting firm of Andrew Low and Company. It took only a few months of this tedious work to convince Kell that the profession of accounting was not for him, and in the spring he returned to Darien. It was a most opportune time for him to return, for the brig *Consort,* under the command of Lieutenant James Glynn, was anchored in Sapelo harbor while engaged in surveying the Georgia coast. Handsome young officers, immaculate in their dark blue uniforms, were frequent guests at the Kell home, hoping to court the favor of John's lovely sisters. The tall seventeen year old visited the *Consort* frequently, making friends with her officers and crew. It was from these visits that Kell determined what he would do with his life. He was now resolved to serve his country as a career naval officer.[3]

Kell's mother wrote to Congressman Thomas Butler King, petitioning him for an appointment for her son in the United States Navy. In September of 1841, she received a reply:

HOUSE OF REPRESENTATIVES, WASHINGTON

September 11, 1841

My Dear Madam: After many and repeated efforts I have at length obtained a midshipman's warrant for your son. He now belongs to his country. That he will bear himself gallantly and honorably in the service to which he belongs I do not doubt. That he may attain its highest and brightest honors is the sincere wish of your faithful friend

And obt. servant,

THO. BUTLER KING.

To Mrs. KELL,
    Darien, Ga.

On September 27, 1841, Kell, at eighteen years, appeared before a justice of the peace in Darien to take the oath of allegiance as an acting midshipman in the United States Navy. During his more than twenty years of service, this oath would be twice severely tested, and each time it would have a profound effect on the life of John McIntosh Kell.

Kell's orders soon followed. He was to report to the sloop of war *Falmouth* which was being fitted out at the Brooklyn Navy Yard for a cruise. The *Falmouth* was under the command of Kell's cousin, Commander James McKay McIntosh. After some delay, during which time Kell acquired his uniform, sword, and quadrant, the *Falmouth* was recommissioned and assigned to the "Gulf Squadron." Kell, along with eleven other midshipmen, went aboard on February 9, 1842, to begin his first cruise, and on February 14, the *Falmouth* sailed for Pensacola, Florida.[4]

As a young midshipman, Kell and the other "reefers" on the *Falmouth* had much to learn. This was in the era prior to the establishment of the Naval Academy at Annapolis, and each midshipman was expected to learn everything an officer needed to know about seamanship by serving on board a warship. Large Federal men-of-war usually employed a professor on board to teach the middies the basics of what they needed to know. On the *Falmouth* the teacher was William S. Fox, and Kell considered him "a very smart professor...I get him to show me everything that I want, and he is very kind." Kell was fortunate, for Professor Fox, unlike most who

An Acting Midshipman, circa 1850
Harper's Weekly

were assigned, seemed to be the exception to the rule. Most often, in spite of having a teacher on board, new midshipmen were mostly on their own in learning such things as entering and leaving a harbor, shortening and making sail, tacking and the handling of the ship in stormy weather, etc. In addition to their studies, each midshipman was required to keep a daily journal of everything that transpired on board, and to submit it to the captain once per week for his inspection.[5]

Kell seemed to enjoy his new life as a naval officer in training and considered his duties important as illustrated by a letter to his mother:

> Our pay is 40 dollars a month. We pay our mess bill out of that—from 10 to 15 dollars—I find it plenty to clothe me and gives me some pocket money in the bargain. Our duty in port and at sea is very different. At sea we have four hours watch to keep, except the dog watches, so we are 4 hours on duty and 12 hours off. You may judge that the mid-watch is the most disagreeable of all. I mean the midnight watch. On shore we do not have dog watches but have all of the day's duty to keep from 8 in the morning till 8 at night. They keep four hours at sea. Then we have 2 liberty days and one boat duty. Then comes the days' duty again.[6]

After a short cruise in the Caribbean, the *Falmouth* finally arrived at Pensacola in late July. By September, she had sailed again, this time to the island of Sacrificios off the port of Vera Cruz, Mexico, to pick up a cargo of silver and convey it to New Orleans. By spring the *Falmouth* was back at Pensacola, and Kell wrote that he was now performing the duties of a master's mate. The *Falmouth* made another Caribbean cruise and then on June 18, 1843, she anchored at Savannah, and Kell was able to visit his home for the first time in nineteen months.[7]

On August 25, 1843, Midshipman Kell was ordered to his next tour of duty which was aboard the newly launched frigate *Savannah*. The *Savannah* was one of nine warships which had been laid down after the conclusion of the War of 1812. She was armed with forty-four guns and carried a complement of 480 officers and men. In October, she sailed from New York with a destination of Callao, Peru, and Kell was thankful for his experiences on the *Falmouth*, for now he had the confidence to perform his duties well on a full size man-of-war.

The *Savannah* stopped at Rio de Janeiro, and Kell and the other midshipmen were given the opportunity to visit the bustling Brazilian city. Christmas was spent here, but soon the American frigate was ready to sail:

> After taking in water and provisioning ship, we continued our voyage around the Horn, encountering rough weather, heavy gales, boisterous seas, and a very low degree of temperature, being nearly frozen for three weeks off the pitch of the Cape. The violence of the gales forced us down to latitude 62 degrees south. After rounding the Cape we shaped our course northward in the broad Pacific, and welcomed the more temperate clime of the lower latitudes.[8]

The *Savannah* finally arrived at Callao on February 17, 1844. There was not much for a young midshipman to do in the small Peruvian town, but Kell made the most of his shore leave. Taking the time to travel the six miles to Lima, he paid a dollar to view the supposed remains of the great conqueror of Peru, Francisco Pizarro. On April 9, Kell was transferred for temporary duty on board the schooner *Shark*. Although it was the smallest vessel of the squadron, Kell gained valuable experience on the *Shark*, acting in the capacity of a lieutenant as she made several coastal runs between Callao and Panama. As the deck officer in charge of the watch, he still had much to learn, however:

> The *Shark* was ordered to take some of our officers leaving the squadron to Panama on their way home. While on this voyage we passed quite near the Lobas group of islands, or really a group of rocks, where seals and sea lions reared their young in great numbers. We were running with a free wind with our square sails set, and the course given me took us quite near the rocks. Upon the near approach of the schooner the seals set up a great roaring as they rolled into the water from their rocky beds and frolicked around in the water in our wake. It happened to be just at dinner time, and the officers taking passage were at table with the captain. I put my head down the hatchway and called to the captain to "come and see the seals playing around the vessel." He replied: "Will be up as soon as I finish dinner,"

but one of the officers came up at once. Calling out, he said: "Howison, come on deck!" As the captain came up he was surprised to see our nearness to the rocks; still I was keeping the course given me, but there was evidently a current setting us on toward them. The captain at a glance took in the situation. He directed me to "put the helm down and haul on the wind and give good distance in passing the rocks," remarking, by way of pleasantry, "Mr. Kell, you must think you are in a coach and four, driving round a street corner." I was strictly carrying out my orders, but was wanting in experience as a watch officer. For a long time after that I heard a great deal of "those seals and my coach and four."[9]

After enduring several voyages on the *Shark* to Panama and back, Kell was once again on the *Savannah* by May 11, 1845. A few weeks later the frigate sailed for Honolulu, Hawaii. Kell was hoping for a more extensive cruise among the Pacific islands, but after spending only four weeks at Honolulu, the *Savannah* sailed for Mazatlan amid rumors, which most did not take seriously, of an impending war with Mexico. Arriving in the Mexican seaport on November 18, Kell and the other officers of the *Savannah* were surprised when word reached them on June 1, 1846, confirming that a state of war then existed between Mexico and the United States.

John D. Sloat, commander of the Pacific Squadron, had received unofficial word back on May 17, that fighting had begun between Mexico and the United States, but now that the "unofficial" news had been confirmed, it was time for action. Earlier he had been instructed by Washington that in the event of war he was to sail his squadron to San Francisco, seize that port, and capture as many other California ports as possible. Accordingly, Sloat pulled out of Mazatlan and headed north. On July 2, 1846, the *Savannah* dropped anchor in the harbor at Monterey.

Sloat was anxious to convey to the Mexican residents of California that he came as a friend, and pledged to the people that their local governments, homes, and private property would be maintained and respected. Sending armed sailors and marines ashore

Commodore John D. Sloat
Commander of the Pacific Squadron at
the beginning of the war with Mexico
Library of Congress

to maintain order, his instructions were quickly carried out. With no organized opposition among the Californians, the American flag soon floated above Yerba Buena (San Francisco), Sutter's Fort (Sacramento), Sonoma, Bodega, and San Jose.

In all of this activity, including the armed contingents who went ashore, Kell had played no part; he chafed at his inactivity on board the *Savannah*, but his turn would soon come. On August 31, Commodore Stockton, who had replaced Sloat, appointed Captain Archibald H. Gillespie as commandant of the southern region of California. Gillespie imposed harsh control over the residents of the area, however, and soon Los Angeles was in open revolt. Within a few days, Gillespie, lacking supplies, fortifications, and equipment, surrendered his few sailors and marines thereby handing the Californians their first real victory. Learning of the American defeat, Stockton ordered the *Savannah* to sail for San Pedro, and assist Gillespie in the retaking of Los Angeles.[10]

On October 7, Captain William Mervine, who now commanded the *Savannah*, landed over three hundred sailors and marines who along with Gillespie's marines, marched on Los Angeles. Kell continued to pace the deck of the *Savannah*, however, for he was not included in the team that went ashore. Through a succession of inept maneuvers and faulty decisions on Mervine's part, the expedition met defeat at the hands of approximately fifty Californians. On November 19, the *Savannah* returned to San Francisco.

Kell's opportunity had arrived. On December 29, 1846, he and Acting Master William F. DeJonge were detached from the *Savannah* and ordered to accompany an expedition consisting of one hundred-one sailors, marines, and rangers. This force was commanded by Captain Ward Marston of the marines and had as its objective the destruction or capture of a group of insurrectionists led by Francisco Sanchez. Writing years later, Kell vividly recalled his introduction to combat:

> From sources apparently reliable we learned that the enemy were in force in the neighborhood of Santa Clara Mission. We made easy marches, coming to camp about sunset, always sending some cavalry ahead to select a camping ground and butcher beeves in readiness for our arrival. After the fatiguing march of the day we would arrive at camp thoroughly prepared in appetite to enjoy the California beef. The cattle grazing on the rich grasses and wild oats of the fertile valleys were superbly fine. "Jack Tar," with his brother marines, would sit round the camp fires and roast his rib of beef with as much zest and pleasure as though he were native to the plains.
>
> The second morning after leaving the ship the courier came in and reported the enemy in camp in a piece of redwoods up in the hills. As it was a rough road ascending the hills, the artillery piece and the infantry were

ordered to keep in the plains, while the cavalry were detailed to reconnoiter and ascertain the exact locality and force of the enemy. Being mounted myself, I obtained permission to accompany the cavalry. We were armed with carbines and revolvers. At early dawn we started on the march. A thick fog enveloped the hillsides, and here occurred one of those strange phenomena—an optical illusion. Three of us were riding abreast, somewhat in advance of the column. Simultaneously each of us cocked and raised our carbines to our shoulders to fire upon what seemed to be a few cavalrymen of the enemy coming toward us down the hill. The next instant the fog cleared and instead of the cavalry we found only a clump of bushes! We proceeded up the hill, using great caution, and in silence. Upon reaching the summit we discovered the camp of the enemy, just abandoned. We followed their trail, down into the plains again, and soon rifle shots were heard and our scouts

**Commodore Robert Stockton
Commander of the Pacific Squadron
at the time of the Battle of Santa Clara**
Library of Congress

came in and reported the enemy just ahead of us, in large force, mounted. We had by this time joined our infantry and field piece. We advanced upon them, they firing indiscriminately from their horses, and retreating as we advanced. They evidently meant to draw us on to the open prairie beyond, where they could maneuver their cavalry to greater advantage. As we emerged from the timber land the enemy surrounded us, and dismounting from their horses, were completely hid by the tall prairie grass and commenced a rapid fire upon our body of men. We returned the fire, aiming only at the smoke from the discharge of their guns, for neither men nor horses could be seen. I now worked the field piece to great advantage, loading with grape and canister, and trained the gun on the point from which came the greatest discharge of the foe. The grape and canister tearing through the high grass would flush the fellows from their cover like a covey of partridges before a fowling piece, when they would mount their horses and ride to a more respectful distance. In this way we carried on a running fight till we neared the old Mission of Santa Clara. The occupants, who had crossed the mountains and taken refuge in the old mission, came out joyfully to join us in the fight. Very soon the Californians were routed and dispersed in all

The Battle of Santa Clara, California, January 2, 1847
This was Kell's only opportunity to participate in the Mexican War.
Library of Congress

directions. We were received with great joy by our countrymen from the East who had crossed the plains and the mountains. Early the next morning a courier came in from the enemy to treat for peace. The offer was accepted, on condition that they deliver up all arms and horses that had been unjustly taken from the people and that they retire to their homes and become peaceful citizens. These terms were accepted, as that distant territory of Mexico had little in sympathy with the government. The large drove of horses captured were driven into a corral and we saw for the first time the dexterity with which they used the lasso. Citizens coming in and claiming their horses, such animals were immediately lassoed and turned over to the owners. It is said that the California boy, as soon as he can run around the yard, uses his lariat in catching chickens, dogs, cats, and all the domestic animals for their infantile sport, as the American boy would play marbles. The guns were all stacked up in piles, and presented a motley appearance of ancient fowling pieces that would have done credit to Falstaff's ragged regiment, and were calculated to do more harm to the persons using them than to those against whom they were directed. This no doubt accounted for the fact that only one of our men was wounded in the engagement of the previous day. We remained at the Mission of Santa Clara several days, till all hostilities were quieted, amusing ourselves hunting wild geese that covered the plains around Santa Clara in such numbers that when they rose for flight they almost obscured the sun like a cloud. We found them excellent food, and took numbers of them on board the ship. A courier was dispatched to the commodore reporting the treaty made with the Californians and their quiet retirement to their homes. Boats were then sent to the head of the bay, where we embarked our artillery piece and infantry forces, and returned to our ships, the cavalry returning by land to San Francisco. Thus ended our military operations against this peaceful people, who cared more for tending their flocks and herds and sitting "in the shadow of their own vine and fig tree" than they did for warfare.[11]

Thus ended Kell's participation in the Mexican War. On March 25, 1847, the *Savannah* was at San Diego preparing for the long trip home. The next morning, she raised anchor and sailed south, her ultimate destination: New York. The passage around the Horn was particularly difficult, for this was the winter season in the Southern Hemisphere, and the *Savannah* encountered freezing gales and heavy snowstorms, which, Kell wrote, kept the sailors busy shoveling the snow from her deck. Finally on September 9, 1847, the frigate arrived in New York harbor, and several days later, Kell boarded a train for the overland trip to his home in the South.[12]

After only a few weeks at his home in Georgia, however, Kell was ordered to report to the naval school at Annapolis, Maryland. The United States Naval Academy had been established in 1845, and in September of that first year, Commandant Franklin Buchanan welcomed the school's first class of midshipmen. On November 2, 1847, Midshipman John McIntosh Kell reported for instruction at the Academy. Kell was of the "date of 1841," as the class was designated, because he originally had been appointed as an acting midshipman in that year. The 186 members of the "date of 1841" proved too large for the old army facilities which had been acquired by the navy, and Kell's class was separated into two divisions. Kell found himself in the second division in which he was expected to spend eight months, after which examinations would be given at the school in June of 1848.

While regulations were strict at the Academy, the "date of 1841" was composed of veteran midshipmen who had learned most of the skills of their profession on the open sea. They looked with disdain on the faculty's attempts to discipline them, and Kell's class soon earned a reputation as mischief-makers and pranksters. Many of the midshipmen's late night slumbers were rudely awakened by the sound of 32-pound round shot rolling along the second floor piazza and then thundering down the stairs. Although liquor was officially prohibited, late night parties that left the merrymakers severely hung over the next morning were frequent.

Kell's roommates were, like himself, veterans of Pacific cruises. They were Alexander R. Abercrombie from Maryland, Robert D. Minor of Virginia, and Robert C. Duval of North Carolina. The four friends shared a room in the old Fort Severn hospital building now appropriately known as "Rowdy Row."

**Old Fort Severn at Annapolis, Maryland, site of the
United States Naval Academy**

U.S. Naval Institute Proceedings

**Captain Franklin Buchanan, USN,
Commandant of the United States
Naval Academy, 1845–1847**

Naval Historical Center

Commander George P. Upshur, USN
Upshure was secretary of the navy when
Kell secured his appointment as an
**acting midshipman. When Kell was
assigned to the Academy, Upshur
succeeded Buchanan as superintendent.**
U.S. Naval Archives

The courses of instruction included Mathematics and Navigation, Natural Philosophy, French, Spanish, Chemistry, and English Literature. Several of the instructors Kell considered very good, but some he rated as only "fair." The middies were initially divided into four sections alphabetically, but after a short time they stood formations and attended lectures according to their class standing. Kell persevered, and in early July of 1848, the Board of Examiners convened at Annapolis. Kell and the other members of his class were tested on their knowledge of mathematics, and then they were subjected to a "long, exhaustive" oral examination. Kell's experience on the Pacific cruises paid dividends, for he had little difficulty with the questions on seamanship. On July 10, 1848, he was notified that he had passed his exams, standing twenty-seventh in a class of two hundred.[13]

Passed Midshipman Kell was granted a three-month leave of absence, and he spent the balance of the summer at his family's home in Georgia. Shortly before his leave was to expire, Kell wrote to the Navy Department requesting to be assigned to the Mediterranean Squadron. With cruises to South America and the Pacific now behind him, he had hopes that the much sought after Mediterranean cruise would now be his. He was to be disappointed, however, for the department had already assigned him to the USS *Albany* which would cruise the West Indies. Little did Kell foresee when he joined the ship in Norfolk, Virginia, on October 28, 1848, that his upcoming service on the *Albany* would change his life forever.

The *Albany*, which was commanded by veteran Victor M. Randolph, had been launched in 1846, and was considered a first-class sloop of war. She carried twenty-two guns and was manned by a complement of two hundred ten men and officers. Although Kell had hoped for the coveted Mediterranean assignment, he was overjoyed to find that three of his classmates from the Academy, Passed Midshipmen Francis A. Roe, Charles P. Hopkins, and Francis G. Clarke, were also aboard the *Albany*.

Several acting midshipmen were also assigned, one being seventeen-year-old John R. Eggleston, who many years later would fondly recall his impression of John McIntosh Kell:

> Kell was a man of splendid physique, well formed in every respect, his face the mirror of his character, filled with benevolence and goodness, but stern to all that was mean and unprincipled. Of the many people with whom I have been associated in the course of a long life, for what may be good in me I owe more to Kell than anybody else. All loved him.[14]

The *Albany* sailed from Norfolk, and the passed midshipmen soon found to their dismay that Commander Randolph and the other senior officers treated them no differently from the youngsters who had just shipped as acting midshipmen. This treatment grew steadily worse until it reached the breaking point, as Kell explained:

> We were some months in fitting out the ship, and by early fall sailed for the West Indies, a delightful cruise through the Windward Islands. This cruise, however, was destined to be of short duration. While we were anchored at Fort du France—the memorable home of Josephine in the Island of Martinique—there was a want of harmony between the lieutenants and the passed midshipmen which resulted in an order that we should perform strictly the duties of midshipmen, such as "calling the watch, and lighting the candle of the lieutenant who had to go on duty." It so happened that the first order was given to me. I declined to obey it, stating that the duty had been previously performed by the quartermasters, I considered it a menial service, and would not do it. The lieutenant of the watch urged me strongly to do it, or he "would have to report me for disobedience of orders." I replied that "I had made up my mind fully to perform no menial duty and that he was at liberty to report me," which he did. I was then summoned into the presence of a very irate gentleman, Captain Victor M. Randolph, of Virginia. He stormed at me violently; said he "would have me court-martialed and dismissed from the service." I very quietly told him "I would not obey the order."
>
> Thereupon he directed the lieutenant to "suspend me from duty and report the case to the first lieutenant of the ship in the morning." The three other passed midshipmen in like manner refused to obey the order and were also suspended, making a very strong case of "mutinous insubordination." We continued our cruise along the south side of San Domingo and Cuba, stopping in at various ports, which we, however, under suspension, were never allowed to visit. This continued for three months, when the confinement so affected our health that the kind old surgeon, Dr. Spotswood, reported that the "passed midshipmen must be permitted to visit the shore for exercise," which requirement was granted and our health improved. From Cuba we ran down to Vera Cruz, where we met the flagship of the squadron, and charges were preferred against us without delay. The Commodore ordered our ship immediately to the Pensacola Navy Yard, the rendezvous of the Gulf Squadron, he following soon after. On arriving at Pensacola a court-martial was ordered for our trial. Here at Pensacola I made the acquaintance of Lieutenant Raphael Semmes, who had just been admitted to the bar of Alabama. He had shortly before this obtained a leave of absence from the Navy Department for the purpose of studying law. He little dreamed then the important part this knowledge of international law would bear on his future life, so thoroughly fitting him for his work in after years while in command of the world-renowned Confederate States Steamer *Alabama*.[15]

Kell was confident that he had acted appropriately, and in a letter of June 4, 1849, to his sister Mary, he explained his conduct:

I am very much indebted to my family, especially my dear Mother for upholding me in disobeying that most outrageous order. I cannot think of it without feeling injured that a man should dare give me such an order! I sincerely wish it was the spirit of our service for an officer to allow no imposition but it is too often the case that a Captain is allowed to do as he chooses, and younger officers are afraid to protest against his conduct on account of his being court-martialed. Of course a young officer gets the worst of it in disobeying an order, but I do not think this should influence one to allow such persecution, and it is an injury to the service. The grade of Passed Midshipman is such that there is no duty allotted to them, and a narrow-minded Captain may enforce an officer of 25 and even 30 yrs. of age the same duty that was required of him when he entered the service a mere youngster. I think it an ill contrived law of our navy that gives to a Commander despotic sway and such is my case. It has long been customary for Midshipmen to take a lantern below, certainly as a favor, but never as a duty required, for it cannot be a duty of one officer to be a menial of another, and it is nothing less in getting a light for him to dress by. I have done it as a favor. I never will as an order, unless the Navy Dept. decides it is my duty, then I think the matter should be referred to higher authority still and Congress made to decide if one officer shall be menial to another. I am confident that such is not the spirit of the Country.[16]

At 10:00 a.m. on July 20, the court, comprised of nine senior officers, convened on board the *Albany* at Pensacola. The first case to be heard was that of Midshipman Roe, one of the four, the others being Kell, Clarke, and Hopkins. Roe was considered the "ringleader" of the four midshipmen and had three charges filed against him, whereas the other three were charged only with "Willful disobedience of a lawful order from his superior officer." The specification of the charge was that they each had refused to carry a light.

Semmes, agreeing to represent the four as counsel, called and examined witnesses for the defense of Roe, while Commander Randolph acted as the prosecutor. After ten days the case was concluded, and Roe was given one day to prepare a statement. On July 30, he read his lengthy address before the board, contending that any officer had a right to disobey an order that was illegal regardless of its source. Nevertheless, the court found him guilty of two charges, including their specifications, and his sentence was "dismissal from the service." Midshipman Kell was next.[17]

Acting upon Semmes' advice, Kell pleaded "guilty" to the specification, meaning he admitted that he refused to carry a light, but "not guilty" to the charge of willful disobedience of a lawful order. The court overruled his plea and he then pleaded "guilty" to both specification and charge. Semmes, with the precedent having been set in the

**The USS *Albany* on which Kell and three other midshipmen refused
to obey an order to light their lieutenant's candle**

Library of Congress

case of Roe, knew that it would be an uphill battle to convince the
court that Kell acted appropriately, and he proceeded to call several
witnesses who all testified that they held a high regard for the midshipman as an officer and a gentleman. As prosecutor, Commander
Randolph called several officers who testified that, as midshipmen,
they had been given such an order, and that they had not resented nor
had they felt it was illegal.

On August 1, Kell was given the opportunity to read his own
statement:

> Mr. President and Gentlemen of the Court:
>
> There is but a single question presented by the charge and specifica-
> tion under which I have never contraverted any of the facts material to the
> issue which has been raised between my Commander and myself and
> would, if I had been permitted, have saved the Court the labor of an inves-
> tigation by my plea. I did disobey the order of Lieut. Reid directing me to
> take a light below and light the candle of the relief.... If I have committed an
> error at all the most that can be said of it is that it is an error of judgment.

Acting upon the principle which is unquestionably a sound one, that an officer of the Navy has the right to disobey any and every order which he may judge to be illegal, I have resisted obedience to the order in question on my responsibility to the Government, believing this to be the proper means of bringing the issue which has been raised between my Commander and myself, before a proper tribunal for adjudication.

...I trust you will bring to the decision of the question, minds free from any prejudice of rank or station. I desire that each one of you will place himself in imagination in my position and ask himself the question whether if at my age such duty had been required of him specifically and peremptorily, under an order, he would not like myself have felt bound to decline obedience in defense of his self-respect. I do not pretend to say whose fault it is—whether it is the fault of the Government or of the Superior officers of the Navy, that the Passed Midshipmen find themselves in the anomalous position they at present occupy, but certain it is there is a fault somewhere. I have now spent the best years of my life in the Service. I have been examined and found qualified for promotion. I have reached the age of mature manhood. I belong to an honored and honorable profession all the members of which are or should be gentlemen and what is my position? Have I any of the rank or authority which should belong to my years, to my social standing in the community, or to my attainments, poor as these are? None whilst nature proclaimed me a man and at the age when man in such a profession as ours is or should be most useful—with all of my faculties developed both physical and mental—the position which I am still constrained to occupy denies me any of the privileges which should belong to my time of life. I am still confined to the steerage, regarded as a mere messenger and required to perform acts which would shock the ideas of propriety of any one in civil life who has passed beyond the leading strings of boyhood. Now that I have the most capacity to be useful to the Government, I am rendered by the Government of least use to it. Instead of performing the duties which I have been declared competent to perform—instead of handling a ship of war as an officer of the deck, I am degraded into a bearer of messages and a lighter of candles. This is a wrong system whoever may be the author of it. It may not be in your power, Mr. President and Gentlemen of the Court, to change this system, but you may do much towards ameliorating it. You should not hold the reigns of authority too tightly. Whenever it is possible to relax them without injury to the Service, you should do so. The more you release the Passed Midshipmen of the Service from the drudgery which in former years has been required of them, the more you will increase their self-respect and the better officers you will make of them. Employments, like associations of men, have a powerful influence upon their characters. You do not find the high-toned gentleman as a rule under the leathern apron of the mechanic any more than you can draw an accomplished officer from before the mast. Men who are made menials of soon learn to feel and act as menials and it is well worth the consideration of the Government and of every officer of the Navy whether Passed Midshipmen should not be removed from the false position in which they are at present placed. I do not wish the Court to infer from these remarks that because I regard my position as a hard and unnatural one, that therefore I would array myself in opposition to undoubted authority, for the sake of ameliorating it. This not only would not answer the end in view, but no officer could be justified in such a course. He should rather appeal to the sympathies of his brother officers and to his government for the removal of the grievances under which he lives, than undertake to redress them in this manner. But what I mean to say is, that my position should be regarded as a sufficient justification of any attempt on my part to resist by legal and proper means any restraint put upon me, or compliance with the well settled laws and customs of the service. Instead of being regarded *a priori* as a wrongdoer, I should on the contrary have the sympathies of my brother officers, and this Court instead of seeking industriously for ground on which to convict me, interpose if possible to save me harmless. It is no part of my intention, Mr. President and Gentlemen of the Court, to argue my case over again to you today, since it is only day before yesterday that it was argued at great length in another trial. All the arguments that were then used, I adopt as a part of my defense and respectfully refer you to them.

It will be sufficient for me to state briefly the several points on which I rest my case. First. The illegality of the order. I insist that the order is illegal on the two following grounds, to wit: First. It is not sanctioned by any law. Secondly. It is not sanctioned by any custom, for although it be admitted that custom requires Passed Midshipmen to call the relief, it does not *require* them to light the candles, the latter act never having been demanded of them heretofore, but always performed *ex gracia* as a piece of politeness, and acts which men perform not under the obligation of an order, but freely and of choice, can never in justice be cited against them to saddle them with a duty. Secondly. The charge is defective, it not stating that the Superior whose order was disobeyed was in the execution of the duties of his office—which words are essential to describe the kind of disobedience punished by the act for the better government of the Navy. Thirdly. The act of refusing to take a lantern below, the only act of disobedience stated in the specification, was not the act objected to by me on any fair interpretation of my motives. My object in declining to take the lantern was to decline lighting the relief's candle, which was the real order given to me—the taking of the lantern being merely an incident of the act of lighting the candle.

The Court should therefore acquit me under the specification, since it does not raise the issue which was raised in fact between the officer of the deck and myself. Reminding the Court of my long confinement on board a small ship in a tropical climate and of the very exemplary character as an officer and a gentleman which it has seen I have borne from my entry into the Service to this time, a period of eight years, I submit my case with all confidence to their hands believing they will do equal justice to their government and myself.[18]

In spite of Kell's argument, and Semmes' able defense, the court found him guilty of both the charge and specification. His sentence: "Dismissal from the Navy of the United States."

Midshipmen Clarke and Hopkins were found guilty also and dismissed from the navy. Kell did not give up hope, however, for the decision would have to reviewed by the department and signed by the president. Departing immediately after the trial, Kell left for his home in Georgia, but unknown to him at the time was the fact that he had made a favorable impression on his defense counsel. Raphael Semmes would one day write: "The relation of counsel, and client, as a matter of course, brought us close together, and I discovered that young Kell had in him, the making of a man. So far from being a mutineer, he had a high respect for discipline, and had only resisted obedience to the order in question, from a refined sense of gentlemanly propriety."[19]

As Kell waited on his family's rice plantation near Darien, Georgia, he still maintained hope that the department would overturn the verdict. In the late fall, he received a letter from Washington dated November 3, 1849. President Zachary Taylor had signed the order. It was now official — Kell was out of the navy.

This was a difficult time for Kell, for although he still maintained that he had acted correctly, he was embarrassed by his dismissal and longed for the sea and the status of a naval officer. After a tour of Georgia in the company of a friend, Kell settled restlessly at the family home in Darien. At his family's suggestion, Kell went to see Thomas Spalding, a prominent Georgian who was active in politics. After listening to his explanation, Spalding agreed to write the senior senator from Georgia, John MacPherson Berrien, to ask that the case be reviewed. Kell traveled to Washington with the letter and was courteously received by the senator. After a careful examination, Berrien promised to see what he could do, and Kell journeyed back to Georgia.

Berrien was a man of his word, and with a new administration in Washington and a new secretary of the navy in office, it was not long before Kell received a notice that he and the other three midshipmen had been reinstated at their full rank and salary. In December 1850, Kell received orders to report to the steam frigate *Susquehanna* at Philadelphia. His ordeal was over.[20]

The *Susquehanna* was captained by Commodore John H. Aulick, commander of the East India Squadron, who was under orders to

Commodore Matthew C. Perry, USN
Library of Congress

negotiate a treaty of commerce with the closed nation of Japan. Kell missed the ship in Philadelphia, but joined her in Norfolk where she sailed on June 5, 1851, bound for the Far East. After a long and tedious voyage, including stops at Rio de Janeiro, Cape Town, and Singapore, the *Susquehanna* finally arrived at Hong Kong.

Kell was pleased with his assignment aboard the steam sloop, for two of his friends from before the court-martial, Bob Minor and John Eggleston, were also serving on the *Susquehanna*. Kell also became close friends with the ship's surgeon, Charles F. Fahs from Pennsylvania, and together they made many trips ashore to explore the mysteries of China. Caution had to be exercised, however, for this was during the period of the Taiping Rebellion (1850–1864), in which the Manchu Dynasty struggled to maintain control while facing expanding Western imperialism. Westerners were increasingly resented, and at times their lives were threatened on the streets of the Chinese cities. With the *Susquehanna* anchored just down river from Canton, Kell and Fahs visited the ancient Chinese city often, but not without being well armed.[21]

Meanwhile, on March 24, 1862, Commodore Matthew C. Perry had been appointed to succeed Aulick as commander of the Japanese Expedition. In reality his was a dual purpose which included protecting American rights in strife-torn China and opening Japanese markets, forcibly if need be, to American trade. Perry left the United States in November aboard the steam frigate *Mississippi*, and while the men and officers of the East India Squadron awaited his arrival, they contemplated the dangerous possibilities of becoming embroiled in the volatile Chinese conflict.

Margery Kell had written her son voicing her concern of such a prospect, and Kell tried to reassure her:

> We would rely more on the formidable show of such a squadron of steamers, to a half civilized race of people who have no idea of steam or the

size of our ships, than coercing them by force of arms. Should we be obliged to act in a hostile way it does not follow that we must invade their country for that would be madness. As you say, they have millions to bring against us, who would fight perhaps to desperation but with our single steamer we could sink and destroy every fishing boat and trading vessel they possess. They have no vessels of any size so that with a squadron we could batter down their Seaport towns, cut off their fish trade which is very great, thus annoying their Coast without their being in any way able to do us the least harm. They would soon be reduced to come to terms and make such reasonable treaty as our Government could desire, but I apprehend nothing of the sort. I do not for a moment believe there will be a hostile gun fired, should the Expedition come out for I know it is the earnest desire of the Government to obtain peaceably a depot for coal for our steamers running between California and China. It needs [to] be on one of their uninhabited Islands and thus by establishing on, or near the coast of their Empire, leave time, and intercourse to effect their civilization.[22]

On November 10, 1852, Captain Franklin Buchanan arrived to take command of the *Susquehanna*. Buchanan, who had been the first commandant of the Naval Academy at Annapolis, would later rise to the rank of full admiral in Confederate service. During this time the *Susquehanna* was moved to Shanghai, and in May of 1853, the *Mississippi* bearing Commodore Perry arrived at the Chinese city. Perry quickly moved his flag to the *Susquehanna*, and Kell was appointed to his staff.

Perry was a wise choice to lead the expedition to Japan. He was an impressive individual, proud and arrogant, and he knew how to impress the Japanese by utilizing pomp and ceremony. On July 1, 1853, the squadron sailed for the Japanese mainland. By the afternoon of July 8, the "Fire-vessels of the Western Barbarians" were anchored in Tokyo Bay. The Japanese had constructed a special building in which to receive the "Barbarians," and on July 14, Perry went ashore. John McIntosh Kell was an interested participant to this historic event:

The next day the squadron got under way and steamed up to this anchorage, where we saw the new building. Coming to anchor (as our squadron did) in line of battle, presenting our starboard broadside to the shore, with springs on our cables to cover the landing of our forces, and in case of treachery that our batteries might play upon the enemy, we presented a formidable array. All boats were now lowered and preparation made for landing the forces, the Commodore and his staff (of which I had the honor of being a member) bringing up the rear. The boats pulled up in column to the shore. As the forces were landed the boats would drop out to the right and left of the landing. The marines forming on the right and the blue jackets on the left, presented an unbroken line from the shore to the building, keeping the Japanese out of that space. The Commodore then landed, presenting a fine appearance, being a large and fine-looking man, in new full-dress uniform, accompanied by his staff. Following this, a striking feature in this body were three stalwart Negroes, neatly dressed in their muster suits, armed cap-a-pie, and carrying in rosewood boxes the credentials of the Minister Extraordinary. This was an imposing spectacle, and the American flag waved for the first time on the soil of Japan in the history of that nation. Each company carried a handsome new flag of the American Union. Thousands of Japanese witnessed this spectacle and observed the strictest order and decorum, while a few of the highest in rank were permitted to approach and witness the ceremonies. The Japanese flags decorated the building and many were carried by the standard-bearers of these officials. As the Commodore and his staff drew near to the entrance of the building he was met by the officer of the Japanese Government and his suite, making the salaams of their country, after which we were conducted into the building; the Japanese were seated on one side and the Americans on the other. The interpreter (Japanese) took his position between the two, down on his knees, not daring to look at either party, but merely repeating the communications as an automaton or a machine might have done. Our grand old Commodore, with his imposing presence and gigantic stature, delivered with great dignity and solemnity the credentials empowering him to treat with the Japanese nation, doing honor to his country by his impressive bearing, both martial and soldierly. After this formality was gone through with some attempt at pleasant intercourse was passed between the two parties, and this great occasion, which proved the wedge that opened Japan to the civilized world, was brought to a close. The Commodore and his staff withdrew from the reception and returned on board ship in the same order with which we had landed. Nothing occurred to mar the very imposing ceremonies in behalf of our country. The fleet got under way and dropped down the bay to our former anchorage, which was better suited for operating our railroad and the telegraph wires brought out by the Commodore to display to these secluded people the vast improvements of the age.[23]

Perry had insisted that he be allowed to negotiate with a high government representative, and that the vice governor of Uraga, with whom he had met, was not sufficient. The Japanese insisted that it would take several months to arrange such a meeting, to which Perry replied that he would retire his fleet to the China coast and return the following year for the high level negotiations.

During the winter of 1853–1854, the *Susquehanna* alternated between Canton and Hong Kong. In February of 1854, Perry led his fleet back to Japan and negotiations were successfully concluded. In the Treaty of Kanagawa the United States obtained two open ports—

Commodore Perry and his staff go ashore, July 14, 1853.

Shimoda and Hakodate. Also included in the agreement were coaling rights, the appointment of consuls, and a guarantee of Japanese protection for Americans who might become stranded in Japan. It was a historic treaty and opened Japan, for better or worse, to the trade and commerce of the Western world.

Kell was not present for the formal signing of the treaty, however, for the *Susquehanna*, at the request of the American minister to China, Robert M. McLane, was dispatched to Shanghai. The Taiping Rebellion was continuing, and McLane feared for the safety of the Americans in the strife-torn country. Kell enjoyed Shanghai in spite of the warring factions because of the companionship of the many American missionaries who resided there. One of these was Emma Wray of Augusta, Georgia, a recent recruit to the mission field. Miss Wray, who considered herself something of a "matchmaker," was quite impressed with the imposing figure of Midshipman John Kell. Writing to her closest friend, Miss Julia Blanche Munroe in Vineville, Georgia, she pleaded with her to make no commitments for marriage until she should have an opportunity to meet the dashing young naval officer.[24]

Perry now prepared the ships of his squadron for the return trip to the United States, and part of this preparation entailed the transfer of Kell to the USS *Mississippi* as an acting master. The vessels of the squadron rendezvoused at Hong Kong, and on September 4, 1854, the *Susquehanna* sailed. A few days later, the *Mississippi* hauled up her anchor and headed for home. Years later a now aging Kell would write that while at Shanghai he had seen a photograph of the "beautiful and feted Miss Munroe" and that "he determined to win her for his wife."[25]

The *Mississippi* arrived in New York in the latter part of April 1855, and Kell immediately left by train for Darien. It was not long before Kell and his future bride came face to face.

> In June of this year I made a visit to the city of Macon. On this visit I met for the first time my future wife. Beautiful city of Macon, within your suburbs I found love and happiness in the long years gone by! And now the life within me thrills when I breathe your flower-laden air, and the memories of the past sweep over me with loving benediction![26]

In September, while awaiting orders, Kell received two important letters from the Navy Department. The first announced his appointment to the grade of master as of September 14, and the second contained a commission as a lieutenant dated September 15, 1855. After all his years of service, his court-martial, dismissal, and reinstatement, he was now *Lieutenant* Kell.

The courtship of Miss Munroe came to a temporary halt on November 24, when Kell received orders to report to Lieutenant Edwin J. DeHaven at Pensacola for duty on the USS *Arago*, a coast survey schooner. The schooner soon departed for Galveston, Texas, where Kell spent the winter, much of the spring, and early summer surveying the Texas coast. During this period he and Blanche corresponded by letters, and their romance developed into an "ardent love, a love that was to crown our days and lighten our path to Heaven."[27]

Returning from the coast survey, Lieutenant Kell and Blanche Munroe were married at Christ Church in Macon, Georgia, on October 15, 1856. After a week in Macon, which included a grand reception and numerous balls given in their honor, the newlyweds left for Kell's family home in Darien. Here the festivities continued with "elegant dinner parties, dances in the evenings, a regatta in our honor by Hon. Thomas Forman, of Broughton Island, and a ten days' entertainment of seventy guests at the estate of Randolph Spalding on Sapelo Island."[28]

Not hearing any word from the Navy Department, Kell traveled to Washington to see about his orders. He was delighted to learn that he had been assigned to the receiving ship *Pennsylvania* at the Gosport Navy Yard in Norfolk, Virginia. On April 20, 1857, he and Blanche arrived in Portsmouth across the Elizabeth River from Norfolk where they set up housekeeping in a boardinghouse near the navy yard.

Kell's duties aboard the *Pennsylvania* were not arduous, and he would recount in later years that the five months he spent there were among the happiest in his life. In August, Kell was disappointed to learn that he was detached from the receiving ship and posted as a second lieutenant to the store ship *Supply* at the Brooklyn Navy Yard.

USS *Mississippi*
First steam-driven ocean-going capital ship. Commissioned in 1841, Kell served
on this ship on his return from China and Japan.

His disappointment was intensified by the fact that Blanche was now expecting their first child. He was consoled, however, with the knowledge that the *Supply's* cruise to the Cape Verde Islands and Rio de Janeiro would be of a short duration.

On December 6, ten days after Kell and the *Supply* had sailed, Blanche gave birth to a son, Nathan Munroe Kell. As the *Supply* plowed its way through the gray Atlantic on Christmas Day, 1857, Lieutenant Kell was writing to Blanche expressing his hope that, "God has preserved our beloved child to comfort and ever make you happy upon this day....If our lives are spared, what joy awaits my return to behold in your arms our little one so dear to us both." Blanche had suggested before his departure that they begin reading the Bible through, starting on Christmas, so that every evening they would each be reading from the same section of Scripture. Kell wrote that he prayed that if their child had arrived safely, that he might "from this day become more worthy of the mercies and blessings that have attended me through life."[29]

On February 20, 1858, with the *Supply* anchored at Rio de Janeiro, Kell finally received the blissful news for which he had been waiting. By the end of July the *Supply* had returned to the Brooklyn Navy Yard and Kell was on his way home. His homecoming was marred, however, by the crushing news only hours before his arrival of the death of Blanche's mother. Kell had visited her in Philadelphia on his way south and had promised to return with Blanche and the baby, but now it was too late.

Even though Kell had obtained an extension of his leave in order to be with his wife and son, he was determined to secure additional time from the Navy Department. In August he left for New York to tender his request in person to his commanding officer on the *Supply*, and along the way poured out his heart in letters to Blanche. His correspondence at this time reveals a man who now considers home as the "dearest spot on earth," and even more so now that God had blessed him with a son. Kell, too, was more conscious of his relationship (or lack of) to his God, and he expressed his earnest desire to "Bannie" that this would change in the future:

> I hope, dear Bannie, through God's mercy, at the earliest period to unite myself with the church and trust that He will sustain me in so doing. I have long desired it, but have felt myself too prone to sin and now do still so feel, but will trust in Him to sustain me, and then should we be separated by broad oceans and continents there will be that great comfort to each of us that he watches over us as one, and our united prayers will ascend for the guidance of our beloved child.[30]

Kell was unsuccessful in obtaining a detachment from the *Supply*, but because the vessel was not yet ready to sail he did succeed in obtaining a short extension. He returned to Georgia where he saw his son baptized, and by September, Lieutenant Kell was again at the Brooklyn Navy Yard. The *Supply* sailed shortly after his arrival, but this cruise would not be a normal supply expedition. There was a threat of war with Paraguay which had fired on an American warship, and Kell's vessel was carrying supplies for the Brazilian Squadron. If war erupted between the United States and Paraguay, he might not return home for months or even years. Finally, in February of 1859, much to his relief, negotiations were concluded between the two countries and war was averted. Kell, of course, was overjoyed, for now he knew they would set sail shortly for home. On May 8, 1859, the *Supply* dropped her anchor once more at the Brooklyn Navy Yard and Kell was soon on the train to Georgia.

Prior to leaving New York, Kell had been advised by his cousin, Captain James M. McIntosh, to apply for a reassignment to the Warrington Navy Yard near Pensacola, Florida. McIntosh had just been given command of the Florida yard, and Kell was eager to transfer there where he could bring his family also.

After applying for the assignment and reaching his home in Georgia, Kell remained true to his promise to Blanche and was confirmed by Bishop Elliott at Christ Church in Vineville, Georgia. This time, Kell had returned in time, for on June 2, a second son, named after his father, was born.

His request for transfer being granted, Kell reported for duty at the Warrington Navy Yard on July 29, 1859. On his off-duty hours, he began working to provide facilities for his family. He planted a vegetable garden, and in September, moved into a house designated for junior lieutenants. Finally in November, he was able to bring his wife, two sons, and two Negro servants to Florida. Blanche would later recall that the short time they spent at the Warrington Navy Yard was "*one* brief blissful year."[31]

While the Kells settled into their delightful home near Pensacola, Florida, the storm clouds of war were spreading their ominous shadow over the nation. The coming war between North and South would change their lives forever, and Kell felt so strongly about this turning point in his life that he divided his memoirs into two distinct sections. What follows here, in Lieutenant Kell's own words, is Part Two of *Recollections of a Naval Life*.

PART TWO

Recollections of a Naval Life

RECOLLECTIONS

OF A

NAVAL LIFE

INCLUDING THE

CRUISES OF THE CONFEDERATE STATES STEAMERS "SUMTER" AND "ALABAMA"

BY

JOHN MCINTOSH KELL

EXECUTIVE OFFICER OF "SUMTER" AND "ALABAMA"

WASHINGTON
THE NEALE COMPANY, PUBLISHERS
431 ELEVENTH STREET
1900

Chapter One

"A long remaining glory
Of things that now are old!"

CAPTAIN MARRYAT in one of his very entertaining books tells his hero to "give his memory leave [or opportunity] to take a stroll." This advice I often take to myself, having arrived at the age when one loves to dwell upon the past, especially its brightest scenes, and people the halls of memory with friends and pictures that seem more dear and bright than the panorama that is daily passing before our eyes, for pictures graven on the heart need no camera to revive them or make them live again. The year 1860 (and some months of the year before) passed at the Pensacola Navy Yard are very dear to memory. There with the sharer of my destiny we presided over the first home we called our own. We had many little experiences that were very amusing to us, and frittered away a great deal of money on pineapple jam, brandy peaches, elegant preserves, jellies and pickles, which, adorning our storeroom shelves, were the next winter to find their way into the Confederate soldiers' hands at the surrender of the Yard. My wife still rejoices that they fell into their hands instead of the enemy's, and hopes they enjoyed them! We often talk of the back country that fed the Pensacola Navy Yard as a veritable "Land of Goshen," and its remembered luxuries seem as did the "flesh pots of Egypt" to a famishing, exiled people. We there rejoiced in all the dainties and good living of land and sea. Our fish car never became empty; the oyster boats were daily replenished; the country people brought in wild turkeys and venison occasionally, domestic fowls of every kind, with splendid fruit in season; and the little schooners brought the West India fruits to our wharves. We kept "open house" and hospitality knew no limit, for with the best old Negro cook that Georgia could produce our housekeeping was an endless pleasure. The cook was very ambitious that her young mistress should equal, if not surpass, the oldest housekeepers in the Yard, and she was the youngest! Her energy was untiring and her zeal wonderful. She listened patiently to the reading of "Soyer," and if she could not understand his French dishes, she at least tried to rival them, and soon learned to make the Spanish omelettes, filled with the sweet bell peppers chopped into mincemeat, to perfection. We found we had something to be proud of in our cook and our housekeeping.

Bob Minor, Jack Cooper, John N. Maffitt, Willie Whittle, "Youngster" Eggleston, and many others, dear friends of the past, were daily with us, and unless Bob made our baby boys sick with too much candy or his favorite "gum drops," we had nothing to disturb the brightness of our home. Occasionally we "showed off" in a grand dinner in honor of some of my senior officers.*

But these pleasures were doomed to be short lived, as the cloud of war was rising above the horizon and we were nearing conflict that we little dreamed would plunge us into the dreadful war of four long, bitter years; when the South would fight the world, with no hand stretched out in friendly sympathy to aid, and at last give up, unconquered, from sheer exhaustion and despair!

The 20th of December, 1860, found me on my way to Macon, Georgia, where my family had preceded me to spend the coming holiday season at home. The 19th, as I was journeying, news came over the wires that the State of South Carolina had upon that day seceded from the Union.† To some it seemed appalling. To others, burning with patriotic zeal, the step seemed none too hasty for resenting our sectional grievances, and in all there seemed a desire to do one's duty by one's own home and State. Mississippi soon followed the example of her plucky sister State, withdrawing on the 9th of January, 1861. Alabama two days later passed her ordinance of secession, and upon the same day—January 11—Florida withdrew from the Union.‡ At this news I

---

* Two other occasional guests at the Kells was the U.S. senator from Florida, Stephen R. Mallory, who would later become the Confederate naval secretary, and Captain David G. Farragut who became known as the conqueror of New Orleans and Mobile in Federal service.

† Kell is mistaken, South Carolina seceded on December 20.

‡ Florida's ordinance of secession was passed on January 10.

returned to the Pensacola Navy Yard for the gathering up of my house-hold effects, for we had left our home with the pictures hanging on the walls, everything as we had occupied it, and our faithful old cook, Maria, in charge of the establishment she and Poll, the parrot, having a very lonely time. I found great changes. Our house, being untenanted, was made headquarters for the Confederate officers, for the Yard had surrendered in my short absence. Commodore Armstrong had retired and Commodore Victor M. Randolph had taken command. Our neighbor, Mrs. Farrand, had gone into our house and, with motherly care, removed the pictures and bric-a-brac, taking all to her own home, including our silver and valuables. The Confederate officers were very civil and polite to me. I got permission to remove all that was mine from the house, but much had to be left and sacrificed for want of transportation. The uncertainty of the future movements of those still in the Yard made purchasers scarce, though I did sell the good cow, that had been a great comfort to us, for a twenty dollar gold piece. I bade adieu to this beautiful home, its frames and verandahs covered with evening glories in fullest bloom, and the conservatory filled with rare exotics, with a feeling of lingering regret. We had been so happy there, and the future, with its lowering clouds of war and turmoil, promised no compensation (though fortunately we could not foresee its disasters and woes!) for our vanishing happiness.

On the 19th of January, 1861, I attended the State Convention of Georgia, witnessed her withdrawal from the Union, went to the hotel and wrote my resignation (within an hour from her secession) to the Government of the United States, waited its acceptance, and then offered my services to Governor Joseph E. Brown. If not the very first, I was among the first to take this step. Commodore Tatnall was in command at Sackett's Harbor.[*] He being the senior naval officer in the State of Georgia was of course later, on his return, put in command of her naval forces; but just now there was no Navy.

Governor Brown accepted my services, and commissioned me to proceed to Savannah, purchase a steamer, take command of her, and hold myself in readiness for harbor and coast defense. The secession movement of Georgia drew her sons to her soil, and soon all were within her borders. The gallant Tatnall, Charles Morris, my intimate friend and senior; the young Armstrong brothers,[†] Wilbourn Hall, Graves, Stone, all came home to abide by the decision of their State and to share her fortune for good or ill!

---

[*] Josiah Tatnall, sometimes spelled Tattnall, had resigned from the U.S. Navy on February 21, 1861.

[†] Richard F. and Aeneas.

Through old letters of daily correspondence at this time (February, 1861), I find this item: "The *Everglade* returned to Savannah to-day. She has her papers correct, so that the purchase will probably be closed to-morrow, when I will take command. She is to be called the *Savannah.* I have twenty-five men shipped, and hope to make up the fifty men required before I leave."*

On the 28th of February I write: "I took command of the Steamer *Savannah* this afternoon, with officers and men numbering forty-five. I have only three watch officers—Midshipmen Armstrong, Hooper and Meriwether, but I hope to have Lieutenant Armstrong before we sail. I am making every exertion to leave here by Monday or Tuesday next, but find so many repairs and outfits to be made that it will be as much as I can possibly do to be ready by that time. I am occupied every moment of time, but hope in a few days to get things regulated." My first duty was to go to Fernandina, and with permission of Governor Perry, of Florida, to take two guns from that point to Fort Pulaski. On March 22d I write: "I have just arrived in Savannah and find that Commodore Tatnall is here. I shall report to him in the morning. Charles Morris's steamer, the *Huntress,* has arrived.† He will probably get off for duty in a week or ten days." March 25th: "The Commodore visits this steamer to-morrow, and will take a trip down to Fort Pulaski." Early in April I find this item: "While at Brunswick to-day, received orders from Commodore Tatnall to proceed to Savannah without delay." The Monday previous to this date I record: "A very black and threatening cloud making its appearance in the western sky late in the afternoon, and rapidly covering the heavens, by 8 o'clock it became so very dark I had to anchor under the north point of Capelo Island. Finding it bright and clear the next morning I got under way, and at 3 o'clock in the afternoon I anchored off old 'Sunbury,' the home of my childhood. The terror-stricken inhabitants were sure the 'Yankees were upon them.'" One man took to the woods, and not until I went on shore and made myself known would they believe themselves safe. I was then welcomed heartily, and a Mr. Anderson, whom I found living in our old house, kindly offered his vehicle and proffered to drive me to Captain Abiel Winn's (whose wife was my relative). I spent a very pleasant evening with the family and the venerable Colonel Maxwell, much beloved in that county. Upon my return to Savannah I received orders from Commodore Tatnall "to go at once to St. Simon's Island and take the Jackson Artillery from that point to Savannah." This company were from Macon, commanded by Captain Theodore Parker,

---

* Side wheel steamer, 406 tons, one 32-pounder.

† Side wheel steamer, 230 feet, 500 tons, 1 to 3 guns. Later became blockade runner *Tropic.*

First Lieutenant Charles Nisbet. Officers and men were the flower of
chivalry of Georgia's central city. In these later years I have heard many
amusing anecdotes related of the members of this interesting company.
To meet Dr. Mataner, then its efficient young surgeon, and Judge James
T. Nisbet, an honored member of the company, and hear them "spin
yarns," as I am told they do in memory of those patriotic days, must be
a genial social treat. The handsome Lucius M. Lamar, one or both of
the Blooms, and many others of Macon's favorite sons belonged to this
company and were "illustrating Georgia" at this time. I landed them
with guns, equipment, and baggage in safety in Savannah. Captain
Parker received orders to leave the guns, and his company were granted
one week's leave of absence. The following day I received orders to
proceed to Sunbury, taking on board my little steamer to that point the
remains of Commodore James McKay McIntosh, which had been
brought from Pensacola (where they had been temporarily interred)
by his nephew, Lachlan H. McIntosh, and which, through the interest
of his native State and by Act of the Legislature, were to find a final
resting place in the burial ground of his ancestors in old Midway
Churchyard, Liberty County. His relatives, Major William McIntosh,
Lachlan H. McIntosh, Judge McQueen McIntosh, of Florida, his nephew,
John McQueen McIntosh, of Darien, and myself were privileged to accompany these remains as escort. In honor of this event the Savannah
Morning News correspondent, of date of April 18th, says:

> The remains of the late Commodore McIntosh arrived in Sunbury, Lib-
> erty County, the place of his nativity, on Tuesday, the 16th inst., for final
> interment in his native county. The body was conveyed from Pensacola by
> railroad to Savannah, in charge of his nephew, Lachlan H. McIntosh, and
> thence in Steamer *Everglade* (or *Savannah*), Captain Kell, commander, to
> Sunbury, accompanied by the relatives of the deceased. It was here received
> by the Liberty Independent Troop, with appropriate remarks by Mr. W. C.
> Stevens, a member of the corps, and briefly responded to by Captain Kell.
> After the ceremony of reception was over it was escorted by the L. I. Troop
> to the cemetery at Midway, nine miles distant, its final resting place.
>
> An impressive and appropriate prayer was offered at the grave by Rev.
> C. C. Jones, D.D., and after interment a wreath of roses and olive branches,
> entwined by the hands of Mrs. Jones, suspended from the headstone of the
> grave. I herewith transmit copies of the addresses, a publication of which in
> your columns would no doubt be gratifying to the friends of the lamented
> dead.

ADDRESS OF MR. STEVENS.

Captain Kell: Permit me as the organ of the Liberty Independent Troop
to express to you their just appreciation of the service which brings you to
these shores, and their heartfelt cooperation in the funeral obsequies of the

occasion. In the social relations of life, loved and esteemed by his friends for his kindness of heart and manly qualities, Commodore McIntosh was to most of us personally unknown, but history has recorded his public career and his grateful countrymen are ready to award that meed of praise which is the just tribute to merit. By reference to an excerpt of his life we find that he entered the naval service of the United States, September, 1811, and for a period of forty-nine years continued in the active exercise of different vocations, passing through the various grades of service—midshipman, passed midshipman, master, lieutenant and commander—as rapidly as the service would admit. Although never engaged in actual hostilities (if we except the first period of initiation into service) we find him during a reign of national prosperity in offices of important trusts and great responsibility, requiring the exercise of sound judgment and a character distinguished for fearlessness of danger. In 1821 he was attached to an expedition under Captain Kearney for the extermination of pirates on the West India coast. In 1851, after receiving his commission with the rank of captain, he was ordered to the command of the U.S. Frigate *Congress,* attached to the Brazil Squadron under the command of Commodore McKeever. Soon after this he was removed to the command of the Naval Station at Sackett's Harbor, where he remained till 1857, when by order of the President of the United States he became flag officer of the Home Squadron. This command was conferred at a time when British fleets in Southern waters became exceedingly troublesome by attempting to board and search American vessels, but by prudence, judgment, a dignified courtesy, and firm determination, he vindicated and maintained the position his country had ever taken against the right of search, and received for his conduct his country's unqualified approbation. Subsequent to this period Commodore McIntosh was placed in command of the Navy Yard at Pensacola, in which station he expired on the first of September, 1860. Here closed his earthly career, almost up to the point of the dissolution of the Government which he had always served with fidelity and honor, and upon the eve of a great and momentous revolution. Had Commodore McIntosh survived to see this day it is not difficult to surmise what would have been his position in the recent inauguration of political events. Had he lived to behold the Confederate flag of these Southern States thrown proudly and defiantly to the breeze, his ardent and true Southern heart would too surely have reflected the sentiment of its emblematic colors— valor, purity, and truth. But, sir, while we may regret the necessity that sunders the bonds of earthly existence and view with sorrow from life's circle its gems drop away, we must bend to an inexorable fate and bow with submission to the Will of Providence! "The boast of heraldry, the pomp of power, all that beauty, all that wealth e'er gave, await alike the inevitable hour. The path of glory leads but to the grave." And now, sir, with hearts alive to the duties of the occasion we bid you welcome here, and thrice welcome the mortal remains of the gallant Commodore James McKay McIntosh to a final interment in the soil of his native State, and the county of his birth!

To this I replied:

Gentlemen of the Liberty Independent Troop and Citizens of Liberty County: In behalf of the widow and children and the relatives of the deceased I tender you their warm and heartfelt acknowledgments of the consideration and respect thus shown to his memory. It would have been a satisfaction (melancholy, it is true) to his old comrade-in-arms, and brother friend, the gallant Tatnall, to have responded to the kind words that have been spoken. It was his intention and earnest desire to accompany the remains of his deceased friend to their last resting place, but danger threatens our people and he stands at his post ready to meet it. His duty to his State alone prevents his being here, and I know that the noble spirit of his late comrade looks down from Aloft with responsive sympathy and approval. Again do I thank you in behalf of the family and friends of the gallant departed, and beg to present as one of his relatives my own warm appreciation of your sympathy and consideration.

My command in the service of my State was destined to be a very short one. I had two or three more trips southward, including a very pleasant Sunday, when we anchored off Cumberland Island, and I spent a few hours with my friend Mr. Nightengale and family. On returning to Savannah, headquarters for reporting my movements, the last week in April, I received "confidential orders" from the Confederate Government at Montgomery to "report to Captain R. Semmes, at New Orleans, without delay."

Lieutenant Kell, immaculate in his blue Confederate uniform (the switch to gray came later) and neatly trimmed beard, sat for this portrait in New Orleans one day before the sailing of the CSS *Sumter*.

Kell is pictured here standing to the right-rear of Semmes (seated in the center) on the deck of the *Sumter* just prior to her sailing from New Orleans.

Captain Raphael Semmes, CSN
Photographed just prior to the sailing of the CSS *Sumter*

Naval Historical Center

Chapter Two

THE first day of May I parted from my family at Macon, Georgia, as I thought for a few short months, but as it proved in the Providence of God, and in the line of my duty, for three years and four months of the most eventful period of my life. Fort Sumter had surrendered and the times were assuming a warlike aspect, foreshadowing our years of deadly strife. Of this great war I do not propose to write a history. Abler pens than mine have undertaken this work, some satisfactorily. The book written by my great commander and senior, Admiral Semmes, — worthy an honored place in the library of every cultivated American, — discussed the questions of national and political significance of those troublous times.[*] I only wish to give to posterity and to history in these recollections of my life the part it was my duty and my privilege to act in the great drama of the War Between the States. I trust I have in some measure outlived the animosities of those "times that tried men's souls," at least sufficiently so to hold the impartial pen of truth, without which history (no matter how sensationally or attractively adorned or bedecked) must be utterly valueless!

Arriving in New Orleans on the third day of May, I reported for duty to Captain Semmes, who had preceded me by a week or ten days.

---

[*] Semmes' book, *Memoirs of Service Afloat,* was published in 1868.

During a long talk with him I found that a steamer had been purchased by the Confederate Government, which he was to command, and that at his request I had been ordered to this vessel as executive officer. I found her a neat, fast passenger steamer that could be converted into a vessel of war, but many alterations were required for this purpose. The captain had immediately upon arrival commenced this work of remodeling. I found her at Algiers, the shipyard across the river, and as many workmen as could be employed were cutting away the light passenger cabins, strengthening decks for supporting the battery, and shaping her for her destined work. This was no easy task to perform with the appliances at our command. Our pivot gun, whose unique carriage and circles was constructed of railroad iron, — the ingenuity of whose construction was due to the inventive genius of Mr. Roy, — proving the truth of the trite old adage, "necessity is the mother of invention." Our 32-pounders (four in number, as broadside guns) were furnished us from the Norfolk Navy Yard, but the gun carriages had to be improvised, and were very creditably gotten up by our mechanics at the shipyard.*

In a few days all our officers reported for duty and were detailed for superintending work in the different departments. With the great disadvantages under which we labored our work progressed slowly, and consumed much more time than we anticipated. During this detention in fitting our ship for sea the enemy had secured a blockade of the mouths of the Mississippi River, quite effectually making the hope of our escaping lessen day by day, but the delay was unavoidable. About this time we had a sad accident, resulting in the loss by drowning of one of our young officers, Midshipman John F. Holden, of Tennessee. While performing the difficult task of taking out an anchor for the *Sumter,* as she lay in the swift current of the Mississippi, his boat capsized, and before assistance could be rendered three of the crew, with himself, were drowned.†

On the third of June work had progressed sufficiently for us to put the *Sumter* in commission. Our colors were presented by some fair ladies of New Orleans. After completing our outfit we invited on board a number of prominent citizens of New Orleans, together with the ladies who had presented our flag, to accompany us on a trial trip up the river, when we tested the speed of the ship and the quality of

---

* The vessel Kell refers to was the screw steamer *Havana* which had become stranded at New Orleans when Federal blockaders appeared in the Gulf. She was 470 tons, 180 feet long with a 30 foot beam. She had one vertical direct-acting engine driving a single screw, and was capable of only 10 knots.

† Holden had resigned his position as Acting Midshipman in the United States Navy on March 5, 1861.

our battery, both of which proved quite satisfactory. On the 18th of June we steamed down to the barracks below the city to take in our powder, and that night, with a beautiful moon shining, we continued our passage down the river and by daylight next morning came to anchor off Fort Jackson. Here we remained several days, exercising our crew with the battery.

Although our crew were most of them fine sailors, they were not "men-of-war's men," and had to be drilled at the guns. Our crew at this time consisted of 92 men, 20 of whom were marines. Our officers were as follows:

Commander, Raphael Semmes; First Lieutenant, John M. Kell; Lieutenants, Robert T. Chapman, John M. Stribling, William E. Evans; Surgeon, Francis L. Galt; Paymaster, Henry Myers; Captain's Clerk, W. B. Smith; Lieutenant of Marines, B. Howell; Midshipmen, Richard F. Armstrong, William A. Hicks, Albert G. Hudgins, Joseph D. Wilson; Engineers, Miles J. Freeman, William P. Brooks, Mathew O'Brien, Simeon W. Cummings; Boatswain, B. P. Macasky; Gunner, Thomas C. Cuddy; Sailmaker, W. P. Beaufort; Carpenter, William Robinson.

On the 21st of June we hoisted anchor and dropped down to the Head of the Passes for the purpose of taking advantage of the movements of the blockading fleet. The Frigate *Brooklyn* was at Pass á la Loutre and the *Powhatan* was at Southwest Pass. To our great annoyance we had some difficulty in getting a pilot. Captain Semmes dispatched an officer to the pilot's station with a written demand that a pilot be sent immediately on board the *Sumter*. They furnished a very inefficient one, who, when the opportunity offered, declared that he knew nothing of Pass á la Loutre. Captain Semmes, realizing that the opportunity could not be allowed to pass, sternly ordered him to "take us out, and if he ran us ashore or put us in the hands of the enemy he would swing him to the yardarm as a traitor." This threat convinced the pilot that Captain Semmes "meant business" and could not be trifled with, and alarmed him very much, but at the same time we hoisted a pilot signal. This opportunity was given us by the *Brooklyn* giving chase to a vessel off the harbor. All hands were called to "up anchor," and the engineer ordered to get up steam. This was eagerly obeyed.

Our crew had been so tormented with the heat and mosquitoes in the river below New Orleans that they begged to go to sea and fight the enemy, rather than endure such torture, with consequent loss of sleep and rest. We were soon on our way. As we approached the pilot station we saw a small boat shove out from the shore, and in less time than it can be told the boat was alongside of us and a line thrown out to pull it to our gangway without stopping our headway, and the next moment a stalwart young fellow jumped over our side and took his position at our pilot stand, saying, "give her all the steam she can carry." During this time at the pilot station handkerchiefs were waving and all eyes turned in that direction saw the pilot's young wife and sister were waving him and us God-speed and success! This was the last we were to see of the South and our native shores for long months and years!

As we approached the bar there was a vessel ashore with hawsers across the stream to haul her off, which by signal of the pilot were slackened up to allow us to pass. As we rounded this point of the bar the pilot said: "Captain, she's all free; give her hell and let her go." Ordering his little boat to haul alongside, the next moment he and the old pilot (now supremely happy) jumped in, cast off their lines, and pulled for the shore. The *Brooklyn* was now approaching us (having given up her chase) under full steam and sail. We shaped our course to the east, hugging the wind as close as our yards could brace, and putting on all the steam we could carry. We had the advantage of the *Brooklyn* in laying closer to the wind and thus eating to windward of her. With a smooth sea we held our own, and after a chase of forty miles she fired a gun, which fell short, and putting up her helm and clewing up all sails, she gave up the chase and steamed quietly back to her anchorage at the mouth of the passes.*

Seeing our advantage, and being greatly relieved, we manned our yards and gave "three cheers for the Southern Confederacy!" All hands were ordered down to "splice the main brace," in other words, to take a drink to the success of our cause. The next order was to secure our guns and anchors for sea, always keeping a bright lookout for sails, as of course we were now in the track of the enemy's cruisers. We made a pleasant run that night, and the next morning, the second day of July, was a lovely day. We shaped our course to pass to the south side of Cuba, not sighting any sail, for which we were thankful, as we wished to pass out of the land-locked waters of the Gulf.

On our third day out a sail was reported from the masthead standing to westward. As she approached her lines and sails satisfied us that she was the enemy's ship. We rapidly neared her and fired a gun and hove her to. Captain Semmes sent a boat on board, with which the captain returned, bringing his papers. She hailed from Maine, "way down East," and was named the *Golden Rocket*. She was in ballast on her way to Havana for orders.†

The captain upon being told that his ship would be burned expressed great sorrow, which touched our hearts. He stated "that he

---

* The *Brooklyn* carried 21 guns and could do 11.5 knots.

† July 3, 1861.

had lost one ship, and now to have this one destroyed he would be a ruined man, and could never hope to have another command." He was told to return to his ship, gather up the goods and chattels of his own and the crew, and the officer in charge of the boat directed to set fire to the ship. Seeing his ship in flames he shed tears, and we were so sympathetic we at once made up a purse for him. It was a sad sight to sailors' eyes, the burning of a fine ship. We had not then grown accustomed to the sight with hardened hearts. Some weeks afterwards we read through the Northern papers his account of the capture, in which he denounced us as pirates, etc. This proved a check to our unappreciated generosity and closed our sympathetic hearts to future expressions of woe on the part of our enemies.[*]

The following day, continuing our course eastward, we descried two sails, apparently brigantines. We fired blank cartridges to heave them to. They proved to be American, loaded with sugar for English ports, one named the *Cuba* and the other the *Machias.* We placed a prize crew on one and took the other in tow. We could not burn them, as their cargo was neutral, so we determined to take them to Cienfuegos[†] and place them in the hands of a prize master till their capture should be proved legal. Our midshipman, the prize master in charge of the *Cuba,* inadvertently went aloft to look out for land, and a portion of his crew proving treacherous, he was shot and wounded and had to surrender. The other brig we had to cast off (and put in the hands of a prize master) to accelerate our movements to make other captures. The same afternoon we took the *Adams,* of Massachusetts, and the *Ben Dunning,* of Maine.[‡] We put prize crews on board and directed them to hold on to the light-house at Cienfuegos till daylight. At that time, as we anticipated, several other sails came out with the land breeze. We allowed them to pass beyond the marine league, which is the limit of neutrality by international law. By 10 o'clock a. m. we had captured three more ships, two barks, named, respectively, *West Wind,* of Rhode Island, and *Louisa Kilham,* of Massachusetts; also the brigantine *Naiad,* of New York. When we set sail we had quite a little fleet proceeding to Cienfuegos. On passing the fort the commanding officer fired over our heads two ball cartridges from muskets and directed us to come to anchor, our prizes going on. We dispatched an officer to the fort to demand an explanation of this conduct. The officer replied that "our flag was a strange one among the nations of the earth, and having never been seen in these waters before he could not let it pass." In a short

---

[*] The Lincoln government, refusing to imply any legitimacy to the Southern government, continued to brand all Confederate naval activity as "piracy" for the duration of the war.

[†] Cienfuegos, Cuba.

[‡] The *Albert Adams* of Massachusetts.

time the commandant at the fort called upon Captain Semmes, with permission from the Governor of Cienfuegos to proceed to the town. We ordered one hundred tons of coal to be brought to us in launches, and in thirty-six hours we were ready for sea. The captain visited the shore to take observations to test his chronometers, taking with him the junior lieutenant. Upon their return on board we made ready for sea, leaving about midnight.

Our course was now shaped for the Island of Barbadoes, from there for Cape St. Roque, where we hoped to intercept the northern trade for the Pacific and the East Indies. The trade winds, however, were so strong against us, as well as the current, that after seven days out, finding our coal nearly exhausted, we had to resort to sail, and hoisting our propeller* we sailed with the wind a point free for the Island of Curacoa, which lay to leeward of us. We encountered some very rough weather on this passage, but on the 17th day of July got up steam and reduced sail to enter the port. We made signal for a pilot, who came off to us late in the evening, but after ascertaining our nationality he informed us "that it was too late to get up to St. Anne (the little town), but he would come the first thing in the morning to carry us in." Upon his return to shore and advising the American Consul of our nationality, the consul entered a protest against our being allowed to come into port, regarding our war as a rebellion. Captain Semmes, feeling justly incensed, wrote a letter to the Governor of the Island asking that he give a written statement that Holland had closed her ports against the Confederacy. If such were the case he wished to report the same to his Government. Lieutenant Chapman delivered this letter in person. A parley of all the Island officials was held, and in two hours Chapman returned, with the news that we could enter port. We steamed in, passing through a small entrance, almost like a canal, with hotel and stores on either side, opening into a little lake. We rounded to, let go our anchor, hoisted our boats and spread awnings and a few minutes after were surrounded by bumboats ready to supply us with fruits, vegetables, and everything pertaining to the tropics. Our purser was dispatched to purchase, and we at once set to work, with lighters alongside, to coal ship. The water here is so beautifully clear and transparent that one of the amusements of our men was to throw silver coin of the smallest size in the water and see the little boys—the street "gamin" of the town—dive for them and bring them up from water fathoms deep before they reached the bottom.

The American Consul gave us some trouble here, tampering with our men and trying to induce them to "desert from the piratical craft."

---

* Kell evidently was thinking of the *Alabama*. The little *Sumter* had no lifting screw.

After coaling, watering ship, and laying in fresh stores, we left this little land-locked harbor, trying our course to the eastward, against the strong trade wind and equatorial current. We stood over to the Spanish Main to intercept the trade with that coast. Early on the morning of the following day "sail ho!" was cried from aloft, and by half-past six o'clock we had captured the schooner *Abby Bradford*, loaded with flour and provisions, bound for Puerto Cabello. There was no mistaking the "cut of her jib" — she was a "down Easter." We took her in tow and proceeded to port. In the evening we cast off the *Bradford*, with orders for her to hold on to the light, as we did. There being light land breezes and no current, we easily held our position all night. The next morning Captain Semmes communicated with the governor in regard to leaving the prize in the port till properly disposed of. The governor objected most decidedly to this, whereupon the captain concluded to run the risk of sending her in to the Confederacy with her cargo of provisions, placing on her an intelligent quartermaster, who had some knowledge of navigation. He was to take her in by the western passes to New Orleans. In making this attempt, approaching too near the passes, she fell into the hands of the enemy, and our prize crew were taken prisoners, but were not long in being released or exchanged.* We got clear of the harbor, and it was not long before we discovered a sail in sight. We chased her seven or eight miles and finally captured her. She was a bark bound for Puerto Cabello, a part of her cargo belonging to a Venezuelan merchant of that city, and was named *Joseph Maxwell*. Captain Semmes hoped to induce the governor to allow the vessel to remain as a prize till lawfully adjudicated, he giving up the neutral portion of the cargo. The governor, being influenced by the American Consul, disputed the capture as within the marine league. This being so foreign to the truth or facts, Captain Semmes decided to place a prize crew on board, with Midshipman Hicks in charge, to take her to a Cuban port to be placed in the hands of our agent there, then with his crew to make the best of his way to the Confederacy.†

We now put out under steam to continue our voyage eastwards and to avoid the current setting westward we hugged the coast of Venezuela with its high mountains running up from the sea. By this track we avoided the trade winds and partook of some of the influence of the land breeze. In making this trip we encountered heavy rain with violent thunder storms and vivid lightning. In these waters we passed over the coral reefs surrounding the islands called the "Friars," from

---

* The quartermaster was Eugene Ruhl.

† Midshipman William A. Hicks.

their resemblance to monks' heads. Looking down in the pellucid waters one sees exquisite landscapes and fish of every brilliant hue. I am sure that Jules Verne could never have visited these enchanted waters, or we should long ago have been treated to a description of them from his marvelous pen. The next land we sighted was the "Dragon's Mouth," three islands so called from their peculiar shape. Through these we passed and entered the Port of Spain on the Island of Trinidad. On this island is that wonderful freak of Nature, a lake of pure asphalt, a liquid almost as black as jet, which since that day commerce has made wonderfully useful.

Upon my visit to the shore with a brother officer, walking in the principal street of the town, what was my surprise to be greeted by name. A former resident of Savannah, Georgia, whom I knew in my early youth, had become a resident of this island. Mr. Cunningham was very cordial in his greeting and invited us to his house to tea. There we had the pleasure of meeting his sister, who was making a home for him on the distant Island of Trinidad. Their comfortable house was literally embowered with vines, and sat enthroned in the most beautiful and luxuriant tropical foliage. We enjoyed the evening with them very much, and they no doubt enjoyed the talk of old friends and their loved former home in Savannah, for I was able to give them late news, having had my headquarters in that city when in command of the little steamer *Savannah,* I being on duty there when ordered to the *Sumter.* We were allowed to coal here, which delayed us only a day or two, after which we continued our course to the eastward, passing through what is called the "Mona Passage" from the Caribbean Sea into the broad Atlantic.

The coast of Trinidad is very picturesque and mountainous, one might almost say precipitous, and Nature there seems evergreen, so bountiful and beautiful is the foliage of shrubs and trees. As is usual in such countries and climates, bird life is very abundant and the plumage gorgeous and beautiful. Water fowls, pelicans, etc., and in the interior parrots and paroquets and the brilliant little humming birds fill the air. We were told that there was a small species of deer on the island, but we had no time in our busy cruise to devote to the pleasures of hunting, and the chase to which we were to devote ourselves was the chase of ships, and not of the harmless denizens of the forest!

We pursued our course, contending with wind and current (which were both against us and increased daily), with a clear sky overhead. Thus we ran on for some days, when it became evident (our coal running short) that we would have to seek a port to leeward. Captain Semmes ordered the fires banked and sail to be made, shaping our course to Cayenne, in French Guiana. There we hoped to re-coal, and from there continue our course to our desired cruising ground for intercepting the trade which passes around Cape St. Roque from the Pacific and East Indies — in other words, all the trade south of the equator bound to Northern ports. As we approached Cayenne, the Capital of French Guiana (also a penal settlement of France at that time), we found a pilot-boat waiting to take us to a suitable anchorage. Shortly after we arrived we heard salutes being fired, and upon inquiry found it was in honor of the birthday of the French Emperor, Louis Napoleon, it being the 15th day of August. We found Cayenne and its people rather inhospitable, and we could make no purchase of coal, so we proceeded down the coast in the direction of Dutch Guiana. The water on this coast is very shallow, averaging from three to five fathoms. We passed some beautiful islands. On the crown of one of the islands were some guns mounted, and a fine looking building, which we learned was a French hospital or sanitarium for sick soldiers and sailors.

On Sunday, the 18th of August, we approached the mouth of the Surinam River, when the lookout reported a steamer standing towards us. We at once got up steam and beat to quarters, to be ready for a fight if necessary. All the indications were that she was about our size and battery; but our anxiety was somewhat relieved by her coming to anchor about nightfall. We now came to anchor and the crew were allowed to leave their quarters and turn in for a rest, not knowing "what a night might bring forth." The next morning we got under way at daylight. We exchanged colors with the steamer. It proved to be a Frenchman, bound up the river for Paramaribo, as we were. They got a pilot from the light-boat and we followed close in their wake. We steamed up the river, the scenery of which resembling that of Southern rivers, with sugar plantations on either side, but far more tropical, even, than our Southern waters.

Paramaribo is the capital city of Dutch Guiana, and what strikes one most about the city is the growth of the tamarind tree, of which there are beautiful avenues on every side. It somewhat resembles the live oak tree, though it does not grow to such size or spread its branches to the extent of that grand tree. While at Paramaribo we had a ball given in our honor by the "merchant princes" of all classes, without even the distinction of color. Indeed, the coal merchant who favored us most was a quadroon, and quite a gentleman, having been thoroughly educated and cultivated in Holland. The daughters of this man were among the prominent belles and beauties at this ball, bedecked with diamonds and attired in handsome Parisian gowns, and were very graceful in the dance as they were led through its mazy intricacies by our brass-buttoned, lace-bedecked young officers. "When one is in Rome one should do as Rome does," etc. One striking feature of the ball, as the evening and exercise grew warm, was the waving of perfume holders, which was very refreshing. At a late hour we repaired on board ship, feeling that we had enjoyed rather a novel experience at the hands of our hospitable entertainers. But "variety is said to be the spice of life," and life has many phases.

The CSS *Sumter* prepares to sail from New Orleans, June 18, 1861.
Naval Historical Center

The CSS *Sumter* running the blockade out of New Orleans, June 20, 1861.
Naval Historical Center

Chapter Three

HAVING completed our coaling, we made sail the following day, coasting prudently along to avoid the currents as well as the coral reefs, that are so dangerous on that coast, taking advantage of the winds as much as possible to save our coal. We felt our way to the southward and eastward, making for the port of Maranham in Brazil. We rounded Cape Garupi, off which we found very uneven soundings, causing us to draw out as the soundings shoaled, and came to anchor that night in the open sea. The next morning, upon heaving up our anchor, we found it broken from the pitching of the ship and the surging of the windlass. Not seeing any pilot boat, we continued our course under constant use of the lead and line, drawing off as we shoaled the water. Suddenly we ran upon a reef, which gave a shock to all on board. The engine was stopped and reversed, when the influence of the tide in this reversed condition swung us clear. Some fishermen about half a mile from us made attempts to warn us of our danger, whereupon we at once came to anchor and sent a boat for one of them to come and pilot us. To our great relief he did so, and with this aid we hove tip anchor and stood in for the town of Maranham.* There we arrived safely, through an

---
* Semmes in his memoirs records this stop as the Brazilian city of Sâo Luis.

52

almost miraculous escape from wreckage on the coral reefs. Our little ship showed no evidence of injury.

We arrived in Maranham on the 7th of September, a gala day to Brazil,—as the 4th of July is to America,—the day of Brazilian independence and establishment of an empire. The customary official visits were paid, and here Captain Semmes took a little needed rest in a refreshing visit to the shore, while we coaled, provisioned, refitted and repainted ship. The men were given "liberty days," and the officers enjoyed their strolls ashore, where they were hospitably received and entertained at the various city clubs and met many pleasant people. The middle of September found us ready for sea, and getting a pilot on board we left the harbor under favorable auspices, and with pleasant recollections. The following day found us out of sight of the coast of Brazil, and in a favorable position to intercept the trade, which had been the object of our cruise for some months past.

We now let the steam go down and uncoupled the propeller and cruised under sail.* After some days sailing we encountered some most remarkable phenomena in tidal waves and currents, which would occur at certain hours of the day. Like a wall of water, roaring and foaming in its approach like a cataract, it would toss the little ship about like a plaything, making it difficult to keep one's footing. As often as I had crossed the equatorial line I had never before witnessed these tiderips. As they rolled to the northward and westward all would become calm again. After remaining in this latitude and longitude for a few days, one morning the cry of "sail ho!" was reported from the masthead—a very welcome cry, for the quiet of the calm belt was growing very monotonous. Hoisting the "Stars and Stripes" from our peak they were replied to by the same flag.† As the brigantine approached near enough to hail we hauled down the United States flag and hoisted our own, requiring him to "heave to." We found the vessel the *Joseph Parke,* of Boston. We kept the *Parke* for awhile, putting Lieutenant Evans and a prize crew on board, to be used as a scout. To our astonishment we found the ocean almost devoid of the enemy's flag, and after keeping the *Parke* a day or two longer we concluded to make use of her as a target before burning her, which was her final fate. It was a great disappointment to us to find this highway of trade almost deserted by the Federal vessels, for we had long looked forward to reach this cruising ground, with hope of great success. The neutral ships were abundant, but the enemy had grown wary. One little English brigantine, the *Spartan,*

---

* While the *Sumter* did not have a lifting propeller, it could be uncoupled which would allow it to "freewheel" thus reducing drag somewhat.

† It was a common practice in nineteenth-century navies to display the enemy's flag as a means of deception.

resembled the Yankee so closely that we gave her a long stern chase. We made her "heave to" with the American flag at our peak. Upon boarding her we found her a Nova Scotian, with clean hull and long, tapering mast. The captain (no doubt out of patience with the chase we had given him and not in the best of humor), upon being asked the latest news, told us "we [he supposed we were Yankees] had been whipped like the devil at Manassas"; and he did not seem at all sorry for it! Our boarding officer remarked upon his apparent "want of sympathy," when like a true Briton he replied, "I like pluck, and never like to see a bully try to whip a little fellow." Of course we enjoyed the joke, and so did he. We continued in this latitude some days and encountered more of the tide-rips, and some very tempestuous weather as we were nearing the northeast trade winds. We passed through a curious phenomenon of Nature in a cloud of yellow dust, being precipitated apparently from the skies on our decks.

On Sunday, the 27th of October, while enjoying a fine morning and a smooth sea, "sail ho!" was cried from the masthead, reporting a gaff topsail schooner, with taut mast and white sails, showing her Yankee build. As soon as we could get up steam we began chase. We found her very fast and the chase was a long one. When near enough we fired a blank cartridge across her bow, which brought her to with the "Stars and Stripes" flying at her masthead. Upon boarding her she proved to be the *Daniel Trowbridge,* from Connecticut, with a cargo of provisions for the Spanish Main. This capture gave us a full supply of the nicest provisions, of which we were much in need, — beef, pork, all the canned vegetables and fruits from the Northern markets, with crackers and breadstuffs of the finest quality, and a deck load of live stock, such as pigs, sheep, and geese. The transfer consumed a day or two, but was very welcome work to Jack, and gave us several weeks' provisions.

We now steered for Martinique, and soon after entered the harbor of Port de France.* After coming to anchor an officer was dispatched to pay the official call on the commanding officer of the port, the French Admiral Condé, governor of the island. He received our officer very courteously, and showed a kindly disposition to the Confederacy and our struggling cause. The next day Captain Semmes called upon him and obtained permission to land prisoners and get a supply of coal. This being a military port we had to go to St. Pierre to purchase from the market, having sent our purser ahead to secure the same on reasonable terms. We weighed anchor and stood for St. Pierre, where we came to, close in shore, with our anchor in deep water and a hawser securing our stern to the shore, where we lay comfortably to coal and

---

* November 9, 1861.

have some necessary repairs done to our machinery. After coaling ship and waiting for repairs we heard from recent newspapers of the capture of Messrs. Mason and Slidell, forcibly taken from the English Steamer *Trent* by Captain Wilkes, of the United States Steamer *San Jacinto*. Such a high-handed measure on the part of the United States Government elated us with the belief that war with England would ensue, not supposing for a moment that Seward (the shrewd statesman) would apologize or give up his prisoners after the approval and commendation of the people of the Federal States and Congress, and by the Honorable Secretary himself, of this action! This act was too flagrant a violation of the laws of nations to pass. Earl Russell was very positive in his instructions to Lord Lyons to "demand an apology to be made within seven days, or return with his legation and papers to London." This act of course would mean a declaration of war, and England would have been sustained by the European powers, but the Secretary of War humbled himself and the Nation and he made the apology demanded. The Confederate ministers and their secretaries were given up and the South lost the opportunity of recognition and an ally, much to our disgust.

But to proceed with our cruise. I leave history to record the facts that led to the immediate restitution of the Confederate ministers, Messrs. Mason and Slidell.[*]

---

[*] The two Confederate ministers were released on December 27, 1861.

The CSS *Sumter* captures the brig *Joseph Parks*, September 25, 1861.

Chapter Four

MARTINIQUE is one of the Windward group of islands, is of volcanic formation, running from north to south, and is in a higher state of cultivation than the islands that surround it of that group. Its harbors are indentures in the land formed on the west side, and protected entirely from the trade winds. St. Pierre, its mercantile port, runs from the top of the mountains down to the sea, and the streets being paved so as to leave a gutter in the center of the street, shower of rain washes them clean. In the rear of the city are fine botanical gardens, filled with tropical plants. The grounds are beautifully laid out, with inviting springs here and there, charming grottoes, and everything to please the eye and taste. Twenty-four hours after we arrived at St. Pierre the Federal steam Sloop of War *Iroquois* came in, evidently in search of us.[*] She came near enough for us to see the great excitement on board when she found us in port, with the Confederate flag flying at our peak. We saw the telescopes brought to bear upon us, and their evident delight at what no doubt seemed to them their nearness to a long-desired capture. On board the little *Sumter* there was a fiery spirit of resistance manifested. Every man looked after his side arms, and made application for putting in order their short Roman swords with which

---

[*] The *Iroquois* was commanded by James S. Palmer.

they were armed as boarders. It was remarked on board that "so nice an edge was put upon these swords that they might have been used to shave with," and by sunset every man was anticipating, if not desiring, being boarded. The *Sumter* was snugly moored with a long scope of chain ahead and the stern fast to a tree on shore. The *Iroquois* anchored and communicated with the shore. Upon being informed that if she anchored she would have to remain in port twenty-four hours after the departure of the *Sumter,* in accordance with international law, she got up anchor and stood out of the harbor. As night advanced, however, she drew in to the shore, and about 11 o'clock made evident demonstrations of boarding us, as she was heading for us under a low head of steam. All hands were called to quarters on the *Sumter,* the guns were cast loose and trained upon the enemy, and boarders called away. At this time the *Iroquois* rang a bell from her engine room and sheered off from us. It was only a feint, or possibly a change of purpose upon seeing we were not to be surprised, but ready to resist. She rang her bell as signal to go ahead slowly, and steamed out of the harbor. This was our first night's experience, and in the morning Captain Semmes communicated to the governor her strange proceedings. The governor then communicated to Captain Palmer, of the *Iroquois,* that he should require him to observe the neutrality of the port and keep beyond the marine league. We noticed the boats of the *Iroquois* plying between that vessel and an American schooner at anchor in the harbor, and learned from acquaintances on shore during the day that an officer from the *Iroquois* was stationed on the little schooner to give signals of our movements. This was also reported to the governor, but no action taken on it, and the espionage continued.

We were now through with our coaling ship and repairing and were anxious to get to sea. Every evening at sunset all officers and men were required to be on board and steam gotten up, in readiness to make good our escape if the opportunity offered. We had one drawback, the moon and stars were not in our favor, and not until the ninth day of waiting did we find that the night would be sufficiently dark for us to attempt to get out. On the night of the 23rd of November everything was in readiness and all hands called to get the ship under way—the armorer with tools for slipping the cable, the quartermaster with ax to cut the hawser from the stern, and the engineer with steam up, the firing of the 8 o'clock gun being the signal to go ahead. All this was promptly done, and at firing of the gun the little *Sumter* bounded off like a thing of life. Captain Semmes had a little stratagem of his own to carry out. He steamed across the city lights so that he could easily be seen at full speed steering south. Our lookout, instructed to report signals from shore, now reported two red lights, which we interpreted as going south. After running a short distance out southward we got under the shadow of a very prominent boulder, stopped the engines, and while so concealed changed our course to the northward. Our glasses on the *Iroquois* showed her steaming rapidly southward, and before morning we were many miles apart! Poor Palmer, we heard, paid for his want of success by being relieved of his command. After this night of great anxiety we shaped our course for the broad Atlantic. The enemy's cruisers in the land-locked waters of the Gulf were active in pursuit of us, as we found from captured papers, and Captain Semmes now decided to make our way to European waters.

Our frail bark was built and intended for only one night at sea in the run from New Orleans to Havana and the voyage across the Atlantic was a severe test of her seaworthiness. Our course was now to the northward and eastward, which soon put us in the track of commerce between Europe and the West Indies. We were changing from the temperate to the tropic zone, in which latitude we experienced much changeable weather. The second day out we sighted a large ship standing in our direction and evidently of American build. We fired a gun across her bow and hoisted the American flag. She hove to, with Stars and Stripes at her peak, and upon the captain being brought on board with his papers she proved to be the *Montmorency*, of Bath, Maine, from England, loaded with coal for the English mail steamers that touch at St. Thomas. She was bonded and allowed to proceed on her way, as she was carrying neutral property from a neutral port.

The following day we took the *Arcade*, a schooner from Portland, Maine. There being no papers to prove the property neutral, we applied the torch to her and she burned finely. By this prize we learned of "Dupont's grand naval victory at Port Royal," where a fleet of war vessels nineteen in number, with at least thirty transports containing fifteen thousand men, captured two mud forts and a few hundred raw recruits! We now let our fires go down, lowered the smoke-stack and uncoupled the propeller, and put the *Sumter* under sail, as our coal was becoming exhausted and we were not halfway across the ocean. On the 3rd of December we sighted another prize. As she was running down to us we had no chase to make, and hoisted the French colors. When under our guns we hove her to with a blank cartridge, and sending an officer on board she proved to be the *Vigilant*, of Bath, Maine. We got late papers from the North by this ship, containing full accounts of "the blockade of the pirate *Sumter* by Captain Palmer," but no account of his want of success! There was also a graphic description of Commodore Hollins'[*] gallant exploit in introducing the ironclad ram

---

[*] Captain George N. Hollins.

at the month of the Mississippi (in October) into the enemy's fleet, which consisted of the *Preble,* the *Water Witch,* the *Richmond* and the *Vincennes.* While these vessels all escaped except the concussion to the *Richmond* (which was the ship assaulted), the experiment proved of great benefit to the enemy, whose unbounded resources enabled him to introduce the *Monitor* with more favorable results later in the war.[*] The crew of the *Vigilant* were equally divided as to color, and were messed accordingly, all seated at the same mess-cloth. This making no distinction as to color was very amusing to our crew, but seemed to make no difference to our prisoners.

Our next prize was the *Eben Dodge,* from New Bedford, a whaler, bound for the Pacific Ocean.[†] From this prize we took a good supply of fresh water, of which we stood greatly in need, also took stores, clothing and provisions. We took her two fine whaleboats during a rough and tempestuous sea, and after the arduous work of transferring cargo, burned the ship. The weather continued changeable and the falling barometer indicated a coming storm, which we prepared for by sending down light spars and sails, and on the night of the 11th of December the gale broke upon us in all its fury. We now put the *Sumter* under close reefed top-sails and try-sails. The wind and fury of the storm increased to such a degree that I was called by the officer of the deck. Some of our bow ports were being stove in. I summoned the carpenter and his crew and barricaded the ports, and strengthened her in such a manner as to resist the violence of the waves and prevent our gun deck from being flooded. For several hours the gale was furious, but as day dawned the wind and sea moderated sufficiently for us to bear away under our fore-sail, and we ran before a fast following sea. This experience in the *Sumter*, from the unseaworthiness of the little craft, surpassed in danger even the violent typhoon I experienced many years before in the China Seas in the United States Steam Frigate *Mississippi,* of which I was master at the time. The bad weather continued and we were buffeted about with heavy westerly gales, and spent our Christmas Day in mid-ocean, nothing to mark it to poor Jack but an extra "tot of grog," which is known to the sailor as "splicing the main brace." It was so disagreeable that we did not even have muster and inspection, holiday occasions on board ship. After passing through

---

[*] The Confederate vessel Kell refers to was the CSS *Manassas*. She had been built as a privateer but seized by the Confederate Navy and incorporated into their fleet at New Orleans. On the night of October 12, 1861, the *Manassas* under the command of First Lieutenant Alexander F. Warley attacked the Federal vessels at the Head of the Passes at the mouth of the Mississippi River. Although suffering some damage, all of the Union warships escaped.

[†] December 8, 1861.

about two weeks of this monotony we had a change of wind from the eastward. Being in the track of the European trade, we sighted and boarded a number of vessels bound west, but not an American among them. On the 30th day of December we spent the entire day boarding ships of various nationalities. The only compensation for this trouble was that we learned what was going on in the outside world, from which we had been so cut off of late, and through the courtesy of the many ships we received many late and interesting newspapers. The "*Trent* affair" was largely discussed in most of them. American war news was occupying the press of the world. We then learned of England being called upon to mourn the sudden death of "Albert the Good," the lamented Prince Consort.[*]

---

[*] Francis Charles Augustus Albert Emmanuel, husband (consort) of Queen Victoria, died of yellow fever.

The CSS *Sumter*, outwitting the USS *Iroquois*, steams out of St. Pierre, Martinique, November 23, 1861. In reality the departure occurred in the dead of night.

Naval Historical Center

The CSS *Sumter* stops two merchant vessels while flying what appears to be an Argentine flag.

Naval Historical Center

Chapter Five

OUR next port of entry was the beautiful and commodious harbor of Cadiz, which we reached early in January, 1862.[*] We put the ship under steam, and after getting a pilot on board proceeded up this beautiful bay, passing a strong fortification on our starboard side. We had our colors flying, and were saluted by many vessels at anchor in the harbor. We were soon boarded by the health officer, reporting our ship clean and our men well. Captain Semmes communicated with the United States Consul through letter conveyed by the health officer, that we had a number of prisoners on board, crews from the different ships we had destroyed, and he desired, after paroling them, to turn them over to his care. The consul at first refused to take them, but after communicating with the American Minister at Madrid he was instructed to receive them. We were glad to free our decks of the additional numbers that crowded and inconvenienced us.

After getting rid of our prisoners, Captain Semmes applied for permission to go into dock, as we were in a leaky condition. This was refused, with peremptory orders to "leave the port within twenty-four hours." The captain positively declined to do this, and urged that he be allowed to put his ship in seaworthy condition before venturing to

---

[*] The *Sumter* arrived at Cadiz, Spain, on January 4, 1862.

sea again. Another communication with Madrid, and we were allowed to go into dock. Next day we proceeded up the bay about eight miles, where we found everything in readiness, and in a very short space of time we had the little *Sumter* in dock. Upon close inspection we were pleased to find we had not suffered as much as we thought from running on the reefs entering Maranham. There was no injury done to her bottom except displacing a portion of her false keel and rubbing off some of her copper. The troublesome leak proved to be at the journal of the propeller, and was soon repaired. While in dock we had a great deal of trouble with our crew. Cadiz proving very charming, and the inveterate Yankee Consul putting in his work, several of our crew were induced to desert, and we left the port of Cadiz minus half a dozen men. On our return to our anchorage off the city the captain made application to the authorities for the return of our men, as we were informed that they were sheltered at the American Consulate; but we could get no satisfaction, and on the 17th of January we set sail for Gibraltar. As we left the port of Cadiz we saw a Spanish boat with an officer in her bow waving a formidable looking yellow document. It was reported to Captain Semmes. He gave orders to take no notice of it, but increase the speed of the ship. We had been so coldly received in Cadiz that we cheerfully took leave of that port, with no regret at leaving. During the night we ran far enough out to hold on to the light, but after midnight we got up steam for our run to Gibraltar. In all my cruises in the old Navy it had never been my good fortune to enjoy the charming cruise in the Mediterranean. The Pacific, the South American waters, the Gulf, and the far-distant China Seas,—all but the very enjoyable Mediterranean,—had fallen to my lot. As we passed the Pillars of Hercules before entering the strait, I found much to interest and charm me.

We made the light at Gibraltar just at day dawn. As soon as we had light enough to use the telescope we scanned the horizon to see in what company we might shortly find ourselves—whether friend, foe, or neutral. We soon discovered two sails that looked very inviting for a chase—too inviting, indeed, to be resisted. We chased one for about two hours. It proved to be the Bark *Neapolitan,* of Kingston, Mass., with a cargo of sulphur for Boston. The cargo was protected in a measure by being consigned by Baring Bros. to their agent in Boston, but sulphur was contraband of war, and possibly the reputed agent a partner. So Captain Semmes very wisely decided to burn the ship. We transferred the prisoners as quickly as possible, for there was another sail in sight, of Puritanical whiteness, the "cut of whose jib" we thought we recognized. We took time, however, to transfer some of the beautiful fruits belonging to Baring Bros. to our various messes. Figs, raisins, oranges, and other fruits fresh from Sicily were very tempting! The second sail was the Bark *Investigator,* of Maine, her cargo iron ore. She was bound for Wales. Finding her cargo British, we released her under ransom bond. The chase of these vessels had consumed many hours, and lured us away miles to the eastward of Gibraltar.* Between two and three o'clock we turned our head in the direction of the rock, and about seven o'clock in the evening, under the full blaze of Europa Point light, we steamed in and anchored under the shadow of the renowned historic rock. It had been a day of fatigue to all on board, and we were only kept up by the excitement of chase and our surroundings of activity, so the night of rest was gladly welcomed. If I may be forgiven the liberty, instead of using my own descriptive powers (which are poor, at best), I will here give a pen picture of this point in the words of an eminent divine, Rev. Robert Barrett, of Atlanta, who is also a great traveler, and I imagine a great lover of Nature:

> We entered the Bay of Gibraltar at daybreak. Jupiter seemed to rest on the crown of the great rock that loomed above the sea. Below, like sleeping sea birds, lay the dark hulls of many a steamer, ship, and gunboat. I was amazed at the marvelous beauty of Gibraltar. Grim as it appeared from the water, we found it a flower garden where we began to drive along the tortuous road that winds up to the top. Every crevice in the rock seemed to blossom. Such fuchsias, such geraniums I never saw before! At the foot of the rock is a town of 20,000, Spaniards and Moors. The shops and streets present a most novel and interesting appearance. The garrison is composed of 6,000 red coats. This great rock, 1,400 feet high, is hollowed out. A series of galleries or tunnels are cut on the inside, about ten feet back from the outer wall of the precipice. These galleries are pierced every forty feet, for cannon and for light. Still further in the rock are great chambers full of ammunition and provisions sufficient for five years. Thus while this vast mountain of stone is covered with flowers, it fairly bristles with unseen guns. Between Gibraltar and Spain is a strip of neutral ground, flat, unused, barren, useless, like all neutrality! The view of the bay and of the sea from the top of Gibraltar is quite as fine as the Bay of Naples. The snow-crowned summits of the Sierra Nevadas are distinctly seen. The solemn, far-off mountains of Africa suggest mystery. The Mediterranean seems to say, "I mean History." The Atlantic, vast and majestic, stretches toward the West.

If Cadiz tried to freeze us out and gave no hospitable hand to "the stranger at her gates," we were fully compensated for the mortification by the warmth of our reception at Gibraltar. Our "English cousins" warmly welcomed us. Even while obliged to observe a strict neutrality,

---

* The destruction of the *Neapolitan* took place in full view of many interested observers at Gibraltar, but was still in international waters. The *Sumter* anchored at the British base on Januray 18, 1862.

this did not interfere with the social enjoyment of our sojourn among them. We were not unexpected visitors at the port of Gibraltar, for the news of our trouble at Cadiz had preceded us, and the chase we made for the *Neapolitan* had drawn crowds to the signal station to witness the capture, and subsequently our little bonfire had created a great excitement. Soon after anchoring we were made the usual tender of service from the admiral of the port, and had sent a boat to report ourselves to the health officer. By ten o'clock the next morning officers of the Army and Navy, and citizens, began to call on us. At an early hour Captain Semmes went on shore to pay his respects to the military commander of the rock, Sir Wm. J. Codrington, K.C.B. He gave permission to land our prisoners, who were paroled and sent on shore immediately. We were treated with all the courtesy due to our rank, and but one stipulation made, "that we should not pursue the enemy from British neutral territory." This, of course, we could not do in the face of international law, in which our leader was so well learned. Communicating with our minister in England, Mr. Mason (he had just relieved Mr. Yancey, who from ill health gave up his position), we were allowed to draw upon Messrs. Fraser, Trenholm & Co. for repairs to our little craft, sadly in need of them. We then entered heartily into the enjoyments of the port. The clubhouses were opened to us, and we made many pleasant acquaintances. It gives me great pleasure here to record that in those days of recreation I formed a very pleasant friendship, which has not ceased (but grown warmer with the passing years), for a young Canadian, an Army officer, Brown Wallis, a lieutenant in the "Prince of Wales 100th Regiment of Royal Canadians," then stationed at the Rock. Here we also met Major Fremantle, who afterwards, later in the war, visited our Southern States, and was a warm Confederate sympathizer, writing and publishing very interesting accounts of the same.* In writing of my friend, Captain Brown Wallis, a late English paper makes this statement: "Mr. Brown Wallis was one of the original Canadian officers of our regiment. His commission in the 100th bore date July, 1858. During the time he served in the old 100th he was one of the smartest officers and a thorough soldier. He took the greatest possible interest and trouble in promoting and furthering everything for the welfare of the regiment. He left the 100th to take a very responsible and highly important appointment under the Government of Canada. His retirement from the old corps was universally regretted by his brother officers and the rank and file, amongst whom he

---

* Lieutenant Colonel Arthur J. L. Fremantle, a member of Her Majesty's Coldstream Guards, traveled the Confederacy from Texas to Virginia in 1863. His widely read book, *Three Months in the Southern States*, was published the following year.

was so deservedly popular. That he should some years before have given up the profession of the law, for which he was studying, the comforts and luxuries of a home of affluence, to embrace the military profession, won for him the admiration of his friends, and are the best evidence that the spirit of loyalty and patriotism is as strong in the hearts of Young Canada as in any portion of Her Majesty's dominions." He is still a faithful and loyal subject of Her Majesty, being in the Department of Interior, at Ottawa, Canada, and still faithful and loyal to the friendships of his youth, — a noble, earnest English gentleman. Some of my happiest hours of leisure were spent with him at Gibraltar and I review that time with unfeigned pleasure in memory.

The *Sumter* capturing two merchant vessels within sight of the English base at Gibraltar.

Illustrated London News

The immense British bastion of Gibraltar, the finale anchorage of the CSS *Sumter.*

Illustrated London News

Chapter Six

A few days after our arrival at Gibraltar we were invited to partake of one of their greatest sports and pleasures, a grand fox chase. An English nobleman, who owned them, allowed the 100th Regiment to keep his pack of fifty hounds at the Rock of Gibraltar, and it was worth seeing these splendid creatures in twenty-five couples, under full control of their keepers, — hunters, keepers and all in gay attire and eager for the chase. I had often heard and read of the vigor of English women, but saw proof of it at that time. Sir Wm. Codrington, with Lady Codrington and their two young daughters, joined our party.* We crossed the little narrow strip of land that joins the Rock to Spain, and a few miles' ride brought us into the cork woods. The early part of the day we enjoyed the chase through this forest, the echoes of which resounded with the baying of the hounds. The ladies entered keenly into the sport, rode their horses beautifully, with no apparent fatigue, though it must have been a ride of between thirty and forty miles, and returned quite fresh to a seven o'clock dinner! Imagine an American lady doing the same! The cry of the fifty hounds was music, and although on so grand a scale it brought to memory other fox hunts over the red clay hills of Georgia. The dogs ran so admirably

---

* Sir William J. Codrington was the governor general of Gibraltar.

that, to use the huntsman's parlance, you "could cover them with a blanket." We got up two or three of the wily, treacherous, little beasts, but carried none in as trophies. Our ride was over a very broken country. We were fond of riding through the cork woods, but were warned to avoid them. The rough men who barked the trees for the cork of commerce were a set of banditti willing to venture anything for money. They would not have scrupled to capture us had any reward been offered for our heads by our enemies. The cork tree somewhat resembles the oak, though it does not grow so large or have as luxuriant foliage.

After a few days in Gibraltar, and much effort made to procure it, we began to realize the impossibility of securing coal. The captain decided to send the paymaster, Mr. Henry Myers, to Cadiz for it. In accomplishing this duty he was accompanied by a friend, a former United States Consul at Cadiz, Mr. Tunstall. They took passage on a little French steamer that plied between the Rock of Gibraltar and Cadiz, stopping at the Moorish town of Tangier on the route. Arriving at Tangier, they found the steamer would be delayed an hour or two, and so decided to walk up to the hotel. Upon their return to the steamer the ever-watchful Yankee Consul informed the authorities that there was a pirate on shore for whom a large ransom would be paid, thus arousing their cupidity. The two unfortunate gentlemen were set upon by a Moorish mob of soldiers, overpowered and seized, placed in double irons and imprisoned at the American Consulate.

As soon as the news of this high-handed and unjust act reached the Rock, Captain Semmes made every effort for their release. He wrote to the English Minister, asking his immediate influence in the name of civilization and humanity! Mr. Hay refused to interfere, simply declaring the neutrality of his government, and Messrs. Myers and Tunstall were hurried off on board the enemy's Sloop of War *Ino*. From this vessel they were transferred to the Federal Merchant Ship *Harvest Home*, on board of which they were treated with the greatest insult and indignity. Their heads were shaved like felons; they were heavily ironed, and put below hatches and kept in this condition till they reached Boston. There they were imprisoned for awhile, but treated as prisoners of war, and finally released on parole. Paymaster Myers was a most efficient officer and a high-toned gentlemen. The treatment he received aroused in the hearts of his brother officers and shipmates a feeling of righteous indignation. I have at times the pleasure of extending to him the hand of friendship in these more peaceful days.

The career of the doughty little *Sumter* was drawing to a close; dangers seemed to beset her at every turn. We were unable to purchase coal, and could not make the necessary repairs. It would have been absolutely necessary to have had new boilers put in to make another cruise or prolong this one, and we could not have done this short of the shipyards of England. In the face of all these difficulties, — to say nothing of being watched by from three to six Federal cruisers, each one greatly her superior, — Captain Semmes made up his mind, after much deliberation, and with much regret, to lay up the *Sumter* in ordinary, in charge of Midshipman Armstrong, Master's Mate Hester, and ten seamen. To pay off his officers and crew, with instructions to make the best of their way to the South and report to the Government at Richmond, was his next step, and the hour of parting came, upon which we need not dwell.

I have always felt that the little *Sumter* has never had full justice done her, or been accorded her high meed of praise! She was the first vessel to unfurl the flag of the young Confederacy to the nations of the world on the high seas. Frail and unseaworthy at best, her career was a marvel. In the bands of a commander as daring as any Viking in seamanship, she swept the waters of the Caribbean Sea as she moved silently on her career of triumph. No ship of her size, her frailness, and her armament ever played such havoc on a powerful foe! Within the six short months of her brief career she had captured, ransomed, or destroyed seventeen of the enemy's ships, and so alarmed the commercial world as almost to drive their flag from the thoroughfares of the ocean. When Captain Semmes made known his intention of giving up the little craft there was a feeling of sadness among officers and crew. Of course she had done what she could, and there was pride and satisfaction in feeling she had accomplished a great deal, but it seemed to sailor hearts like desertion and abandonment to leave her to an unknown fate! There was no use, however, in the face of the frowning circumstances, to attempt to run the blockade. After consulting by telegram our minister, Mr. Mason, and coming to a decision, the captain gave orders to disband and seek other work for their cause and country. In less than a couple of months the little *Sumter* was sold, and sailed under the British flag as a merchant ship. We afterwards heard she had gone into the port of Charleston, South Carolina, as a blockade runner, the new owner having given her the name *Gibraltar*. After some little time and service she found a watery grave in the North Sea, where two years later her far-famed successor, the *Alabama,* was doomed to sink after an unequal combat, to be seen no more "till the sea gives up her dead!"[*]

---

[*] The *Sumter* was purchased by the Liverpool firm of Melchir G. Klingender which was secretly representing the Fraser, Trenholm and Company. Finally, on February 6, 1863, during a howling gale, the *Sumter* now named the *Gibraltar* escaped to sea. She ran the blockade into Wilmington, North Carolina, in July of 1863, but because of her slow speed waited five months before conditions were favorable for her departure. Shortly after the war had ended the *Gibraltar* foundered in the North Sea and was lost.

About the middle of April we took passage on the English mail steamer for Southampton. She was on her regular trip from India, and had as passengers many Englishmen who had worn out health and strength in the East in search of fortune, and were now returning to Old England with well-filled pockets to recruit broken health and spend their declining years in affluence and comfort. The steamer was fitted up with every luxury and comfort for the East India traveler and we made ourselves very comfortable. As we passed out of the harbor of Gibraltar we cast a lingering look at the little vessel that had been our "home on the rolling deep" during those last exciting months. Many of our hospitable friends and entertainers of the regiment at the Rock were there to wish us a very pleasant voyage home. We were fully prepared to enjoy the voyage as passengers, and not actors, on the magnificent mail steamer, and were delighted with the beautiful scenery on the coasts of Spain, Portugal and France. After six days' pleasant steaming at this charming season of the year, we entered the harbor of Southampton, and after a few hours' rest took rail for London.

An actual photo of the CSS *Sumter* after she had been sold and converted into the blockade runner *Gibraltar*.

Chapter Seven

CAPTAIN Semmes and I took rooms together in Euston Square, a very convenient and central part of the great city. A parlor and two bed-rooms furnished our suite, and we gave ourselves up to rest and enjoyment for a few days. While in London we met many brother officers, some resident in England at the time, and others, like ourselves, birds of passage. We also learned all the Confederate naval news and plans on this side of the water. The new Gunboat *Oreto* (afterwards named the *Florida)* had just sailed, without armament, under the British flag for Nassau, New Providence, where her brave and gallant commander, dashing John N. Maffitt, was waiting for her.* Another new ship, the *290*, was nearing completion, but no officers were yet assigned to her command.† We were all delighted with our minister abroad, Mr. Mason, who had succeeded Mr. Yancey (who on account of failing health had returned home). Mr. Mason was a typical Southern gentleman, a fine representative of the old Virginia school of that day. When we called on him to discuss affairs we were invited to clay pipes and old Virginia tobacco, with true Southern hospitality.

---

* Commander John Newland Maffitt would compile an enviable record with the *Florida*, destroying or bonding 24 Northern vessels between January and August of 1863.

† The "290" was the code designation used by the Laid Shipyard in Liverpool for the vessel that eventually became the CSS *Alabama*.

While in London we had the pleasure of attending Mr. Spurgeon's tabernacle, by invitation of one of his church dignitaries. He offered to provide seats for us. According to appointment we met him the following day (which was the Sabbath) at the door of the tabernacle. He escorted us into the building by a private way, and up a flight of stairs, which opened upon Mr. Spurgeon's platform, in the rear of which were a number of pews. In one of these pews sat Mrs. Spurgeon and family. Opposite them we, with the church officials, took our seats. The enormous building was filled to overflowing, but the greatest order and decorum prevailed. The wonderful speaker was listened to with breathless silence. I was more impressed with his earnestness than his eloquence. I had so lately heard the celebrated Dr. Palmer, of New Orleans, that I think I was mentally comparing the two speakers and giving the palm of eloquence to the latter. At the conclusion of the services the immense throng quietly dispersed. We had heard that Mr. Spurgeon preached to the masses, the working classes of London, and if this was true it was a pleasure to witness their reverence in the tabernacle and upon retiring from it.

At our boarding place in Euston Square we had the pleasure of a visit from a genial English clergyman, Rev. Francis W. Tremlett, in charge of the church at Belsize Park. He was an ardent sympathizer with the South and her cause. He invited us to his house, a beautiful English home presided over by his mother and sister. We accepted this kind invitation and met there many Confederate and English Navy officers. The friendship for Mr. Tremlett and his family here formed has been earnest and life-long.

There was no apparent work for us abroad, and we resolved to turn our faces homeward to the Confederacy. For this purpose, late in May, we took passage in the steamer *Melita* for Nassau, intending to run the blockade from that point into Norfolk, Virginia. The *Melita* was loaded with arms and ammunition and belonged to the English firm of Isaac Bros. Accompanying us on our passage to Nassau was my friend and relative, Hon. John E. Ward, returning from China, where he had been as United States Minister. He had left his family in Europe and was making his way into the Confederacy. He was full of his late mission, and very entertaining. I recollect an amusing anecdote of him in this connection. At his first reception in China, having no official dress (indeed, none was required) yet wanting to impress the high Celestial officials with his personality, he donned his Chatham Artillery uniform, of which honored company he had been captain in Savannah. Through the interpreter the Chinese wished to know the meaning of the letters "C. A." on his belt. With ready wit he told them "China and America." This satisfied their curiosity and their sense of honor and dignity. They were very much flattered, and it had the effect the minister desired.

Arriving at Nassau, we found it a live seaport town, crowded with blockade runners and shipping. The hotels were swarming with Confederates and Federals, the latter driving a lively trade in furnishing arms and equipments to the Confederates. Here we met the gallant Maffitt at work before the Colonial Court getting the *Oreto* cleared of the charge of violating English neutrality, which he was at last, after much effort, successful in doing.* While here Captain Semmes gave up one of his officers, Lieutenant Stribbling, to become the executive officer of Maffitt's ship.† Among the guests at the Victoria Hotel were many ladies from the North and South. Among them shone conspicuously Maffitt's young daughter, handsome and just grown up. The inspiring war song, "Maryland, My Maryland," we heard for the first time from her young lips, and sung with great expression and pathos it made one of the events of the evening at the hotel, and always met a round of applause.‡

Maffitt after great delay got his ship out of this harbor and proceeded to his appointed rendezvous to receive his armament. He had many misfortunes. Yellow fever attacked his crew and he lost many men; poor Stribbling died; his young stepson, Laurence Reed, died; he had the fever himself and his life was given up by all on board. As he lay apparently unconscious (as his physicians thought) he opened his eyes, and, looking around him, said feebly: "Don't give me up; do all you can for me; I haven't got time to die now, there's too much for me to do." He recovered to do grand service in the *Florida*. Maffitt seemed to hold a charmed life — he dashed through the nine ships of the enemy's blockading squadron, and flew into Mobile like a meteor, and when recovered and recruited as to health and acquisition of men, dashed out again, meteor-like, fearless and brave. His notable career on the high seas belongs to the history of the War Between the States. Maffitt lived in his life the truth of the lines:

> "The bravest are the tenderest,
> The loving are the daring."

Though I may have cause to refer to his career again in these annals, I cannot help now saying, with a benediction: "Peace to the ashes, and rest to the soul of one so brave and true!" Maffitt lived many years

---

* The *Oreto* had been detained by British authorities on the pretext that she was receiving arms on board in violation of the Foreign Enlistment Act. It took several long months and a trial in Her Majesty's courts to finally gain the ship's release.

† The unfortunate Lieutenant John M. Stribling died of yellow fever on September 12, 1862.

‡ Florie Maffitt.

after the war, and has left a very interesting family to inherit his virtues and his great name.[*]

While at Nassau Captain Semmes received a letter from Mr. Mallory, Secretary of the Confederate Navy, brought by an officer just from the South, assigning him to the command of the new steamer just finished in England, the *290*. He had instructions to gather up the officers of the *Sumter*, but this it was not possible to do, as they were now too widely scattered and some of them assigned to other duties. We were to make our way back to England, resigning on the altar of patriotism, when almost within sight of home, all hope of reunion and domestic happiness, for another and longer cruise of danger and peril, and, as it proved, with loss of everything save life and honor. But I will not anticipate.

---

[*] Maffitt died at Wilmington, North Carolina, on May 15, 1886.

Stephen R. Mallory, Secretary of the Confederate States Navy
Library of Congress

Commander John Newland Maffitt, CSN Kell met Maffitt in Nassau when he and Semmes were on their way back to England.
Editor's Collection

The CSS *Florida* photographed while in the harbor at Brest, France.
Naval Historical Center

Chapter Eight

I HAVE been perusing some of a batch of old letters written from Nassau and England at that most stirring and enthusiastic period of my life. It makes an old man's pulses quicken and the fires of pride and patriotism rekindle on the altar of a dear lost cause. Under date of July 2d, 1862, Nassau, N. P., I write:

As two steamers leave to-day I will write by each, hoping some among them all may reach home safely. Cousin John Ward left here a week ago in the *Memphis.* He promised to see you and tell you of our movements. We were going to link our fates together, when, as I have written in previous letters, the severe trial came to me in the orders to return to Europe and give up all hope of seeing home and loved ones! God grant it may be for the best! At least the sacrifice is made for our beloved country, and it must be done with a good will and a cheerful spirit. The fortitude with which you and my dear mother bear this separation sustains me through it all, and for every duty. We have just received news of a great victory for us near New Orleans, with the capture of 8,000 prisoners. We can but hope the city has been recaptured, for the feeling of the people must have been intense against the brutal Butler, and cries aloud for vengeance! We anxiously await news from Richmond, as the near approach of the two armies must ere this have resulted in a battle. I leave for Europe in a few days now, in company with Captain Semmes and some other officers, and as soon as practicable after our arrival across the water we will take charge of our new vessel (said to be a superior one), and we will be better able to do good service for our country, than in the little *Sumter.*

We have just heard of the capture of the *Cecile,* by which I sent letters, a package, and late English papers. It is truly disheartening to see so many of our arms, and ammunition falling into the enemy's hands. We risk a great deal to obtain small advantages. I have just had returned from England yours of the 19th of March, the first and only letter since running the blockade, now wanting ten days of being a year! Could we have run the blockade, what compensation in the joyous home-coming! But it is ordered otherwise, and a cheerful acquiescence must be given to our duty. Our beloved Southland requires my services abroad, and they must be given. I would not be worthy of your love if I could ever flinch from duty. As I have written (but you may never have received the letters) two months ago, we laid up our good little ship, the *Sumter,* at Gibraltar as unfit for further service. We left Midshipman Armstrong in charge of her, with ten or a dozen men. All other officers detached with orders to make the best of their way home to report for duty. The captain and I came on together and reached this place a week ago. To our surprise he has received orders transferring him with his officers to a superior new ship, in which I trust we will be able to do good service for our country and her sacred cause. Do tell Mrs. Armstrong that her son is in fine health, left at Gibraltar in charge of the *Sumter* on account of his efficiency. He will be promoted, and join us in our new ship with the rank of lieutenant. Congratulate her for me. I enclose her letters to him from England to Gibraltar.

Under date of Liverpool, August 12th, 1862, I write:

We sailed from Nassau on the 13th of July and arrived here on the 5th of August. Met here the news of several blockade runners getting safely into Charleston and Wilmington. I hope you have my many letters, the boxes and packages. I will try to write from the unfrequented ports into which we go, but I can not even hope to hear from home again till the close of this dreadful war. We go on board ship in two hours, and sail early to-morrow morning to meet our new ship at the appointed rendezvous. She is said to be a beautiful gunboat, and very fast. I hope before very long you will get good accounts of us and our work. She will be christened the *Alabama.* Young Armstrong is to be second lieutenant, tell his mother. I am glad of his promotion, as he is very efficient. God grant this war may close this winter, but should it continue longer we must be brave and bear up cheerfully till we have driven the invader from our soil and established our beloved Southland free and independent among the nations of the earth. God grant it!

We were three weeks on our passage from Nassau to Liverpool, where we were detained some days in making arrangements for our cruise. Our ship had preceded us on the voyage, and we hoped was now safely anchored off the Island of Terceira, our rendezvous, where a sailing ship with our battery and stores had gone before her, and both should be awaiting us if no accident had befallen them. Captain James D. Bulloch, who superintended the building of the *290,* as she neared completion was much annoyed with Federal spies. He conceived the idea of running her out as soon as finished on a trial trip, and in order to avoid suspicion he invited a large party of ladies and gentlemen to accompany him, at the same time chartering a little steam tug to follow the new ship out. The gay party made their appearance at the dock for the excursion at the appointed time, and with all on board for the festive occasion the *290* dropped gracefully down the Mersey and steamed across the Irish Channel, shaping her course to the northward. After the enjoyment of a pleasant run, with music and dancing and an elegant luncheon, the new ship being now opposite the Giant's Causeway, Captain Bulloch made signal for the little tug to come alongside, and the merry party, with himself, were transferred to the tug to return to Liverpool. Captain Butcher, a fine young Englishman, in command of the *290,* received his last instructions from Captain Bulloch, and wishing him God-speed and a safe voyage, the ship proceeded on her way around the north end of Ireland, bound for the Western Islands.[*]

On the 13th of August we left Liverpool in the Steamer *Bahama.* Captain Bulloch felt a laudable pride in his work, and desiring to see the opening of the career of the *290,* accompanied us. We were some days, possibly a week, on our trip to Terceira. On the morning of the 20th of August we sighted the land, and to our great delight we were not long in catching sight of our two ships safely anchored.[†] By 11 o'clock we steamed into the harbor and found the work of transferring had begun. The stores were easy enough to transfer, but the heavy guns were not so manageable, and Captain Semmes quickly decided that we had best go around to Angra Bay, on the western side, to a more sheltered place. The anchorage was very much exposed to the prevailing winds, and the captain communicated with the ships to heave up their anchors and follow the *Bahama* to leeward of the island,

---

[*] Bullock had succeeded masterfully in getting the *Enrica,* as she was now known, out of England. But that night, as he and pilot George Bond sat before the fire in an Irish pub, he was concerned: *During the evening it rained incessantly, and the wind skirled and snifted about the gables of the hotel in fitful squalls. Bond and I sat comfortably enough in the snug dining-room after dinner, and sipped our toddy, of the best colerain malt; but my heart was with the little ship buffeting her way around that rugged north coast of Ireland. I felt sure that Butcher would keep his weather-eye open, and once clear of Innistrahull, there would be plenty of sea room; but I could not wholly shake off an occasional sense of uneasiness.*

[†] Bulloch had dispatched the *Agrippina* loaded with guns and supplies for the *Alabama.* She would continue to be the Confederate raider's supply ship, making several rendezvous with her during her cruise.

and that afternoon we came to anchor with the three ships in Angra Bay. In order to avoid trespassing on the laws of neutrality, the captain decided to take the sailing vessel that had the armament on board outside the marine league. Lashing her securely to the *290,* and providing good fenders to prevent chafing, we got under way and proceeded along the coast to the required distance. We had prepared, before leaving port, heavy purchases for hoisting these large guns out of the hold of the ship to the deck of the *290.* This work required very careful management, for even the natural motion of the sea made it a difficult job. To our great satisfaction it was successfully accomplished in two days, we running in at night to our anchorage, casting off our lashings for the two ships to ride comfortably at their anchors.

The name with which our ship left England was the *290.* This was a mystery in itself, apparently. A Yankee, writing an attempt at history in those times, explains for the benefit of the public that "*290* rebel sympathizers among the moneyed English people had built this Confederate pirate," when in truth she was the 290th ship built by the firm of Laird Bros., shipbuilders, of Birkenhead. I do not know that they took special pride or pains in her construction, but they certainly made "a thing of beauty" in a perfect ship of her! She was built rather for speed than battle, though her means of defense were very good. She was of 900 tons burden, 230 feet in length, 32 feet in breadth, and about 20 feet in depth. Her engine was 300 horsepower, and we carried a condenser by which to get all the fresh water required for the crew. Her sailing qualities were perfect, and when under full sail, from her long lower masts, she had the appearance of being much longer than she really was. Her propeller was so constructed as to be easily detached and hoisted in a well made for the purpose. We could at our pleasure have a steamer or a sailing vessel. She had never the very great speed accredited to her, though when under both sail and steam she could be made to run fifteen knots an hour. Her armament consisted of eight guns — six thirty-two pounders in broadside, one Blakely hundred-pounder rifled gun pivoted forward, and one eight-inch solid-shot gun pivoted abaft the mainmast. The Blakely gun was not very satisfactory. It became easily heated, from deficiency in metal, and the powder charge would have to be reduced on account of the recoil. The crew consisted of about one hundred and twenty men and twenty-four officers that is, the captain, five lieutenants, surgeon and assistant surgeon, paymaster, marine officer, captain's clerk, and three midshipmen. We had four fine engineers, boatswain, gunner, sail maker and carpenter. Chapman, Evans and Stribbling, our lieutenants on the *Sumter,* being out of reach when we arrived in England, we made lieutenants of our midshipmen. Armstrong was called from Gibraltar and appointed second lieutenant, J. D. Wilson, of Florida, was third, John Lowe, of Georgia, was fourth, and Arthur Sinclair, Jr., of Virginia, was fifth. The acting master was Irvin D. Bulloch, of Georgia, a younger brother of Captain Bulloch. Francis L. Galt, of Virginia, was surgeon, and David Herbert Llewellyn, a young Englishman, assistant surgeon. Beckett K. Howell, our marine officer, was of Mississippi, and the younger brother of Mrs. Jefferson Davis. Our midshipmen were Eugene Maffitt, of North Carolina, a son of Captain John N. Maffitt; Edward Anderson, of Georgia, and George T. Sinclair, of Virginia, all mere youths, most of them just out of the Naval Academy at Annapolis. None, with the exception of the captain, the surgeon, and myself, had even reached the prime of life, and while they may not have had "old heads on young shoulders," they had all the alacrity, enthusiasm and bravery necessary for our hazardous cruise and steady, ceaseless work. Our engineers were skillful and efficient. As for the crew, they were a mixture. With some very fine, adventurous seamen, we had also about fifty picked-up sailors from the streets of Liverpool, that looked as if they would need some man-of-war discipline to make anything of them, but we had hope in the old adage, "time will show" (as time did show), that we had some good material to work upon. We were some days transferring battery and stores from the ship sent out ahead of us, and by Saturday night we were ready to take charge of the *290*. We steamed out to sea, six miles, in company with the *Bahama*.

On a lovely Sunday morning (strange fate that Sunday should have been her birthday and also the day of her sad sea burial!) — Sunday morning under a cloudless sky, with the soft breeze blowing upon us across the Island of Terceira — we unfurled from the peak of the ship the banner of the Confederacy. The ceremonies were appropriate and imposing. By order of Captain Semmes all hands were summoned aft to the quarter deck. Mounting a gun carriage the captain read aloud his commission as captain in the Confederate Navy, followed by his orders from the Secretary of the Navy, Hon. Stephen R. Mallory, to take command of the ship we were now to christen the *Alabama*. All officers stood with heads uncovered, as in the presence of Sovereign Authority, and while this ceremony was going on slowly ascending to the peak and royal mainmast head were the ensign and pennant of the new man-of-war. At the conclusion of the captain's words and a wave of his hand a gun was fired, officers and men gave a deafening cheer and the band played "Dixie," the anthem of the new-born Confederacy. The *Bahama* then fired a gun and cheered our flag. The captain in his speech had explained to his listeners the object of the cruise, the war that was going on between the States, also the work and dangers before them; but he offered good pay for the work, and if successful in our cause the extra compensation of the Confederate Government, and invited all who wished to go to the paymaster and sign for enlistment. Of the crews of the two ships — the *Alabama* having taken out sixty and the *Bahama* thirty men — eighty men joined us.

The following day the *Bahama* (Captain Butcher) was to sail for her return to England. Captain Bulloch and he took leave of us, wishing us "bon voyage and Godspeed," and the *Alabama* and *Bahama* parted company. After some necessary work the *Alabama* sailed away to begin her brief but brilliant career on the bosom of the trackless deep!

The Laird Shipyard in Liverpool, England, where the CSS *Alabama* was constructed.

Leslie's Weekly

The CSS *Alabama*

Naval Historical Center

Commander James Dunwoody Bulloch, the genius behind the CSS *Alabama*
Scharf's *History of the Confederate States Navy*

Captain Raphael Semmes, CSN
Editor's Collection

Chapter Nine

OUR new ship was now commissioned, christened, and set sail on a cruise. Of course there was a great deal of work to be done before the *Alabama* would be in shipshape for her memorable cruise in search of Federal merchantmen, with strict orders from the Confederate Secretary to "avoid all engagements with the enemy's ships of war, but to destroy all their commerce that we could in the shortest space of time." We had been out almost ten days and were less than a hundred miles from the point where we put the ship in commission, when we sighted and afterwards captured our first prize—a fine whaling ship, named the *Ocmulgee.** All hands were hard at work with a whale alongside, "trying out the blubber." The amazement of the captain at being taken prisoner was so great as to be really amusing, but he bore it as philosophically as a true sailor could, and that is saying a great deal. We transferred the officers and crew and their personal effects, and burned the ship. We did not do this, however, till the following morning, as Captain Semmes thought that a bonfire at night would proclaim our whereabouts and the work we had begun. We took from her a good supply of beef and pork and some small stores.

We now shaped our course for the Island of Flores, the most western of the Azores. We had spent all our spare time in organizing and

---

* September 5, 1862.

disciplining the crew, messing them, stationing them at quarters, exercising them at the great guns, and all the minor work on board a man-of-war, which is of the first importance, so that we were prepared for an excellent muster, our first since going into commission. This muster was not simply a calling of the roll, but reading the Articles of War, inspection of dress, of neatly trimmed sails, of polished brass and iron works, of white decks, and everything pertaining to the health, comfort and cleanliness of a well-kept man-of-war. The Island of Flores rises like a lone sentinel in mid-ocean, and is very fertile and picturesque. As we approached it there seemed to be a succession of hills with lovely valleys between, and little cottages peeping out from the beautiful foliage, looking very cozy and homelike, and all presenting a high state of cultivation and contentment. I think the habitual cheerfulness on board our ship was due in a great measure to the youth of our officers, and their ardor and patriotism were unfailing. They never flagged or wearied, but were always on the alert to meet every duty, and any pleasure that presented itself was eagerly enjoyed. No matter how hard the day's work, the crew would gather around the forecastle and enliven the evening air with amusing nautical ditties, often of their own improvising, but generally closed the evening's entertainment with the national songs of our own beloved Southland.

Our second prize was the Schooner *Starlight,* of Boston, from Fayal with passengers. She gave us quite a chase, for her captain seemed determined not to submit to capture, but our speed proved too much for him, and a round shot across his bows made him heave to with the Yankee flag flying at his peak.[*] The lady passengers were greatly alarmed, but being informed that they were soon to be landed at Flores, their anxieties were relieved. The following day we ran in so near to land passengers and crew that we were visited by the governor of the Island and most of the prominent citizens. This prize we burned. The same afternoon, continuing our course around the Island, we captured a large whaler, the *Ocean Rover* by name. This ship had been three years out, and was on her return home filled with several hundred barrels of sperm oil. The following morning we captured the *Alert.* She had just left New London with a good supply of winter clothing, and it being just what our crew stood most in need of, it was turned over to the paymaster. Their fresh rations also came in good time to fill our larder. We paroled the officers and crew and sent them ashore. Before sunset of this day we discovered another sail standing in for the Island, a large schooner of Yankee rig. She was about three miles distant, but after half an hour's chase was within range of our guns. We fired a

---

[*] September 7, 1862.

blank cartridge and she hove to, an easy prey. She was the *Weather Gauge,* a whaling ship, six weeks out from Yankeedom.

I have often been asked by persons interested in the cruise of the *Alabama* of the treatment of prisoners by Captain Semmes. The late files of papers taken from these captured ships brought us news of the harsh treatment of our prisoners in Federal hands, among them our former paymaster of the *Sumter* and his companion, Mr. Tunstall, two very innocent victims, and Captain Semmes resolved upon taking some retaliatory measures for this treatment. He accordingly put the captains of the *Starlight* and several other captured vessels in irons, as a counterbalance to the treatment of our officers. The captains were very indignant, as they said, "on account of their positions," but Captain Semmes replied that "Mr. Myers held a high position also, and was a gentleman, an officer of unblemished character and great worth, and should not have been treated like a felon." When opportunity offered, however, they were paroled speedily and released, so their harsh treatment was never of long duration. The prisoners were otherwise well treated, and after six or eight captures the captain concluded to desist retaliatory measures, and treated them only as ordinary prisoners of war. We had a respite of several days before we heard again the welcome cry of "sail ho!" Our next capture was the Whaling Brig *Altamaha.*[*] After taking all her boats and crew we burned her. The following night we captured the Whaling Ship *Benjamin Tucker,* from New Bedford. By ten o'clock we had taken crew and boats and burned this ship. The next morning we made an early capture in the Whaling Schooner *Courser.* These ships gave us seventy or more prisoners, and we were much inconvenienced on board ship in consequence, so we thought best to go back to Flores for the purpose of landing them.

We now stood to the northward and westward, and soon sighted and gave chase to a sail. She proved to be the American Whaling Ship *Virginia.* After three long hours of chase we took her. She bore a proud name, "Virginia," mother of States, mother of statesmen! How dear the name to our Southern hearts, but she (the whaler so misnamed) soon fell a prey to the rules of war. A few hours brought us great change of weather, and our next capture was almost in the face of a storm, but we braved it and took the whaling ship *Elisha Dunbar,*[†] which made our tenth capture in two short weeks! The stormy season was now approaching, and September gales and the later and more to be dreaded autumnal gales made us prudently resolve upon a change of base and new fields of operation. The teeming harvests of the great Northwest

---

[*] September 13, 1862.

[†] September 17, 1862.

would by this time be ready for transportation to Europe, and bountiful Nature had no doubt enough and to spare from her capacious arms, not only for the swarms of Irish, German, Dutch, and other nationalities that had gone over to help in the subjugation of the South, and the establishment of the great and glorious Union (for the money found therein, and not for honor or glory), but also for the trade abroad, so we entered upon the ocean highway of that trade.

It was now October, the most beautiful month of the year, when in the lovely Southland the gorgeous Indian summer sets in, and the skies are blue beyond description, and life seems so beautiful to dream, to love, to live! To the seaman it is often a month of perilous adventure, and especially is it one of danger in the waters to which we were wending our way, and before many days had elapsed we were to experience some very heavy weather off the Newfoundland Banks. Early in October we captured the *Brilliant* and the *Emily Farnum,* both from New York, bound for England, loaded with flour and grain. The *Emily Farnum* showed a neutral cargo, so we made a cartel of her, placing our prisoners on board and sending her on her way. We burned the *Brilliant.* We sighted many ships, but they were all foreigners. We continued our way northward and westward, heading towards New York, where Captain Semmes had planned a surprise for the Board of Trade. He intended to enter Sandy Hook anchorage and set fire to the shipping in that vast harbor. We might have accomplished our plans — we certainly would have tried to carry them out — but for the violent gale, amounting to a cyclone, which we encountered, and which left us in a very disabled condition. But of this hereafter.

On the 7th of October we captured and burned the Bark *Ocean Wave,* and in the light of her bonfire gave chase to another sail. It was a beautiful moonlight night and the chase was exciting in the extreme, and consumed some hours. She was the *Dunkirk,* bound for Lisbon. Two days later we fell in with the *Tonawanda,* of Philadelphia, a large packet ship, which carried a cargo of grain; but she had passengers, mostly women and children. As we had no room for these we were forced to release this ship on ransom bond, but detained her a day or two, lest we should need to put other prisoners on board. This was a prudent move, as we soon took the *Manchester,* a fine ship, grain cargo, bound for Liverpool. We transferred the passengers and crew and burned the *Manchester.* The weather now began to show decided danger of approaching gales, which reduced us to reefed topsails. In this condition our next prize came running down to us under all sail. We fired a blank cartridge across her bow, which brought her to leeward of us. She was the *Lamplighter,* of Boston, with a cargo of tobacco. Captain and crew were brought on board and the ship fired. A wilder scene I never witnessed. The flames ran up the tarred rigging like demons to the mastheads, with burning lanyards flying to the gale!

Each hour of the night the gale increased in fury, and by morning we were overtaken by one of the most violent storms that ever blew across the Atlantic. The wind blew with such force (though we had taken every precaution to have our sails in readiness for it) from southward and eastward as to press our little ship almost under the waves. We battened hatches to keep the seas that were breaking over us from going below, and passed life lines along the decks to keep the men from being washed overboard. Our main brace was carried away, the main yard snapped in two like a pipestem, and the main topsail torn into shreds! It was a time of desperation, but the brave sailors were equal to the work. They secured the main yard and lowered the spars to the deck without loss of life. Suddenly the gale ceased and we lay in a dead calm. Captain Semmes, who was watching the storm, turned to me and said, "Mr. Kell, in a few minutes we will get the wind with renewed violence in the opposite direction." I at once braced the yards and secured the storm staysail to receive the storm from the northwest, and we were prepared to receive the gale that came with greater violence, if possible, than it did before the calm. It lasted two long hours. The little ship labored heavily, but weathered it. In a constant sea service of nearly twenty years I had seen but one gale that could equal this one. That gale we encountered in the United States Steam Frigate *Mississippi,* returning from Commodore Perry's Expedition to Japan. We were out a week from Jeddo Bay. I was master of her at the time. Grand old ship that she was, she rode out that gale magnificently. In the storm to which the *Alabama* was exposed the vortex passed more immediately over us, which made it seem more violent while it lasted.

The CSS *Alabama* sets fire to the *Brilliant* on October 3, 1862.

The *Alabama* in a cyclone, in the Gulf Stream, on the 16th October, 1862

First Lieutenant John McIntosh Kell, CSN
Kell is shown here with the heavy beard that he grew during the war.
Editor's Collection

Chapter Ten

IN our crippled condition we had to abandon our brilliant plans of surprising New Yorkers by setting fire to their shipping, and find our way by sail to milder latitudes. We sailed along the coast of the United States, and two or three days after the gale captured the Ship *Lafayette*, bound for Ireland with grain.* We transferred officers and crew and burned her. On the third day after the burning of the *Lafayette* we sighted to the windward of us a tapering, rakish schooner, of unmistakable American build. We brought her to with solid shot, after a short chase, examined her papers, and finding her a legitimate prize, consigned her to the flames. She was the *Crenshaw*, grain laden, three days out, and bound for Scotland. The weather was still rough and disagreeable, but trade in grain ships was too good to be abandoned for rough weather, and we could not seek our mild latitudes very rapidly. Our next capture was the Bark *Lauretta*, disposed of in the usual way. Our next prize was the Brig *Baron de Castile*, loaded with lumber. We made a cartel of her, as our prisoners were getting inconveniently troublesome again, and sent her to New York. Being in the direct line of trade, and so actively employed, we had to keep our fires banked and be in readiness for the enemy's men-of-war, should any put in an

---

* October 23, 1862.

appearance. Our rather limited supply of coal must soon give out, and it became necessary for us to seek our rendezvous, where by this time a coal ship sent to us by Captain Bulloch should be in waiting to supply us. As we were making our way to the southward, we fell in with a large whaling ship, bound for a long cruise to the Pacific Ocean, the *Levi Starbuck*. She had on board all the necessaries to be desired for such a voyage, besides many articles for trade with the islanders in that distant ocean. After supplying all our wants we burned the ship. We got very late news and papers by her, which were of great interest to us. Our next capture was the *T. B. Wales*, an East Indiaman, bound for Boston. She had on board as passengers the United States Consul to Mauritius, with his wife, three little daughters, and a lady friend. At first the ladies were alarmed at being taken prisoners, but the fright soon wore off, and the children were very contented and happy. They were made great pets of by the officers and parted from us with regret. The consul's wife was an Englishwoman of culture and refinement. We gave up our best staterooms to them, and they fully appreciated our efforts to make them comfortable. We secured from the *Wales* a main yard, which replaced our loss by the gale on the Newfoundland Banks. After getting it aloft in place we were complete again in our sailing capacity.[*]

The *T. B. Wales* had been five months on her homeward journey. Besides getting her main yard, which was almost precisely the dimensions of our ship's lost one, we took a lot of spars, of which we stood in need. We were obliged to destroy some articles of East India workmanship that were highly prized by our lady prisoners, among them some elegantly carved ebony chairs. They seemed deeply to regret the loss of these treasures. They bore us no malice, however, for the fortunes of war. The consul, Mr. Fairchild, after the close of the war, when Captain Semmes was arrested and thrown into a Federal prison, wrote to him and offered to be a witness for him against the many false charges brought against him, among them "cruelty to prisoners." In the admiral's interesting book, written some years after the war, he takes occasion to thank the consul for "this act of a Christian gentleman in those troublous times of malice and unrest." The *Wales* gave us several fine seamen as recruits, and we now numbered about one hundred and ten men, our full complement should have been one hundred and twenty.

We now made our way to Port de France, on the Island of Martinique.[†] As soon as we arrived in this port I was sent by Captain Semmes to call on the French Admiral to present his regards and report

---

[*] November 8, 1862.

[†] The *Alabama* arrived at Port-de-France on the island of Martinique on November 18, 1862.

the arrival in that harbor of the Confederate States Steamer *Alabama.*
The jolly Frenchman received me very pleasantly, but while sending
his very kind regards to Captain Semmes, asked me to say that he advised the captain to bring his ship under the guns of the fort, as the
Scotchman of the *Agrippina* (our coal ship) had, under the influence of
too much Scotch whiskey, communicated on shore that he was there
waiting for the *Alabama,* and that he would not be surprised at any
moment at the appearance of American men-of-war in search of us. I
thanked him, and delivered the message. Captain Semmes summoned
the Scotchman, and in one hour's time the *Agrippina* was under way,
standing out of the harbor with orders to proceed to Blanquilla, on the
coast of Venezuela.

At Port de France we had a most amusing experience with our
men, and at the same time the nearest approach to a mutiny we ever
had on board the ship. Late in the afternoon, having landed our prisoners and received the usual amount of visitors, the "bumboats" put
in an appearance, loaded with fruits, pipes, tobacco, orange water, and
sundries; but as night approached we had reason to believe something
stronger than "orange water" had also been smuggled in. Suddenly
some of the men became noisy and boisterous, a most unusual thing
under our discipline. Upon my going forward to quell the disturbance
on the forecastle, a sailor threw a belaying pin at me that, but for the
drunken aim, might have been serious, and others threatened violence.
Some of the men directed to seize their disorderly comrades refused to
do it, and there was a general defiance of authority. Just at this juncture Captain Semmes appeared on deck. He said quickly, "Mr. Kell,
give the order to beat to quarters." The drum and fife were gotten up
and they fell in mechanically, some of them so drunk they scarcely
knew what they were doing. "At quarters" all officers appear armed
as if going into battle, and twenty-five or thirty armed officers were a
match for a hundred or more men with belaying pins and knives. We
then passed among them as they stood at their guns, the eagle eye of
Captain Semmes pointing out the most disorderly and riotous to be
ironed. There were about twenty of the culprits. He then ordered them
taken to the gangway, and called out for the quartermasters to provide
themselves with draw-buckets, and beginning with the most drunken
culprit to douse them thoroughly with water. The buckets full came
down on them in quick succession. At first they were very derisive,
and cried out, "Come on with your water, we're not afraid of water,"
but before long they began to gasp for breath and shiver with cold.
Then they began to beg for mercy and to promise loudly "never to do
the like again." This ceremony took about two hours, all officers and
men standing at quarters, when the captain turned to me and said,

"Mr. Kell, give orders to beat the retreat." There were none who were not sufficiently sober now to go below and change their wet garments, take to their hammocks, and sleep away their troubles. From that time there was a saying among them that showed the novel mode of discipline was not forgotten (to say the least of it): "Old Beeswax [the captain] is hell when he waters a poor fellow's grog!"

It was well that the captain got the *Agrippina* away on such short notice, for the first call of the lookout in the morning reported a United States man-of-war off the harbor. She was the notorious *San Jacinto,* of Wilkes and Seward fame.* She saw us as soon as we saw her. We were amused at her preparation for combat. Her battery of some fourteen guns, her men double the number of ours, we never for a moment thought of engaging her, or of anything but eluding her giant grasp. We remained at our anchors all day, such of the officers as desired going on shore; the stewards of the different messes all busy laying in fresh stores and fruits. The evening set in dark and rainy. The weather was more kind to us than it was when, almost a year before, the little *Sumter* dodged the *Iroquois* at St. Pierre. Knowing the harbor well, we determined upon taking a southerly direction out. When we had gotten up steam and made all other preparations (having no lights) we passed out without even a glimpse of the *San Jacinto,* but we saw by the papers later that she remained some days off the port, still watching for us, unable to credit the fact that we had really escaped!

After a day and night's run we came to anchor with our coal ship off the barren little Island of Blanquilla, off the coast of Venezuela.† In this out-of-the-way little coral reef we found a Yankee whaling schooner. As we were running under United States colors, the master of the whaler came out to us, delighted to see one of his own gunboats, and offered to pilot us in. He was quite carried away with our guns and battery; said he "thought we could give the Pirate Semmes fits if we met him, and hoped we would." Imagine his state of collapse when he found we were the veritable pirate's ship! The captain invited him to an interview — he was aghast and overcome. The captain told him that "out of respect for Venezuela he had no idea of violating maritime law and jurisdiction, and would not burn his ship (though he had called him a pirate), but he must insist upon his 'making us a visit,'" which meant that he would be detained on the *Alabama* till we were ready to depart. He readily agreed to these terms, and his visit was of some days' duration. During our stay here the mate of the little schooner

---

* Kell is referring to the forced removal of the two Confederate ministers Mason and Slidell from the British mail packet *Trent*. It was Captain Wilkes of the USS *San Jacinto* who carried this out on the high seas.

† November 21, 1862.

sighted a whale off the harbor, and immediately all boats were sent in pursuit of him. They came up with him and had a beautiful chase, which we all enjoyed very much as "lookers-on." In a few hours they had killed him, and taking him in tow brought him to shore, where they tried him out.

We had a pleasant stay here, and took advantage of our opportunity to break out the hold, whitewash, and do many useful jobs, while the officers enjoyed many little fishing frolics, as well as happy sports on shore. Everybody enjoyed the week or ten days' stay at Blanquilla. The crew had liberty days in quarter watches, and bathing on the beach was a favorite amusement. There were flocks of sea birds, flamingo, pelican, gull, sand-snipe, and plover in abundance, and those who went on shore usually came back laden with game. Sharks were not scarce, but being a cowardly fish they seldom attacked a party, usually reserving that sport for a lone fisherman or bather. As a health motive these "liberty days" were always given the crew, and they greatly improved by it. When we had finished coaling and were otherwise ready for sea, we let our visitor depart in peace, but, Captain Semmes cautioned him "not to allow himself to be caught a second time, as it might not fare so well with him." We sent the *Agrippina* to the Arcas Cayes for our next rendezvous, having still a supply of coal on board of her.

Through the capture of late papers we found that General Banks was fitting out a great expedition for the invasion of Texas, to rendezvous at Galveston, which city had fallen into the enemy's hands some weeks before. Our vigilant commander laid his plans accordingly. He knew the Galveston bar, and knew that the transport ships required to carry a vast army of thirty thousand men or more would not be able to proceed far into a harbor that held but twelve or fourteen feet of water. He designed to surprise this fleet, fire into them, set fire to the shipping, and make his escape before they could recover from their astonishment, as the late Northern papers had reported the "*Alabama* on the coast of Brazil on her way to the East Indies." Closely calculating the time, we thought the expedition could not reach the city of Galveston before the 10th of January, and it was now only the last week in November. We had plenty of time to make a few more captures, and possibly we might take a California steamer and fill our strong box with gold enough to help us out!

On the morning of the 29th of November we were coasting along the south side of Puerto Rico, enjoying the beautiful scenery, smooth sea, and gentle breezes, when we passed a large French steamer, also a little English bark, which latter saluted us in passing by dipping her colors to the United States flag at our peak. By nightfall we entered the Mona Passage between Porto Rico and St. Domingo. We did not know but that we should find a man-of-war here, as the papers stated that there were many in search of us. Finding none, we decided they must all be busy blockading the Southern ports. We boarded a little Spanish steamer just from Boston and procured late papers from her. They were filled, literally crammed, with Banks' great expedition, which had given life and activity to all New England, and from revival of trade must have made the war very popular there. We requested the steamer to report us the United States Steamer *Iroquois*. What did it matter? "A rose by any other name would smell as sweet," and we might not arouse such an army of sea hunters if we committed the depredation of a name only! The following bright Sunday morning, while most of the officers were on deck enjoying the atmosphere and scenery so suggestive of history and Christopher Columbus, with his early dreams and realizations, and the men were gathered in groups amusing themselves in their own sailor-like ways, we were startled by the cry of "sail ho!" from the lookout. All eyes were scanning the horizon, and soon discerned the snowy sails and tapering masts of the unmistakable American. A few hours' run brought her within our clutches. The bark was the *Parker Cook*, of Boston, bound for Aux Cayes, south side of St. Domingo. She had everything we needed, Boston bread and crackers of the freshest, beef and pork, cheese and good butter, dried and canned fruits and sundries. With the sun's setting rays we fired our opportune and ample provider and left her to her fate. A little Baltimore schooner was our next capture. She was of little value and her cargo neutral, so we transferred the prisoners of the *Cook* to her and let her go on ransom bond. She had not even given us a chase, and like many things in life what is most easily won is little valued!

Diversions and horseplay for the sailors of the *Alabama*, on shore *(top)*, and on board the cruiser *(bottom)*.

Century Magazine

A romantic drawing by Winslow Homer depicting the fear and trepidation among the passengers of a Northern merchant vessel upon sighting the *Alabama*.

Sketch appeared in *Harper's Weekly*

Chapter Eleven

WE sighted many neutral vessels within the next few days, and one Spanish frigate that at first gave us quite a scare, not knowing but she might be the enemy about to "gobble us up" in the dead hour of midnight. As she took no notice of us we concluded she was a Spanish frigate bound for Cuba. We sighted and afterwards overhauled a French bark, that took no notice of the blank cartridge we fired. The boarding officer asked the Frenchman "why he took no notice of the cartridge, but waited for the shot?" The angry monsieur replied: "I and my government are not fighting anybody! There is no war going on with my people" (a most astonishing fact with his mercurial race!), and he shrugged his shoulders with a Frenchman's disgust. In the early part of December the boatswain had called out "all hands in white frocks and trousers for muster," when suddenly came the prolonged and ringing cry, "sail ho!" "Where away?" cried the officer of the deck. "Broad on the port bow, a large steamer, brig rigged." I took the trumpet and called out, "All hands work ship!" In twenty minutes we were ready. Unfortunately, she was in the wrong direction for a California steamer, such as we wanted. She was northwest instead of southeast. We scrutinized her closely. She had no guns, so must be a packet ship. All her awnings were set, and under those on the upper deck were a crowd of passengers, male and female, and as we drew nearer we could see that there were officers in uniforms and soldiers in groups. The scene was stirring and beautiful. The steamer must have suspected our nationality, and she evidently hoped to reach the marine league, and steered for the Cuban coast. We gave chase, but finding she would not stop we threw a solid shot over her deck. It was an excellent shot and took a chip out of her foremast, and she stopped instantly.* We then steamed up to her and sent a boarding officer on board. He soon returned and reported her the American Steamer *Ariel*, from New York, with five hundred passengers, besides one hundred and fifty marines and some naval officers going out to join the Pacific Squadron. She was a prize of the white elephant style and dimensions, except the prisoners to be paroled. We held her a day or two, in hopes of getting a smaller ship to take passengers and crew, that we might burn her. To secure her we sent our engineer to take out a part of her machinery and disable her temporarily. Our boarding officer, Lieutenant Armstrong, reported all alarm on board among the ladies, but when Captain Semmes sent him back to take charge of her with the promise and assurance that no ill should befall them, they were so won by his courtesy that the fairest among the prisoners began to ask for his bright Confederate buttons as souvenirs of this occasion, and he came back with very few buttons on his uniform and fell into the tailor's hands!

The night we were in company with the *Ariel* we sighted a sail, which proved to be a foreigner, but in returning from the chase, stopping our engine suddenly, a part of the machinery snapped and totally disabled us from moving by steam. This we kept a secret, however, for our prize could easily have escaped us had she known it. At daylight the next morning Captain Semmes sent for the captain of the *Ariel* and told him that the chase we boarded the night before reported to him that the yellow fever was raging in Kingston, Jamaica, where he had intended to land his prisoners and burn the *Ariel*, but humanity forbade his landing helpless women and children in a pest-stricken city, so he preferred releasing him on proper ransom bond, return his machinery, and allow him to proceed with his ship. This he gladly assented to, and the papers were drawn up to that effect. When he returned to the ship the ladies called for "three cheers for Captain Semmes and the *Alabama*," which were heartily given, with a waving of handkerchiefs and adieus. I find the following letter in my old package, written at this time, that may be more graphic than my memory:

> We found no trouble in running clear of the *San Jacinto* the night we left Martinique, from whence we steamed quietly down to an island on the Spanish Main, where we filled up with coals from the bark *Agrippina*, which preceded us, sailing again in a few days. Since then we have captured one

---

* The *Ariel* was stopped on December 7, 1862.

bark and a California steamer outward bound. She had no gold aboard, but we had the greater satisfaction of placing on parole one hundred and fifty United States Marines, besides several prominent Navy officers on their way out to join the Pacific Squadron. Among these officers was Captain Sartori, whom you may remember commanded the little steamer on which my friend Gillis was lieutenant, at the Pensacola Navy Yard. I saw him, but had no talk with him. He was honest enough to tell Mr. Low, who was prize master of the *Ariel,* that he "should state to his Government the erroneous reports in circulation about the *Alabama,* for himself and every passenger on board—amounting in all to about seven hundred—and received the most courteous treatment." Holding the place he does as an officer in the Navy, I am compelled to place confidence in his voluntary proffered statement. We have, however, had statements before of prisoners who, upon reaching their homes, have falsified themselves; but we care not for their report of us, so long as we conscientiously serve the righteous cause of our country. The latest news we have of the war was by that steamer, which brought us dates up to December 1st. The two armies were then on either side of the river at Fredericksburg, our forces under General Lee and the enemy under General Burnside. We doubt if the great battle will be fought there, as it gives the enemy every advantage in ready communication for supplies and reinforcements. That a battle has been fought, and one of great importance, during the past month, I think there is little doubt. The North seem impatient to have their new favorite, Burnside, lead his army into battle, and I hope General Lee will give him a good drubbing (if he has not already done so). I have great fears for our poor seaboard, where their gunboats can operate so effectively. Charleston and Mobile have no doubt been attacked by their ironclads, with what result it is difficult for us to conjecture! I also notice in the papers their raids on our salt-works and lumber mills, when the McIntosh County Dragoons peppered them sharply on two occasions. Once upon going up Sapelo River past Belleville they must have gone within three miles of our place, and perhaps have abducted more of our Negroes; and again I notice they went up to the Ridge in a couple of steamers, landing a hundred or two armed Negroes to reconnoiter (they say) while their boats loaded with lumber. They were fired upon sharply from the undergrowth and the armed Negroes made a masterly retreat to the boats! Upon reading this I concluded that we had no force there, but a few of our friends and relations with shotguns and rifles must have taken shelter in the undergrowth and frightened them off. What an outrage on the civilization of the nineteenth century! Arming our own Negroes to murder our families! We hear that Mr. Lincoln's fiat has gone forth liberating four million slaves on the first day of January. Truly he is a mighty man![*]

---

[*] Kell is referring, of course, to the Emancipation Proclamation which Lincoln issued on September 22, 1862. It was to take "effect" in all areas not under Federal control on January 1, 1863.

Our young boarding officer was struck with the conduct of the male passengers of the *Ariel*. Their watches disappeared like lightning! They flew to their trunks and began overhauling them in the most anxious, secretive manner. "I really believe," said he, "they think us no better than their Northern horde of thieves plundering dwelling houses and robbing defenseless women and children." We spent a day or two at repairs, then being in no hurry we sailed to the southward and westward and carefully feeling our way along the Yucatan Banks we entered the Gulf of Mexico. We sighted a bark standing in the same direction as ourselves. Who should it be but the old Scotch captain and the good Ship *Agrippina*. We had made the voyage from the east point of Cuba without sighting a sail. The ocean seemed lonely indeed. The day after sighting the *Agrippina* we both stood in to the anchorage together at the Arcas Cayes, our rendezvous. It was now the 22d day of December. Here we passed the holy season of Christmas. The time so full of home delights and good cheer was to be to us but a time of memories and work. I find a letter written at that time.

Arcas Cayes, C. S. Str. *Alabama.*
December 25th, 1862.

I take advantage of a quiet Sunday (the last of the old year) to write you, not by a mail steamer, and you may never get the letter; for it no doubt puzzles even the Yankees to fix our whereabouts at the present time, but look on the chart of the world that hangs in your father's library, and in the Gulf of Mexico you can find where I spent my Christmas — latitude 26° 12' north, longitude 91° 53' west — which spot you will find on the Yucatan Banks, west coast. A snug harbor, formed by the little industrious insects of the sea. Three small islands, or cayes, as they are called, form our harbor. Each a few hundred yards only in circumference, and the largest of them not over ten feet above the level of the sea. These coral reefs, although they do not shelter us from the force of the wind which blows violently during the frequent northers at this season of the year, yet form a complete breakwater, so that we may ride safely at our anchors, having a distant view upon the horizon to watch the approach of an enemy. Upon the largest of these cayes is a fisherman's hut, unoccupied at this season, but containing nets and all the implements for taking turtles during the summer, when they abound. We have taken the liberty of using the nets and have succeeded in taking a few turtles. The most interesting sight on shore, however, are the sea birds, which flock here in great numbers to rear their young. It is beautiful to witness the anxious defense the old birds make for the protection of their young ducklings; nor will the old ones be drawn or driven from their nests, unless forcibly removed or killed. This fearlessness, however, is to be attributed in a measure to their ignorance of the depravity or wickedness of man, of which I have no doubt they will be taught a lesson before we leave, for our men, so long at sea, are feasting on fresh eggs and young ducklings, notwithstanding their fishy flavor.

January 1st, 1863. Another New Year has rolled around, but alas, how few the inmates of unbroken homes in our beloved Southland that are permitted to-day to greet each other with the time-honored salutation, "A happy New Year!" Let us not sorrow or despond, but rather lift up grateful hearts that we are still able to defend our homes and firesides from the wicked invasion of the hordes of the enemy and their vandal minions, and God grant that ere another year rolls around our land may rejoice in peace and acknowledged independence!

In one of the early days of the new year, having coaled ship abundantly and gotten everything in trim, we got under way from the Arcas Cayes and began our cruise to Galveston harbor.[*] We gave ourselves five days for the trip, and but for a calm that delayed a day we should have reached our destination on the 10th of January. As it was, the afternoon of the 11th found us with the ship headed for the Galveston lighthouse. The man at the masthead was instructed to look out for an immense fleet anchored there. After what seemed a season of weary waiting to us, the cry came, "Land ho! sail ho!" But what a damper! No fleet; five vessels of war only. Presently a shell or two, thrown by one of the steamers, burst over the city. "Well," said the captain in astonishment, "they would not be firing on their own people. Galveston is recaptured and Banks's great expedition a failure!" And this proved true. General Magruder, with the assistance of Captain Leon Smith and a couple of river steamboats, with a number of sharpshooters on board, had driven the fleet to sea. The recapture of the city had changed the plans of the great expedition. Banks afterwards made the invasion of Texas by the Red River Valley, and was met and repulsed by the gallant Dick Taylor.

While we were talking over the changed condition of affairs, deciding that it would not be safe to tackle five men-of-war, each one of which was doubtless more than a match for us, the lookout cried from aloft, "One of the steamers is coming in chase of us." This was a new role for the *Alabama*! She had done a good deal of chasing, but never been chased before. What was to be done? We must show our heels till we got out of sight of the fleet. In ten minutes we had up steam and started on our decoy. We furled sails and cleared ship for action. We were now about twenty miles from the fleet. The enemy, approaching

---

[*] Semmes' information concerning the Banks Expedition was somewhat in error. The Northern general did indeed sail for the Gulf with a force of 30,000 men, but his destination was New Orleans not Galveston. In the meantime, the Texas port had been recaptured on January 1, 1863 by a combined Confederate naval and land force under General John B. Magruder.

on our starboard bow, took position on our starboard quarter. We were now within a hundred yards of each other, heading in the same direction, when both engines stopped. The enemy hailed, "What ship is that?" We replied, "Her Britannic Majesty's Ship *Petrel.*" We demanded, "Who are you?" but only heard "United States Ship — ," name lost to us. The stranger said, "If you please, I will send a boat on board of you." Captain Semmes turned to me and said, "Are you ready for action?" I replied, "The men are only waiting for the word." He said, "Don't strike them in disguise; tell them who we are, and give the broadside at the name." I took the trumpet and sang out, "This is the Confederate States Steamer *Alabama* — fire!" Away went the broadside. The wind was blowing in the direction of the fleet, and the Federal Admiral must have heard the guns and realized that the vessel he sent in chase had a fight on hand.

The *Alabama* fought starboard broadside and her antagonist port broadside, and with each ship under steam it became a running fight. Our men handled their guns well. The action was sharp and decisive, and did not last long, just thirteen minutes after the firing began the enemy fired an off gun, a signal of defeat. Our men sent up a wild cheer. We steamed close to the vanquished steamer and asked if they surrendered. The captain replied that he did. We then offered assistance, and he said his ship was sinking, and he needed our boats. They were promptly sent. In his report Captain Blake says: "After considerable delay [it no doubt seemed so to him] caused by the report that a steamer was coming from Galveston, the *Alabama* sent us assistance, and I have the pleasure of informing the Department that every living being was conveyed safely from the *Hatteras* to the *Alabama.*"[*]

Immediately after our fight with the *Hatteras* we made sail. When clear of all chances of pursuit we hoisted the propeller and put sail on, as we were running before a northerly gale of wind. The next morning I was on deck very early, looking after the clearing up of ship and putting things in order after the fight, when Captain Blake came up on deck. Having known him in the old service, he saluted me, "How do you do, Mr. Kell? Fortune favors the brave, sir." I thanked him and replied, "We take advantage of all fortune's favors." We ran on with a spanking breeze, and that day sighted and came up with a ship. It was our coal ship, the *Agrippina.* The old Scotchman dipped his colors by way of saluting, and we returned the salute. He little dreamed what work we had accomplished since we parted from him a few days before.

---

[*] The action with the *Hatteras* took place in darkness, but in spite of this, all seventeen officers and 101 men of the Federal vessel were rescued. Two Federal sailors had been killed and five wounded. Six men escaped capture in one of the *Hatteras'* boats.

We continued our course with favorable winds till we approached Kingston, Jamaica, when we lowered our propeller and steamed into the harbor.* Here we met the English admiral of the West India Squadron. Captain Semmes reported his arrival with a number of prisoners. After communicating with the authorities on shore we were permitted to land them which we did after paroling. Captain Semmes, feeling the want of rest and relief from the life on shipboard, accepted the invitation of a friend on shore and visited him at his bungalow on the heights, leaving me in charge of the ship to coal and repair damages received in the fight, which amounted to a few shot holes and some rigging cuts, all of which was soon attended to and the men given liberty. In the company of our recent prisoners all were "hail fellow well met!" Our men, carried away with victory, many of them got gloriously drunk, and gave me a good deal of trouble to get them back and properly sobered. After reporting all things in readiness, Captain Semmes returned on board, quite refreshed from his rest, giving us a glorious description of the difference of temperature he had enjoyed up in the hills. We then got the ship ready for sea and proceeded on our way.†

---

* The *Alabama* arrived at Kingston, Jamaica, on January 20, 1863.

† January 25, 1863.

The sinking of the USS *Hatteras* off Galveston by the CSS *Alabama*, January 11, 1863

The CSS *Alabama* in the harbor of Port Royal, Jamaica, after dropping of prisoners taken from the USS *Hatteras*

Chapter Twelve

WE LEFT Port Royal harbor late in January, about the 25th, bound for the coast of Brazil. We passed through a heavy sea, with a stiff northeaster blowing, but by morning the wind had moderated and the sun rose bright and clear. The first business on hand was a few trial cases and courts-martial of our delinquents and culprits of the few days' stay at Jamaica. These were scarcely disposed of when "sail ho!" greeted the morning air and our listening ears from the masthead. The tapering masts and fluttering sails in the idle breeze proclaimed her nationality. She was the *Golden Rule,* for Aspinwall, and belonged to the Atlantic & Pacific Steamship Company.* We had the satisfaction of burning with this prize a complete set of masts, rigging, etc., meant for the United States Brig *Bainbridge,* that had lately been swept of everything of the kind in a gale off the coast of Aspinwall. We also destroyed a lot of patent medicines. Salt air is very healthy and bracing, and we did not expect to need any of them in our voyage to the distant Cape of Good Hope and the East. The weather was not good at this time; we had head winds to labor against, with diminished speed, and sometimes stiff northeasters blowing, great trials to the mariner. We boarded a brig, but she was Spanish, bound for Havana. Later in the night we

---

* January 26, 1863.

110

hove another sail to with a shot, and sent a boat on board of her. She was the *Chatelaine,* of Boston, just from Guadalupe, where she had discharged a cargo, and was now on her way to Cuba for sugar and rum for the Bostonians. We saved her the trouble of another cargo, and she lit up the heights of Alta Vela, a mountain of rock about fifteen miles from the mainland of San Domingo, and frightened the sea birds, if there were no other eyes to witness the conflagration.

We steamed eastward and anchored off the old town of San Domingo. Here we landed our prisoners of the two captured ships. There is no city in the world of more historic interest than this old city of San Domingo. It was the temporary home of Christopher Columbus, and his last resting place for two and a half centuries. Here his son, Diego Columbus, was sent to enjoy a position of vice-royalty. The ruins of the Palacio of Diego are still to be seen, and also those of the Dominican Monastery, that once sheltered three hundred monks. Who can conjecture at this late period, or what imagination picture, the sorrows of their loveless, homeless, human lives! Yet the self-abnegation with some devout souls must have found its compensation in the comforting love that sometimes fills the hearts of those that "have left all to follow Him." On the cession of the Island of Haiti to France, the remains of Columbus and his brother, Bartholomew, were removed to Havana. San Domingo was founded by Bartholomew Columbus in 1496. The great earthquakes of 1684 and 1691 are responsible for the ruin of the magnificent buildings that once adorned this historic ground, though there has also been much vandalism in later periods, when Sir Francis Drake took the city by assault, and in the years 1822 to 1825, when the Haitians themselves occupied the city for its spoliation and desecration. At the time of our visit its greatness was but a memory and a dream. There were but three craft in its waters, our own one of them. Haiti has been truly called the "Paradise of the Negro." Here fruit abounds the year round. Fish is always abundant. The generous sunshine allows them to do with very little clothing, which the Yankee skipper can supply at small cost, and the people revel in idleness. We tried to make an early start from this land of ease, but the usual supplies of the market, butchers and fruit vendors, all on board for the last refreshing supplies, detained us. Finally getting rid of the motley crowd we turned our head to the eastward and steamed away. The day's run was quiet, and after nightfall we entered the Mona Passage.[*]

Our first capture after leaving San Domingo was the Schooner *Palmetto,* bound from New York for Puerto Rico. We had a chase of some hours to get her, but her papers concealed nothing, made no attempts at neutrality, and her cargo being provisions we helped ourselves to all

---

[*] The *Alabama* sailed from Santo Domingo on January 29, 1863.

articles needed, and burned her.* The next day we descried four sails. The first we gave chase to, but she was to windward and a long way ahead. To secure her we might lose the other three. We abandoned her and gave chase to two of the others. We felt sure they were both Americans, they were so tall and white. One was steering to the eastward and one to the westward. The first was evidently drawing us on to allow the other to escape. Taking her, we put a prize crew on board and started in pursuit of the other. She was less obstinate than her confrère and hove to at the first gun. She was the Bark *Olive Jane*, wine laden from Bordeaux for New York. Not a bottle of brandy or a basket of champagne saw the decks of the *Alabama*! The sea maidens and their lovers must have drunk a libation to the God of War if the flames left any to go down to their seashells and coral homes beneath the waves! We then turned to our first prize. She was the *Golden Eagle*, for San Francisco from the Pacific Islands, cargo guano. We burned her. Though she was the *Golden Eagle*, she (or her cargo) must not be allowed to make the golden grain for our enemies when we had hardly enough for the helpless women and children at home! A day or two after the capture of these two ships we sighted four more sails, all bound for Europe. One was French, the other three English. The next day a lone Portuguese passed us. The following day we came along with a Dutch brig and an English bark, also an English four-master, in none of these did we take special interest. The next morning the lookout reported seven sails, all bound for Europe, all neutral. Truly we were getting into good company. Our dear Maury had so marked the pathways of the sea that they were like the highways of the land, easy to pass by his charts, the lighted lanterns of the deep!

We next, sighted an English ship, and an American almost in her company. The English one saluted us in passing. The American was very chary, and evidently tried to get out of the way. We sent her a shot that made her yield. The boarding officer found her with a cargo of guano from the Chincha Islands, belonging to the Peruvian Government, bound for Antwerp. She was the ship *Washington* (great only in name). We released her on ransom bond on account of her neutral cargo, and put our prisoners on board of her to be landed. On the 1st day of March we found ourselves in the early morning most unexpectedly (for the night had been dark) within a mile or two of a tall American. A gun was all that was required to bring her nearer to us, and we certainly wanted her mail or late newspapers. She was the *John A. Parks*, of Maine, and had lumber on board, bound for Montevideo. We helped ourselves for our carpenter, who was transported with delight. With

---

* February 3, 1863.

all our captures we had never had anything in his line. He had to be remonstrated with, lest he should want it all, as we could not accommodate a cargo of lumber on our little ship all at one time. We burned the *Parks*. The coveted mail both amused and aggravated us. In these papers came news that the "new rebel pirate *Florida* had put to sea to assist the British pirate *Alabama* in her work of destruction to American commerce," etc.[*]

At this time, while the *John A. Parks* was still burning, we came up with an English bark that kindly took our prisoners, the captain of the *Parks*, his wife and two nephews, to land them in England. Our next capture was the *Bethiah Thayer*, from the Chincha Islands, with guano for the Government of Peru. We ransomed her. We were now nearing the equator. We met a number of sails, but all were neutral. About midnight on the 15th of March (the weather was very thick and cloudy) the lookout roused us with "Sail ho, close aboard!" We hailed, but she flew on the wings of the wind. We wore ship and made sail in pursuit, and used all the expedition we could, but by the time our preparations were made she was nearly out of sight. Between three and four o'clock we had gained on her so effectually as to heave her to with a gun. She was the *Punjab*, of Boston; cargo, jute and linseed oil. The cargo being properly certified English property, we released her on ransom bond and sent the prisoners from the *Bethiah Thayer* on board of her to be landed. On the morning of the 23d of March we made two captures, the *Morning Star*, of Boston, and the *Kingfisher*, of Fair Haven, Massachusetts. We released the first on ransom bond and burned the latter. She was a little whaler, and her crew of twenty-five or thirty men all Portuguese. We were now in sight of the commerce of the world and never out of sight of sails. At the crossing of the equator (as all mariners know) the weather is apt to be capricious. Sometimes a thunder storm, followed by light airs and calms. Two days after burning the *Kingfisher* we made two captures, the *Charles Hill* and the *Nora*, both of Boston, bound for Liverpool. We took forty tons of coal and half a dozen recruits from these ships and then burned them.

On the 19th of March we crossed the equator. There was a dense and blinding rainfall, and the great equatorial current was setting to the westward. We had to abandon a chase at this juncture, losing her in the gloom and darkness. The weather continued raining, with fitful gusts and calms, for several days. The 3d of April the clouds lifted in the early morning watch and showed us a tall, fine ship going to the

---

[*] Throughout the war, the Lincoln government refused to publicly refer to the Confederate cruisers as anything but "pirates." This, in spite of the fact, that every nation in the world recognized the de facto existence of the government in Richmond, and its legal right to commission cruisers to destroy Northern commerce at sea.

southward. The wind died away, which was a great help to us, but towards noon a heavy rain set in, when we lost sight of her for a time. We steered in her supposed direction, however, chased all day, and about five o'clock in the afternoon we sent a whaleboat out to find her and halt her, and a boarding officer to take possession. Night was setting in. We hoisted a light to guide them in our direction. In two hours more she was alongside of us, a prize. She was the *Louisa Hatch,* of Maine, with a cargo of coal for the Island of Ceylon. What a godsend in mid-ocean! Hundreds of tons of coal nearing the Brazilian coast, where coal, from its scarcity, always brings from fifteen to twenty dollars a ton. Our old Scotchman and the *Agrippina* were to meet us at Fernando de Noronha, but we could not let the *Louisa Hatch* slip, or destroy her valuable and needed cargo, so we put a prize master on board and directed him to keep in our company. By the 9th or 10th of April we came to our anchorage off Fernando de Noronha. The ship *Agrippina* had never put in an appearance. We concluded the old Scotch sinner had grown to regard us as veritable pirates, or become afraid of our powerful enemy. We knew he had been dispatched to us by our faithful friend Captain Bulloch. No doubt he sold the cargo of coal elsewhere. We now saw the wisdom and foresight of Captain Semmes in holding on to the cargo of the ship *Louisa Hatch.*[*]

---

[*] The "old Scotch sinner," Robert McQueen, did indeed sell the cargo of coal, pocketed the money, and returned to England with, as Semmes later related, "some cock and bull story."

The CSS *Alabama* stops a merchant ship on the high seas.

Chapter Thirteen

TO the mariner in these waters the solid peak of granite that marks and adorns the Island of Fernando de Noronha is nothing new, but it must always excite wonder and admiration as one of the marvelous freaks of Nature in this volcanic region of the earth. The Island is made use of by Brazil as a penal settlement. It is well guarded by troops, and has a Brazilian army officer in command, but having very little trade and little communication with the outside world a more lonely, out-of-the-way rendezvous could not have been chosen for us. It has some little farming interest, worked by the convicts, and we were able to get some fresh supplies. We went through the usual custom of communicating our arrival to the Governor of the Island and he sent an aide to call. The Island is in some parts quite fertile, and I remember that we ate there the young coconut in its custard-like stage, when it can be dipped out of its shell with a spoon, and is very delicious. Captain Semmes and Dr. Galt called upon the governor and found him at a late breakfast, which he insisted upon their partaking of, after which they had cigars, and then horses were ordered that they might accompany the governor in his "morning constitutional." His family were, to say the least of it, "caste," but we were not expected to take notice of so small a matter as that in foreign countries!

It took us some time to coal, and while we were lying in port with the *Louisa Hatch* beside us, two ships (evidently whalers) came in, hove to, and lowered boats. Their object was to barter sperm oil for supplies. As we had no flag in sight they could not know our nationality. They innocently inquired, and our prize master told them "we were a Brazilian steamer bringing convicts." They seemed suspicious of us. We quietly got up steam and moved outside and reconnoitered.* They were outside the marine league. We fired as we drew near, and they made no resistance. One was the Bark *Lafayette,* of New Bedford; we made short work of her. The other was the *Kate Cory,* of Westport. We were going to make use of the latter to convey our prisoners (now quite numerous) to be landed, but a Brazilian schooner that had come to anchor offered to take the prisoners to Pernambuco if we would reward them for their trouble by giving them a few barrels of flour and pork. This we consented to do, and so we burned the *Cory.* We remained some days after coaling, hoping the *Agrippina* would come, but finally giving her up, we went to sea. This was now the latter part of April, and with our bunkers filled and all hands refreshed by a season of rest, we steamed forty or fifty miles to the eastward, let the steam go down, raised the propeller, and quietly began our usual work of watching for the enemy's ships.

We had been but twenty-four hours out when the signal was given, "Sail ho!" Another whaler, thoroughly saturated with oil, returning home after a three years' cruise in the Pacific Ocean. She was the Bark *Nye.* We burned her. The next day we took the *Dorcas Prince,* of New York, bound for Shanghai. The *Prince* was forty days or more out and her newspapers were old. We transferred the master, his wife and crew, and burned the ship. For some days we overhauled nothing. We received through courtesy some papers from a St. John's, New Brunswick, ship, but they had nothing interesting in them. On the 3d day of May we gave chase to a fine clipper ship and took her, the *Union Jack* by name. While we were pursuing the *Union Jack* another sail hove in sight. She also became a prize — the *Sealark,* of New York, bound for San Francisco. Both ships were burned. From these ships we obtained late papers and found that the "Stars and Stripes were waving over half the slave States! In thirty days Charleston would be taken and the Mississippi opened." All very discouraging news to us, but only the greater inducement for vigor in our work. We were making our way toward Bahia with the crews of our prizes, four in number, that must be gotten rid of, as they were more than we could hold with comfort. We reached the anchorage off this city on the 11th of May. The bay and city of Bahia are beautiful and imposing. The city is divided into two parts — upper and lower Bahia. The harbor is so commodious as to take in vessels of any size. Bahia was originally the capital of Brazil, but about

---

* April 15, 1863.

the year 1763 the vice-royalty was transferred to Rio Janeiro. There are few cities of its size that have as many fine public buildings, or as much natural beauty. When one ascends into the hills upon which beautiful residences, as well as public buildings, are situated, the eye takes in the scene below like a vast amphitheater with the lovely bay in front of it. I think the people of Bahia were disposed to be very kind to us, though we had been preceded in our visit there by very condemnatory articles in their papers, complaining of our destruction of the two ships outside the marine league at the island off their coast. The captain with his command of international law soon set them right about that matter. We were a week or more in Bahia, enjoying all the hospitalities of its citizens and the salubriousness of its climate. The men had their runs on shore, and a British merchant gave a very handsome ball to the officers of our ship.

The morning after this entertainment a steamer of war made its appearance in the bay, but showed no colors, it not being the hour for hoisting them. We showed them our colors, and quickly in reply was the Confederate flag thrown to the breeze. It was the *Georgia,* commanded by Wm. L. Maury.* She had come in to meet her coal ship, ordered here to rendezvous. Our old brother officers of the *Sumter,* Chapman and Evans, were on board of her. It was a joy to meet again and hold pleasant intercourse with them in a brotherly way, to exchange our experiences in the time we had been parted, and express our hopes of meeting again at home in brighter times. In a few days we were ready for sea again.

On the 25th of May (a day or two out of Bahia) the shout of "Sail ho!" from the masthead served to remind us that we had regained the track of commerce on the pathway of the deep. We were preparing to chase, when "Sail ho!" rang out again. The ships were in the same direction. We had a rough time boarding and overhauling them. They were the *Gildersleeve,* a New York ship, from London, with coals for some navigation company; the other, the *Justina,* a Baltimore ship. We put the prisoners of the first ship on the *Justina* and released her (as some of her cargo was neutral) on ransom bond and burned the *Gildersleeve.* The next evening we began a chase that consumed the night and amounted to nothing, being only a Dutchman! The next evening we had a successful chase of the *Jabez Snow,* of Buckport, Maine, from Cardiff, with coals for Montevideo. We took provisions and cordage and consigned her to the flames. Our next capture was the Bark

---

* The CSS *Georgia* had been acquired in Scotland by Matthew Fontain Maury, Commander William L. Maury's cousin. The *Georgia* sailed from England on April 1, 1863 for a rendezvous at sea where she received her armament. During her seven month cruise she destroyed or bonded nine Northern merchant vessels.

Amazonian, of Boston, bound for Montevideo. We turned over our prisoners to an English brig to be landed in Rio Janeiro, where he was going, paying well for the courtesy in provisions. The next capture was the Clipper Ship *Talisman,* from New York, bound for Shanghai. She made no pretense at neutrality, and we burned her.*

The coast of Brazil is at all times and in all weathers a dangerous coast, being coral bound, and coasting there can never be a pleasure to the seaman from the amount of anxiety it involves. We were now in the winter season of this country, for their June is as our December, and we experienced some miserable weather. In the middle of June we were compelled to put on our winter clothing to be comfortable. On the 20th of June we captured the Bark *Conrad.* She was a very pretty little vessel, and Captain Semmes resolved to make a cruiser of her. We had captured and taken from the *Talisman* two rifled 12-pounders (brass), which we transferred to our cruiser. Acting Lieutenant Low was made captain; Midshipman George T. Sinclair, first lieutenant; Adolphe Marmelstein, second lieutenant; and two young seamen watch officers, and we gave them ten men. Twenty rifles and half a dozen revolvers completed the armament. We called her the *Tuscaloosa,* being the offspring of *Alabama.* When the *Tuscaloosa* hoisted the Confederate colors three cheers were given by the *Alabama.* The cheers were heartily answered by the small crew of the newly commissioned ship. The youthful captain and crew made sail on their cruise, our first appointed meeting to be at the Cape of Good Hope.†

We now passed some little time of inactivity. We overhauled a good many ships, but all were neutrals. Either our enemy were learning the "tricks of trade," or were too much engaged at home to take care of their commerce abroad, or possibly they were "gaining wisdom by experience" and were daily growing more wary of the few little Confederate cruisers that were trying to do what they could for their blockaded homes and country. It was late in June or the first of July that we next sighted an American. We were actually by this time in search of food. The ship's bread had become both stale and weevil eaten, and we were hoping daily to fall in with a well-provisioned ship. This only could prevent our going all the way to Rio Janeiro for breadstuffs. As Captain Blake, of the *Hatteras,* had once facetiously observed, "fortune favors the brave," and the shot we sent across the bow of our next capture made the ship heave to speedily. She was the *Anna Schmidt,* from Boston, for San Francisco; cargo, sundries, which means everything—food, clothing, medicines all required for the use of man, and

---

* June 5, 1863.

† The *Tuscaloosa* was not very successful, destroying only one prize during her short cruise.

"Boston notions" thrown in for good measure! Such Boston bread, biscuits, and crackers, and all so fresh and good! There was no attempt at protection papers, so we helped ourselves hugely (with thankful hearts) and burned her, after our task of lightening her cargo was finished. We had grown so accustomed to these duties that the days were very monotonous when such work did not present itself. We next took the ship *Express,* of Boston, from Callao, for Antwerp; cargo, guano from the Chincha Islands. The papers were not satisfactory and the ship was burned. The master of the *Express* had his wife and a lady friend on board, and though they were just from Cape Horn there seemed no alternative but that we must take them to the Cape of Good Hope. In the travel of several hundred miles we now made we sighted but one ship.

Captain Semmes thought it best to go first to Saldanha Bay, as we did not know how many Yankee men-of-war we might find waiting for us at the Cape of Good Hope. We arrived at Saldanha Bay on the 28th of July, 1863. Saldanha Bay is in Cape Colony, South Africa, fifty or sixty miles north-northwest of Cape Town. It has a fine anchorage at all seasons of the year, and is the station in this part of the world for the Dutch East India Squadron on the west side. It seems hard to understand or appreciate that it should not hold the place in the commercial world that Cape Town does. It is really a land-locked harbor, where ships of any size may ride at anchor safely, while the gales at Cape Town sometimes cause even the sailor's stout heart to tremble and his cheek to blanch with fear. Arriving at Saldanha Bay we were surprised to find nothing at anchor. We communicated with the shore for supplying the ship with fresh provisions, and sent the seine for securing fish. The fishermen had fine success and reported the bay "grand fishing ground." The original settlers of Saldanha were exclusively Dutch, but the country has for many years past been in the hands of the English. At the time of our arrival there, late in July, we might have expected bad weather, as the month of August would correspond with February in the northern hemisphere, but their winter had not set in, or rather was unprecedentedly mild, and to us delightful. We set to work with a hearty good will to overhaul ship, to look after her machinery, rigging, caulking, repainting, etc. Those not required for the necessary work were given all the delight of going on shore in search of pleasure and amusement, and "Jack" had in turn his "liberty days" to idle and frolic. Although immediately at the anchorage the shore looked barren and rocky, with immense granite boulders and precipices on every hand, proceed a little and Nature asserts her right to deck the earth in verdure, and affords excellent grasses for sheep, that are abundant, and cattle, that are plentiful, but rather undersized. Far back in the interior game is fine and hunting a grand sport. Pheasants are abundant, the deer is native in several varieties, rabbits and quail in bountiful supply, to say nothing of the wilder sport, for the ostrich in its native plains, the lion and tiger in their jungles, and still further inland the majestic elephant is at home.

We were thronged with visitors. All came with extended hands, for the English papers had proclaimed our "piratical deeds," and all seemed anxious to welcome the sea-rover to their shores. The captain had many timely presents to express his gratification over — wild pea-cock to dine on, ostrich eggs fresh for breakfast, one enough for break-fast for the mess; pheasants and quails, and a superb bunch of ostrich feathers (worth several hundred dollars) as a souvenir of his visit. We were kept busy, notwithstanding our other work, in showing the Boers, and sometimes their families, over the ship, to their great pleasure and admiration. When my work was done in superintending the overhaul-ing of the ship I took a little jaunt and recreation, feeling the need of rest and diversion for mind and body.

Having been invited by one of our young visitors (a very promi-nent Boer) to visit him at his home a few miles distant and join him in an ostrich hunt, we made our preparation for the same. Leaving the ship early in the morning, we took horses and rode to his farm, where we found a sumptuous breakfast awaiting us. We had no idea such delicious dishes could be made of the fish which cling to the rocks on these shores, the shells of which we had been collecting as specimens for their great beauty. Everything was abundant and delightfully served, and greatly enjoyed by those who had been three months at sea, and with appetites sharpened by a horseback ride in the early morning. After breakfast we prepared for our hunt. Our friend and host was greatly disappointed that we had brought shotguns instead of rifles. We thought buckshot would be best to secure the birds, but he told us "that they would have very little effect on the hard bones of these enormous birds." Four of us got into what he termed his "Afri-can spring cart" (though we failed to find much spring), he taking the driver's seat and driving four horses. We drove several miles, when he pointed out a little rising ground, where he said he had sometimes seen the birds feeding. We began our lookout and in a few minutes sighted three fine ostriches. He explained to us his mode of approach-ing them. He drove as if to pass them, and made several circles around the birds. They took very little notice of us, only raising their heads occasionally to look at us as they fed. As our circles drew in and nearer to them, he stopped the cart and told us to get out, "as this is a fine opportunity for a shot." We quietly got out, took deliberate aim and fired — without ruffling a feather! The call to "heave to" was disregarded and the majestic birds trotted off, apparently in a slow gait, but making such strides that they covered ground very rapidly in a straight line, and as far as the eye could reach they were going as fast as a horse could run! By this time our "buck ague" began to pass off, and we realized all the disappointment and chagrin of a lost opportunity. We consoled ourselves with shooting at some little spring-bok (a small deer peculiar to those regions), and returned to a grand dinner, after which we drove back to the shore and found our boat in waiting to convey us to our ship-home. If we could have remained long enough our young friend wished to give us an elephant hunt and many other pleasures; but the *Alabama* like "time and tide [and duty] waits for no man," and work gotten through we must ere long leave the beautiful waters of Saldanha Bay.

The CSS *Georgia* which anchored in the harbor of Bahia, Brazil, in company with the CSS *Alabama*

Naval Historical Center

Commander William L. Maury, captain of the CSS *Georgia*

Naval Historical Center

First Lieutenant Robert T. Chapman of the CSS *Georgia*

Naval Historical Center

Chapter Fourteen

THE creeping shadow that throws its gloom athwart the sunshine was in store for us, and grim death (without our knowing it) was soon to look into the face of one of our fine young officers and claim him as his own. Death is at all times a sad and gloomy thing, but when it comes—dreadful, accidental death—in a foreign land, to one young and full of all life's gladness, it is doubly saddening and full of horror! We had faced a great deal of danger, but grim death kept far away till now. Among the last of a party of young hunters to set out for sport and enjoyment on shore was our third assistant engineer, Cummings. The party were just returning at sunset, when in the act of stepping into the boat his loaded gun struck against its side and the load was discharged in Cummings' body near the heart, and he fell back dead upon the shore. His friends and comrades lifted him tenderly into the boat and brought him to the ship to be prepared for his interment. We got permission to lay him to his last repose in the family graveyard of a farmer, who promised that the grave should always be cared for, and with ship's boats amounting to six forming a procession, with funeral stroke and drooping flags we carried his body ashore. I read the beautiful service for the dead over him from my prayer-book, and we buried him and left him to his dreamless rest, the waters of Saldanha Bay his ceaseless dirge till the morning of the resurrection, when the grave (like the sea) "shall give up its dead!" His brother officers raised a subscription among themselves to erect a monument to mark the spot where he sleeps the quiet sleep of death in the land of the friendly stranger.* Many years afterwards I had a call in my office in Atlanta from an uncle of Mr. Cummings, and gave him all these details, which seemed to comfort and gratify him, and he remarked that he would be so glad to recount it to his family, who had mourned long and deeply for the youth who had so sadly passed away from them in his early manhood.

While at Saldanha Bay Captain Semmes received by a little schooner that came in from Cape Town several letters from the merchants there welcoming us to the Colony and offering to supply us with anything we might need, especially coals. Early in August we got under way for Table Bay. I find an old letter in the packet, which I here give, written at that time:

C. S. STR. *Alabama,* At Sea,

July 29th, 1863.

We are now but forty miles from the Cape of Good Hope, and will probably run into Simon's Bay to-morrow to land prisoners, learn the news, etc. I will take the opportunity of writing, hoping some wave of good fortune may attend the receipt in due time of my occasional letters, this one among them. My last was written from Bahia two months ago. It is now over one year since I have heard from home. We have had no news from the United States since the 2d of May. You can imagine our anxiety to learn the result of the spring campaign; how Fighting Joe Hooker fared in his advance upon Richmond; whether our army in the West holds Tennessee, and has beat Rosencrans; indeed, if our arms throughout have been victorious, and conquered a peace. If not, then must this cruel, dreadful war continue till the end of this Administration, when the Yankees may begin to see that the South can never be conquered, and a new President may come in on the popular cry of peace measures.

Simon's Bay

August 12th.

I began this letter two weeks ago, but experiencing a gale of wind that night, we put into Saldanha Bay. Finding we could not do all the repairs

---

* One hundred and thirty-one years later, another funeral procession made its way slowly from Columbia, Tennessee, to "Elm Springs," the headquarters of the Sons of Confederate Veterans on the outskirts of town. Inside the wooden casket, carried on the horse-drawn wagon, were the remains of Second Assistant Engineer Simeon W. Cummings. With the help and assistance of friends in South Africa, including the South African Navy, Cummings' remains had been exhumed and flown to the United States. On Sunday, May 29, 1994, before the eyes of 1,000 attendees singing "What a Friend We Have in Jesus," reenactors of a Confederate Marine Honor Guard fired a twenty-one gun salute, and Engineer Cummings was laid to rest in the soil of his beloved Southland. (From *Gray Thunder* by the editor.)

necessary, and doing all that we could effect within ourselves, we steamed to Cape Town, fifty miles to the southward, and had the good fortune of taking our fifty-sixth prize, the *Sea-Bride,* just as she was steering in for the land bound for the same port as ourselves. We threw a prize crew on board of her, with orders to stand off the coast and meet us at an appointed rendezvous, and continued our way into the harbor. As we approached it was wonderful to behold the people congregated on shore. The hillsides were covered with an excited populace and no sooner was our anchor down than hundreds crowded on board to see the far-famed *Alabama* and Captain Semmes. Their enthusiasm was beyond description, and their hearty welcome and sympathy for our cause truly gratifying. The day following, from early dawn "till dusky eve," was a brilliant, gala day, and our visitors can only be enumerated by thousands! The two days following bad weather prevented as much visiting on board, yet a few of the more daring ones battled with the winds and waves to say they had been on board the *Alabama!* At daylight the next day we got under way and steamed around the Cape of Good Hope to this Bay, where we anchored early in the afternoon (the 9th), and have been busy at work ever since making the necessary repairs; so busy, indeed, that I have not been able to leave the ship, and in consequence have declined many pressing invitations of the most kind and complimentary nature.

August 13th.

The late news of our glorious victory over Hooker near Fredericksburg, and the gallant defense of Vicksburg, is most cheering, and fills our hearts with gratitude to God, and love for our brave and chivalrous brothers of the South. The death of our good and noble Stonewall Jackson must have caused mourning throughout the land, but his last words teach us not to be disconsolate at his loss, since it was God's will that he should be taken from us! We are looking hourly for the steamer from England, which should bring us news from the United States up to the first of July. No doubt important news from Vicksburg, which place has been so formidably attacked by General Grant. God grant us victory! I wrote you all about our putting into commission as a cruiser a little prize we took, naming her the *Tuscaloosa.* Armstrong is well, tell his mother, though I hope she will hear from him at the same time this reaches you.

The capture of the *Sea-Bride* caused a great commotion at Cape Town. She was of Boston, from New York, with a cargo of provisions and notions for trading on the east coast of Africa. We sent an officer on board to procure the ship's papers, and bring on board the *Alabama* the captain and crew, with instructions to "lay off and on the port" till further communication with him. Just below Table Mountain, as it sloped to the sea, the shores were covered with the entire population of Cape Town. We now steered for the anchorage in the bay. As we started for the bay the crowds returned to the wharves in the city to secure boats for visiting our ship. No sooner had we dropped anchor than the visitors began to crowd our decks. The officers and crew took delight in receiving them and in extending to them the hospitality of our little vessel. Captain Semmes sat in his cabin receiving the ovation tendered him by an admiring populace. Bartelli, his faithful and devoted steward, stood at the cabin door and received all visitors with laudable pride. The captain, with pen in hand, was kept busy writing his autograph at the request of his lady visitors. The following day was a gala day. Army officers and their wives, all the city officials and their families called, and we numbered visitors from every class and station in life. The captain took time, however, to arrange for the sale of our prize and cargo for one-third of her value. A speculative Englishman was purchaser, whereupon we got up steam and communicated with our prize, ordering her up the coast to Angra Pequena Bay, situated in the Hottentot country, beyond the limit of the British possessions.

We steamed around the Cape of Good Hope to Simon's Bay, the military station of the colony, where we found Admiral Sir Baldwin Walker's flagship and other English men-of-war. They received us cordially, and we exchanged many pleasant courtesies, they inviting us to dine, etc. We remained in port a few days, and then left to join our prize and conclude our sale. We found her at the place appointed, safely anchored. We went to work to break out the cargo, and took such things as we needed for provisioning our ship. The *Sea-Bride* was loaded with all the luxuries of the New York market. After satisfying our own needs we turned over the remaining cargo and the ship to the purchaser. He transferred the cargo to little coasters, running them into ports in the colony, and no doubt realized a good profit. The ship (as we learned afterwards) was an elephant on his hands. Taking in ballast he ran her around the Cape on the east coast of Africa and tried to get clearance papers from Portuguese ports. Failing at that, or to make sale of the ship, the last we heard of her she was seen as the "Flying Dutchman" off the Cape. So far as we know, thus ended the career of the *Sea-Bride*. We returned to Simon's Bay and received as warm a welcome as upon our first visit.[*]

Admiral Sir Baldwin Walker lived in comfortable style in a neat cottage on the bay. He invited Captain Semmes and I to dine with himself and staff. While at the table the admiral informed Captain Semmes that "if he intended remaining any time he had better change his anchorage nearer the shore, to avoid any conflict with the United States

---

[*] The sale of the *Sea-Bride* was semilegal at best, but Semmes sold the vessel and her remaining cargo for $16,940.

vessel of war *Vanderbilt,* as Captain Baldwin, who had dined with him a few days previous, had stated that he 'was in pursuit of the *Alabama,* and did not mean to fire a shot at her, but to run her down and sink her!'" Captain Semmes quietly replied that "it would take two to play at that game; that the *Vanderbilt* had the speed, being four times as large as the *Alabama,* but he could turn his ship in a very small space, whereas the *Vanderbilt,* from her great length, would require much more room,—which reminded him of the chase of the greyhound and the hare. The greyhound was with his great speed about to overtake the hare, when the hare would turn suddenly and dodge out of the way, and the greyhound would go tumbling on, and lose his game." Admiral Walker, however, impressed upon Captain Semmes that "this was the second time the *Alabama* and *Vanderbilt* had visited his port within a day or two of each other, and possibly the third time they might come into collision." After dinner we joined the ladies of the family, and found the admiral's wife and daughter very charming. At a late hour we took leave and returned on board ship, whereupon the captain gave orders to "get under way and stand to sea." The next morning we were fifty miles from the Cape, and continued under steam and sail that day till we struck the "brave West winds" described so graphically by Commodore Maury in his "Geography of the Sea."

We now hoisted our propeller, banked fires, and the next land we sighted was the Island of Java, in the far East, and we never afterwards heard of the *Vanderbilt* and her various pursuits of us till after our return home. She chased us very persistently, from all the newspaper accounts, but apparently it was a chase to keep up appearances, with no intent to capture. We were constantly hearing of her previous to this time, a day or two ahead of us, or a day or two following after us, sometimes almost near enough to see each other's smokestacks, but the face-to-face meeting did not come! I cannot say that we regretted it, for she was much more than twice our metal, and no doubt had greatly the advantage of us in speed. It was late in September when we left the Cape of Good Hope, I think about the 25th of the month. We had a great deal of trouble with our men here about their "liberty days," and had to leave some dozen or more behind us; but having the offer of some of his "boarders" by a landlord, who was quite tired of them, feeling that he could not well spare so many men, Captain Semmes began to consider how he could make good his losses by accepting the landlord's offer of taking the rollicking gentlemen on a pleasure trip, as passengers on board our steamer, awaiting a chance of their offers of enlistment. We could not, of course, enlist men in Her British Majesty's dominions! We left the Cape in a gale of wind, but then the Cape that divides the Eastern and Western world is acknowledged by mariners to be a very "stormy point."

It took but a few hours' run to find ourselves in the Indian Ocean. Our "gentlemen boarders," when recovered from their drunken debauch and made decent and respectable by a deal of scrubbing and a call upon the paymasters' stores for clothing, made a "virtue of necessity" and gave their valuable services in return for our hospitality and payment of their bills at the Cape, and some of them proved very good seamen. In our voyage to the East (as contradictory as the terms may seem) we struck the "brave West winds" again, had continual rain squalls and thick weather, and were often in danger; but we did not meet the dreadful icebergs which are sometimes in these regions the terror of the sea. Nothing can be more dangerous than to meet these drifts of ice, unless it be the avalanches that come down the Alps, burying everything in their way. In the year 1856 I was associated with Lieutenant de Haven on the coast survey of Texas. He was an officer who had been in the famous search for Sir John Franklin and party in Arctic waters. His thrilling narratives of danger and distress, his snow or ice-blind eyes and frost-bitten hands and feet bearing witness to the truth of his assertions, made on me a strong impression in its sickening detail of suffering! While I had volunteered in every service that had even a dim foreshadowing of a fight, the blood of my Highland ancestry giving me, I freely acknowledge, a love for the same, I frankly say I would never have volunteered as an Arctic explorer, or chosen a death by freezing! But this is a digression.

We missed the icebergs, but rode ahead of two or three threatening cyclones. The constant entries in my logbook (which I am sorry to say found its grave in the *Alabama),* I well remember, had such entries as these: "rough weather," "quantities of rainfall," "furious, turbulent winds," "meeting a ship would be a bad thing for us now; such blinding rains we would run into each other," etc. It is astonishing, the loneliness of the ocean as to sails. In a run of seven or eight hundred miles, as I mentioned before, we only sighted one sail; so in our present run of more than four thousand miles we have met but three or four ships. About the middle of October we passed the little islets of St. Peter and St. Paul, but did not stop, as the weather was very bad. We were trying to make the Straits of Sunda, the passage into the China Seas. Late in October we boarded a Dutch ship from Batavia. They informed us that the United States Ship *Wyoming* had boarded them a little way out of Batavia. As we drew near the Straits of Sunda we fell in with several ships and chased and boarded three English and one Dutch ship. A day or two later, while we were giving chase to two English ships, a third ship hove in sight. It was too American to be allowed to elude us. We fired across her bow, and the flag of the United States went up, our first prize in East India waters. She was the *Amanda,* from Boston; cargo, sugar and hemp.[*] The papers were not satisfactory, so we burned her, after taking off necessary articles for our ship. We soon after came to anchor off the north side of the Strait, a mile or two from Sumatra, where we hoped to procure the fresh food needed for the good health of our crew, for we had been a long time at sea.

---

[*] November 6, 1863.

First Lieutenant John McIntosh Kell on the CSS *Alabama* stands behind his commander, Captain Raphael Semmes. Photograph was taken at Cape Town, South Africa, in August of 1863.

Naval Historical Center

Lieutenant Kell on the deck of the CSS *Alabama* at Cape Town, South Africa

Two of Kell's fellow officers on the *Alabama*: Lieutenant Arthur Sinclair, Jr., *(left)* and Lieutenant Richard F. Armstrong. Photographed at Cape Town, South Africa, August 1863.

Chapter Fifteen

HAVING been warned of her near vicinity to us, we tried to keep "our weather eye" open for the U.S. Steamer *Wyoming*. We took the narrow and most unfrequented channel to the Strait, passing Stroom Rock and the small garrison town of Anjar. Our next prize in these waters was a beautiful new ship, *Winged Racer.** She was a New Yorker, of graceful, symmetrical mold, known in the shipping world as a "clipper." She was returning from Manila with a cargo for New York of coffee, Manila tobacco, sugar, jute, etc. We found just what we wanted, and made havoc in the coffee, sugar and tobacco. We thought the *Winged Racer* too handsome a ship to burn, but what could we do? Our tenders were not a success; our only sale, the *Sea-Bride*, was a failure. We could run nothing into our own ports, and to fire our prizes seemed the only thing to do. We made the master of the *Winged Racer* a present of his boats and all he could stow in them, and he took our prisoners of the *Amanda* and proceeded to Batavia, the little fleet of boats looking very pretty as they pulled away. By the lighted bonfire of the *Winged Racer* we steamed out of sight of Java and Sumatra, made a little island called Lone Watcher, here meaning to wait till daylight for further action. Scarcely was the propeller hoisted when "Sail ho!" rang out, and

---

* November 10, 1863.

135

we made sail in chase. If the breeze had freshened at all we would have lost her, but fortune favored us and the failure of the wind acted greatly in our favor. It made the capture more possible each moment, and finally complete. The speed of the *Alabama* made her shorten sail and heave to. The ship proved to be the *Contest*, from Yokohama for New York, a fine clipper ship; cargo, Japanese goods, curios, etc. Among other things some elegant hand-carved ebony armchairs that it seemed a shame to burn, they were so beautiful. We made the night brilliant with her destructive conflagration. We sighted and boarded a great many vessels in these waters, but American commerce had dwindled into very small dimensions! The sails were mostly Dutch and English, but Dutch predominated.

Of all the waters that cover the face of the earth none are so beset with dangers as the China Seas. The surveying expedition that have been going out to these waters since the time of Commodore Perry's great expedition have seemed to make little headway, and with the best of modern charts to light the ocean a ship stands in danger during the changing of the monsoons, or drifting with the terrible under-currents upon coral reefs so abundant on every hand, and shoals and breakers. Winds, weather and the very elements conspiring against us, we now considered it best to make some point to do our necessary repairing. We were some distance from Singapore, so made for the small Island of Condore (claimed by the French), a very pretty, fertile spot. We had availed ourselves of no rest since leaving the Cape, and not having much fear that the *Wyoming* would find us in this far-away harbor, we anchored and gave ourselves up to enjoyment and relaxation. Here game and fish were abundant, bathing a luxury, and life delightful. Insects, birds, reptiles and the celebrated vampire bat were all here, a deer of small size, and even a small species of bison. Apes, too, abounded, sufficiently fearless and intelligent enough looking to tempt the followers of Darwin into credulity—some looking old and venerable enough to have been patriarchs. I think it was on this island that a party of our men captured a lizard between three and four feet in length. The serpents, we were glad to hear, kept to the jungles. I doubt if they could have been any more dangerous than the rattlesnakes that inhabit the lagoons and sun themselves on the savannas of our own Sea Islands on the Southern coast. But one never grows accustomed to rattlesnakes, or snakes of any kind, and while the mother of mankind in fearless innocence was beguiled into converse with the Tempter "in the form of a serpent," her descendants I have usually found ready to give a wide berth, with a shudder of horror, to all serpent kind.

The young governor of the Island of Condore was a Frenchman about five-and-twenty years of age. He paid us every attention, and enjoyed our visit as heartily as we did. We spent two weeks or more there, and then turned our heads in the direction of Singapore. We crossed the Gulf of Siam, and on the 19th of December anchored under Palo Aor, a little island whose forests are coconut trees and the inhabitants Malays. These people were a merry, careless set, who enjoyed life to its fullest extent, lived on fish and fruits, were too near the equator to care for clothing, and gave no thought to the morrow. Simple children of Nature, knowing nothing of civilization, living their quiet, happy island lives, with no knowledge or thought of the bustling unrest of the great world outside the limit of their horizon. The city of Singapore, our next port of landing, is situated on an island of the same name in the Malay Peninsula, and is the seat of commerce in that section of the globe. It has 100,000 inhabitants, and a more motley, mingled multitude of the nations of the earth could hardly be found anywhere. Persians, Hindoos, Javanese, Chinese, Japanese, Malays, Sumatrans, Tartars, Siamese, Bornese, all mingled in the crowded streets, while the shipping—European and American—made the picture complete. We found here upwards of twenty American vessels laid up. The destruction of the Ship *Amanda* off the Strait of Sunda had decided the American East Indiamen to get out of harm's way, or at least to "lay up" until our departure from the China Seas.[*]

We were treated with great consideration and hospitality by the people at Singapore. They were almost as glad to see us and fête us as the kind people at the Cape of Good Hope had been. The governor of the colony at Singapore was a British colonel. We sent an officer to call upon him and report our arrival and our needs. An English merchant came on board and offered to supply us with everything in his line. Shortly after he urged Captain Semmes to make him a visit (which he did) of a day or two at his semi-English Oriental home. It is astonishing how rich these Englishmen grow in the East, but they never lost their English habits and tastes, no matter where they locate. We had the usual trouble with our rollicking tars, and half a dozen were left behind at Singapore; but their places were supplied by fellows eager to take a trip with us till such time as they could safely enlist without the consent of Queen Victoria, or with no condemnation of her Government for our infringement of neutrality.

The morning we left Singapore, when our little ship was sailing through the Strait of Malacca, "Sail ho!" was cried from the mast, and an American-looking ship being hove to showed us the English colors. Master's Mate Fullam was sent on board to examine papers.

---

[*] The *Alabama* arrived at Singapore on December 21, 1863. The American ships "laid up" were mostly for sale, for no one wanted to ship goods on an American vessel because of the fear of Confederate cruisers.

The master was requested to come on board the *Alabama,* but refused point blank to do so. Mr. Fullam (a young Englishman himself) was very suspicious of the craft. When he returned and reported facts, Captain Semmes, for the first time in the cruise, resolved that he would assume the role of boarding officer under the circumstances, and had rather an amusing experience. He soon satisfied himself that the ship was American, if the cargo was English, or purported to be. When the master of her saw the gleam of decision fatal to his hope of escape in Captain Semmes' eagle eye, he began to remonstrate, and said to him, "You hadn't ought to burn this ship," for such and such reasons. His phraseology was quite sufficient, and the doom of the ship was sealed. She was freshly painted the *Martaban,* but a fortnight previous she had been the *Texan Star.* The master made frank acknowledgment of his change of plan said "all things were fair in war," and rather boasted of the shams and ruses he had used (so unsuccessfully) to save the ship. We ran into the little town of Malacca to land our prisoners, or get permission to do so. It was early morning—the morning of Christmas Day. The little town just waking from its sleep, the friendly lighthouse throwing its light on our deck, all reminded us of distant towns and homes and lights so faraway!

In a little while boats came off to us filled with officers and citizens and a few ladies, all urging us to spend the Christmas Day with them. The captain excused himself, saying "there is no holiday in time of war," and in two or three hours we were on our way, the only outward observance of the day being that the crew "spliced the mainbrace" in honor of festivities consequent upon the season. The following day the lookout called out "Sail ho!" twice very hurriedly from the masthead, and our flag seemed to strike two Yankee skippers dumb, as they were not polite enough to show their bunting in return. They were both large ships, of 1100 or 1200 tons burden, one named the *Highlander,* from Boston, the other the *Sonora,* also from the land of the Puritan. We gave them their boats, and as they were captured at the western entrance to the Strait of Malacca they found it easy sailing to Singapore. One of the captains when he reached our deck told Captain Semmes, with a long-drawn sigh of relief, that "he had been trying to keep out of his way for nearly three years, but now the suspense was over, and he was relieved that there was no more running to be done." Captain Semmes replied that he "was very glad the long search was over."

The last day of the year we cleared the Sumatra coast and crossed to the Bay of Bengal, toward the Island of Ceylon. We doubled this island and found ourselves on the coast of Malabar. The middle of January we captured the *Emma Jane,* of Maine. We took the provisions we required from her, transferred the crew, and burned the ship.

Coasting eastward a short distance, we made the little Portuguese town of Anjenga and came to anchor. There were no English in this town, but a mixture of Portuguese and Hindoo, the presiding official a Portuguese. We arranged to land our prisoners, and the officer sent his son to call upon us. Captain Semmes returned this call of ceremony through one of his lieutenants. This officer was so long in returning that Captain Semmes sent me with an armed boat's crew to rescue him in case of danger. I found it was only a feast or fête day, and all officials were devoutly attending church, which delayed our officer's call of civility. Both Spaniards and Portuguese are great nations for keeping saints' days and religious festivals of all kinds. They never allow worldly business or secular employments to interfere with their religious calendar of saints' days. They seem as happy and exultant in their priest-ridden superstitions and idolatry as the Puritans, who turned their backs on home and country and sought new lands with the privilege of "freedom to worship God" in their own way.

The conquest of India by Great Britain is surely one of the "special Providences" in which we are taught to believe, and the "Empress of India" has a right to think with pride of her vast cotton fields that help so largely to clothe the world; but dearer far must be to her the knowledge of the grand religious influences brought to bear upon her heathen subjects. Schools have sprung up everywhere, the printing press, the railroad, all modern appliances of utility and civilization have usurped the place formerly held by despotism. Now a beneficent Government is displaying the happy rule and reign of justice and humanity!

Having coaled ship at Singapore we left. Passing through the chain of islands adjacent to the Malabar coast, we stretched across the Arabian Sea in the direction of the eastern coast of Africa. The weather was perfectly delightful. For a fortnight or three weeks we had serene skies and gentle breezes, with scarcely even a change of sail; and fleecy, gauze clouds, such as make children dream such "fairy dreams" as Hans Christian Andersen has given in his very charming books to delight the world. The beautiful dolphin peopled the Arabian Sea, passing near the ship in great schools, and some flying fish were caught by the sailors. On the last day of January we crossed the equator, and the latter part of the first week in February we made the Comoro Islands, and getting up steam ran in and anchored at Johanna. This is quite a stopping place for ships passing to and from the East Indies by way of the Mozambique Channel. Johanna at the time of which I write was ruled by an Arab, who called himself a Sultan. The Sultan sent his commanding officer to call upon us, and we made contracts with him for supplies of fresh meats, etc.

We spent a quiet week among the Johanese, and enjoyed it, they being very friendly. Having taken in fresh vegetables, fruits, and plenty of beef, we got under way and turned our faces to the southward. The lovely weather we had in the Arabian Sea did not follow us into the Mozambique Channel, and as we drew near the south of Madagascar we encountered some of the most terrific rain squalls and thunder storms I have ever seen. The lightning played about us with wild fury, as though opening the very heavens above us, and the thunder crashed and rolled with deafening volume till it seemed as if the heavens and earth, the mountains and the deep, were being broken into eternal dissolution! It was a relief to leave the channel and pursue our way, pointing to the Cape of Good Hope. The "stormy Cape," as it is known to mariners, might equal, but could never surpass, the sublime glory of the storms of such frequent occurrence in the waters of the Mozambique Channel. Early in March we took soundings on the dangerous Agulhas Banks, where the ground swell and the angry currents seem to meet each other, and the battling billows fight themselves into fury, like contending armies. "Men who go to sea in ships" can realize in the wonderful power of the elements the hand of Him who guides and rules the storm, and yet whose watchful, tender love "heeds even the sparrow's fall."

After an absence of six months we found ourselves anchored at our old cruising ground off the Cape of Good Hope. We met as warm a welcome as we had received on former visits. Captain Semmes was very indignant to find our cruiser, the *Tuscaloosa,* had been seized under the pretext that she was an uncondemned prize and not a ship of war, and that having been brought into British waters regardless of British neutrality, she should be seized and returned to her original owners. It did not consume much time (with his legal knowledge and ability) for Captain Semmes to set matters right, and after some very spirited correspondence with the authorities the *Tuscaloosa* was ordered released and turned over to Captain Semmes, or his lieutenant in charge of her. But for this useless detention our little cruiser would have done efficient work. Low was an able young officer, who had George Sinclair as his first lieutenant and Adolphe Marmelstein (who had been a quartermaster on the *Alabama)* as second officer, and was fully equal to his duty—loyal and true. By the time, however, that the orders reached the Cape we had left that part of the world, and possession of the *Tuscaloosa* was never resumed. Doubtless she was reclaimed by her owners, or the Federal Government.[*]

We spent several days at the Cape and there met the equinoctial storm March 20th. We had a great influx of visitors, to whom we tried

---

[*] The *Tuscaloosa* was handed over to United States authorities at the end of the war.

to play the part of agreeable host, though we were very busy all the while coaling and provisioning ship. We received a bountiful supply of newspapers at the Cape, and they were very welcome, for we had been cut off from our part of the world for many long months. All news was depressing and discouraging. It was very apparent that our cause was daily growing weaker. We could but see that after the Battle of Gettysburg and the surrender of Vicksburg defeat seemed to stare our struggling people in the face, and with the failing finances and shut-in ports ruin seemed inevitable!

By the middle of April we had reached the track of homeward bound American ships from the Pacific. On the 22d of April we sighted and gave chase to a ship and chased her all night by the light of the moon, on a smooth sea. At daylight a gun brought her to. She was the *Rockingham,* her cargo guano, from the Chincha Islands, bound for Cork. We made a target of her and then burned her.* Two or three days later we took the *Tycoon,* from New York for San Francisco, with a valuable cargo, much of it clothing. We took what we needed, got plenty of newspapers, dates a month back, and burned her. On the 1st of May we re-crossed the equator. We entered the Northern Hemisphere with the usual amount of calms and storms. The late papers made us sick at heart. There was gloom and disaster on every hand, and our poor Southland in her single-handed fight against the world was giving out! We passed through the Azores, bringing vividly to mind the opening of our career, when the beautiful *290,* fresh from her builders' hands, was christened and received her armament, and full of life and spirit was ready for the fray! Now worn and jaded officers, men and ship— what a contrast! We had done valiant work and had nothing to regret in our brief and brilliant career.

I found from his talks with me that Captain Semmes had fully made up his mind to seek rest and refitment of ship in some friendly port where we could go into dock and allow the little ship that had been our home for twenty-two months to be made anew. The mental strain and excitement through which we had lived was really more wearing upon natural energy and powers of mind and body than labor could have been. We stretched over from the Western Islands to the coasts of Spain and Portugal, thence to the historic British Channel; on the 10th of June made Cape La Hague, on the French coast, and a few hours later were boarded by a French pilot, and at noon were anchored in the port of Cherbourg. A few miles from these shores, later in the month, the valiant *Alabama* was destined to sink in mortal combat, to rise no more!

---

* Lieutenant Kell noticed that many of the *Alabama's* shells failed to explode when they struck the *Rockingham*—a forecast of things to come.

A recently discovered photograph of the CSS *Alabama* at anchor in Singapore, December 1863

Lieutenant John M. Kell as he appeared while serving as executive officer of the CSS *Alabama*

The cruise of the CSS *Alabama*

Editor's Collection

Chapter Sixteen

SOON after our arrival at Cherbourg an officer was sent on shore to ask permission of the port admiral to land our prisoners of the two captured ships. This being obtained without trouble or delay, Captain Semmes went on shore to see to the docking of the ship for repairs. Cherbourg being a naval station and the dock belonging to the government, permission had to be obtained of the emperor before we could do anything. The port admiral told us "we had better have gone into Havre, as the government might not give permission for repairs to a belligerent ship." The emperor was absent from Paris at some watering place on the coast, and would not return for some days. Here was an impediment to our plans which gave us time for thought, and the result of such thought was the unfortunate combat between the *Alabama* and the *Kearsarge*. The latter ship was lying at Flushing when we entered Cherbourg. Two or three days after our arrival she steamed into the harbor, sent a boat on shore to communicate, steamed outside and stationed off the breakwater. While Captain Semmes had not singled her out as an antagonist, and would never have done so had he known her to be chain-clad (an armored ship), he had about this time made up his mind that he would cease fleeing before the foe, and meet an equal in battle when the opportunity presented itself. Our cause was weakening daily, and our ship so disabled it really seemed to us our work was almost done! We might end her career gloriously by being victorious in battle, and defeat against an equal foe we would never have allowed ourselves to anticipate.

As soon as the *Kearsarge* came into the harbor Captain Semmes sent for me to come to his cabin, and abruptly said to me: "Kell, I am going out to fight the *Kearsarge*. What do you think of it?" We then quietly talked it all over. We discussed the batteries, especially the *Kearsarge's* advantage in 11-inch guns. I reminded him of our defective powder, how our long cruise had deteriorated everything, as proven in our target-practice off the coast of Brazil on the Ship *Rockingham*, when certainly every third shot was a failure even to explode. I saw his mind was fully made up, so I simply stated these facts for myself. I had always felt ready for a fight, and I also knew that the brave young officers of the ship would not object, and the men would be not only willing, but anxious, to meet the enemy! To all outward seeming the disparity was not great between the two ships, barring the unknown (because concealed) chain armor. The *Kearsarge* communicated with the authorities to request that our prisoners he turned over to them. Captain Semmes made an objection to her increasing her crew. He addressed our agent, Mr. Bonfils, a communication requesting him to inform Captain Winslow, through the United States Consul, that "if he would wait till the *Alabama* could coal ship he would give him battle." We began to coal and at the same time to make preparation for battle. We overhauled the magazine and shell rooms, gun equipments, etc.[*]

The *Kearsarge* was really in the fullest sense of the word a man-of-war, stanch and well built; the *Alabama* was made for flight and speed and was much more lightly constructed than her chosen antagonist. The *Alabama* had one more gun, but the *Kearsarge* carried more metal at a broadside. The seven guns of the *Kearsarge* were two 11-inch

---

[*] There has always been much speculation as to why Semmes wanted to battle the *Kearsarge*. He always claimed that if he had known about the chain armor shielding her sides, he would never have challenged Winslow. Several of his officer, however, in later years claimed that he did know. With the *Kearsarge* guarding the exit from the harbor, and no word yet on when or if the dry-dock would be made available, Semmes was faced with several options. First, he could continue to await the return of the emperor and trust that Napoleon III would grant the needed permission to use the dry-dock. If the *Alabama* was finally put in for repairs, it would take at least a couple of months for them to be completed, and by then most of his crew would be gone, and a score of Federal warships by that time would be patrolling off Cherbourg. A second option was to attempt to steal out on a dark rainy night, slip by the *Kearsarge*, and head for the open sea. But what then? Where could he go? With British and most French ports now looking with disfavor on visiting Confederate vessels, with the *Alabama* desperately in need of repairs, and with the war clouds looming darker and darker over his Southern homeland, it may have seemed to Semmes that it was time for drastic action. It may also have been, and it seems evident that this was Semmes' primary reason, that he was just so very tired of running.

Dahlgrens, four 32-pounders, and one rifled 28-pounder. The *Alabama's* eight guns were six 32-pounders, one 8-inch and one rifled 100-pounder. The crew of the *Alabama* all told was 149 men, while that of the *Kearsarge* was 162 men. By Saturday night, June 18th, our preparations were completed. Captain Semmes notified the admiral of the port that he would be ready to go out and meet the *Kearsarge* the following morning. Early Sunday morning the admiral sent an officer to say to us that "the iron-clad Frigate *Couronne* would accompany us to protect the neutrality of French waters."

Many offered to join us. William C. Whittle, Jr., Grimball, and others; also George Sinclair and Adolphe Marinelstein, officers of the *Tuscaloosa,* and others who were in Paris came down to join us, but the French authorities objected, and they were not allowed to do so. Between 9 and 10 o'clock, June 19th, everything being in readiness, we got under way and proceeded to sea. We took the western entrance of the harbor. The *Couronne* accompanied us, also some French pilot-boats and an English steam yacht, the *Deerhound,* owned by a rich Englishman (as we afterward learned), who, with his wife and children, was enjoying life and leisure in his pleasure yacht. The walls and fortifications of the harbor, the heights above the town, the buildings, everything that looked seaward, were crowded with people. About seven miles from the land the *Kearsarge* was quietly awaiting our arrival.

Officers in uniforms, men at their best, Captain Semmes ordered them sent aft, and mounting a gun-carriage made them a brief address: "Officers and seamen of the *Alabama:* You have at length another opportunity to meet the enemy, the first that has been presented to you since you sank the *Hatteras.* In the meantime you have been all over the world, and it is not too much to say that you have destroyed and driven for protection under neutral flags one-half of the enemy's commerce, which at the beginning of the war covered every sea. This is an achievement of which you may well be proud, and a grateful country will not be unmindful of it. The name of your ship has become a household word wherever civilization extends. Shall that name be tarnished by defeat? [An outburst of Never! Never!] The thing is impossible. Remember that you are in the English Channel, the theatre of so much of the naval glory of our race. The eyes of all Europe are at this moment upon you! The flag that floats over you is that of a young Republic that bids defiance to her enemies, whenever and wherever found! Show the world that you know how to uphold it. Go to your quarters!"

We now prepared our guns to engage the enemy on our starboard side. When within a mile and a-quarter he wheeled, preserving his starboard battery to us. We opened on him with solid shot, to which he soon replied, and the action became active. To keep our respective broadsides bearing we were obliged to fight in a circle around a common center, preserving a distance of three quarters of a mile. When within distance of shell range we opened on him with shell. The spanker gaff was shot away and our ensign came down. We replaced it immediately at the mizzen masthead. The firing now became very hot and heavy. Captain Semmes, who was watching the battle from the horse block, called out to me, "Mr. Kell, our shell strike the enemy's side, doing little damage, and fall off in the water; try solid shot." From this time we alternated shot and shell. The battle lasted an hour and ten minutes. Captain Semmes said to me at this time (seeing the great apertures made in the side of the ship from their 11-inch shell, and the water rushing in rapidly), "Mr. Kell, as soon as our head points to the French coast in our circuit of action, shift your guns to port and make all sail for the coast." This evolution was beautifully performed; righting the helm, hauling aft the fore-trysail sheet, and pivoting to port, the action continuing all the time without cessation,—but it was useless, nothing could avail us. Before doing this, and pivoting the gun, it became necessary to clear the deck of parts of the dead bodies that had been torn to pieces by the 11-inch shells of the enemy. The captain of our 8-inch gun and most of the gun's crew were killed. It became necessary to take the crew from young Anderson's gun to make up the vacancies, which I did, and placed him in command. Though a mere youth, he managed it like an old veteran. Going to the hatchway, I called out to Brooks (one of our efficient engineers) to give the ship more steam, or we would be whipped. He replied she "had every inch of steam that was safe to carry without being blown up!" Young Matt O'Brien, assistant engineer, called out, "Let her have the steam; we had better blow her to hell than to let the Yankees whip us!" The chief engineer now came on deck and reported "the furnace fires put out," whereupon Captain Semmes ordered me to go below and "see how long the ship could float." I did so, and returning said, "Perhaps ten minutes." "Then, sir," said Captain Semmes, "cease firing, shorten sail and haul down the colors. It will never do in this nineteenth century for us to go down and the decks covered with our gallant wounded." This order was promptly executed, after which the *Kearsarge* deliberately fired into us five shots! In Captain Winslow's report to the Secretary of the Navy he admits this, saying, "Uncertain whether Captain Semmes was not making some ruse, the *Kearsarge* was stopped."

Was this a time,—when disaster, defeat and death looked us in the face,—for a ship to use a ruse, a Yankee trick? I ordered the men to "stand to their quarters," and they did it heroically; not even flinching, they stood every man to his post. As soon as we got the first of these shot I told the quartermaster to show the white flag from the stern. It was done. Captain Semmes said to me, "Dispatch an officer to the *Kearsarge* and ask that they send boats to save our wounded — ours are disabled." Our little dinghy was not injured, so I sent Master's Mate Fulham with the request. No boats coming, I had one of our quarter boats (the least damaged one) lowered and had the wounded put in her. Dr. Galt came on deck at this time, and was put in charge of her, with orders to take the wounded to the *Kearsarge*. They shoved off in time to save the wounded. When I went below to inspect the sight was appalling! Assistant Surgeon Llewellyn was at his post, but the table and the patient on it had been swept away from him by an 11-inch shell, which made an aperture that was fast filling with water. This was the last time I saw Dr. Llewellyn in life. As I passed the deck to go down below a stalwart seaman with death's signet on his brow called to me. For an instant I stood beside him. He caught my hand and kissed it with such reverence and loyalty, — the look, the act, it lingers in my memory still! I reached the deck and gave the order for "every man to save himself, to jump overboard with a spar, an oar, or a grating, and get out of the vortex of the sinking ship."

As soon as all were overboard but Captain Semmes and I, his steward, Bartelli, and two of the men — the sailmaker, Alcott, and Michael Mars — we began to strip off all superfluous clothing for our battle with the waves for our lives. Poor, faithful-hearted Bartelli, we did not know he could not swim, or he might have been sent to shore — he was drowned. The men disrobed us, I to my shirt and drawers, but Captain Semmes kept on his heavy pants and vest. We together gave our swords to the briny deep and the ship we loved so well! The sad farewell look at the ship would have wrung the stoutest heart! The dead were lying on her decks, the surging, roaring waters rising through the death-wound in her side. The ship agonizing like a living thing and going down in her brave beauty, settling lower and lower, she sank fathoms deep — lost to all save love, and fame, and memory!

After undressing with the assistance of our men we plunged into the sea. It was a mass of living heads, striving, struggling, battling for life. On the wild waste of waters there came no boats, at first, from the *Kearsarge* to our rescue. Had victory struck them dumb, or helpless — or had it frozen the milk of human kindness in their veins? The water was like ice, and after the excitement of battle it seemed doubly cold. I saw a float of empty shell boxes near me, and called out to one of the men (an expert swimmer) to examine the float. He said: "It is the doctor, sir, and he is dead." Poor Llewellyn! Almost within sight of home, the air blowing across the channel from it into the dead face that had given up the struggle for life and liberty. I felt my strength giving out, but strange to say I never thought of giving up, though the white caps were breaking wildly over my head and the sea foam from the billows blinding my eyes. Midshipman Maffitt swam to my side and said, "Mr. Kell, you are so exhausted, take this life-preserver" (endeavoring to disengage it). I refused, seeing in his own pallid young face that heroism had risen superior to self or bodily suffering! But "what can a man do more than give his life for his friend?" The next thing that I remember, a voice called out, "Here's our first lieutenant," and I was pulled into a boat, in the stern sheets of which lay Captain Semmes as if dead. He had received a slight wound in the hand, which with the struggle in the water had exhausted his strength, long worn by sleeplessness, anxiety and fatigue. There were several of our crew in the boat. In a few moments we were alongside a steam yacht, which received us on her deck, and we learned it was the *Deerhound,* owned by an English gentleman, Mr. John Lancaster, who used it for the pleasure of himself and family, who were with him at this time, his sons having preferred going out with him to witness the fight to going to church with their mother, as he afterwards told us.

In looking about us I saw two French pilot boats rescuing the crew, and finally two boats from the *Kearsarge.* I was much surprised to find Mr. Fulham on the *Deerhound,* as I had dispatched him in the little dinghy to ask the *Kearsarge* for boats to save our wounded. Mr. Fulham told me that "our shot had torn the casing from the chain armor of the *Kearsarge,* indenting the chain in many places." This now explained Captain Semmes' observation to me during the battle — "our shell strike the enemy's side and fall into the water." Had we been in possession of this knowledge the unequal battle between the *Alabama* and the *Kearsarge* would never have been fought, and the gallant little *Alabama* have been lost by an error. She fought valiantly as long as there was a plank to stand upon. History has failed to explain, unless there were secret orders forbidding it, why the *Kearsarge* did not steam into the midst of the fallen foe and generously save life! The *Kearsarge* fought the battle beautifully, but she tarnished her glory when she fired on a fallen foe and made no immediate effort to save brave living men from watery graves! Both heroic commanders are now gone before the great tribunal where "the deeds done in the body" are to be accounted for, but history is history and truth is truth!

Mr. Lancaster came to Captain Semmes and said: "I think every man is saved, where shall I land you?" He replied, "I am under English colors; the sooner you land me on English soil the better." The little yacht, under a press of steam, moved away for Southampton. Our loss was nine killed, twenty-one wounded and ten drowned. That afternoon, the 19th of June, we were landed in Southampton and received with every demonstration of kindness and sympathy.

Semmes addresses the crew of the *Alabama* prior to the battle with the *Kearsarge*. Lieutenant Kell is depicted standing on the deck to Semmes' rear.

U.S. Naval Archives

The CSS *Alabama* engages the USS *Kearsarge* off Cherbourg, France, June 19, 1864.

Naval Historical Center

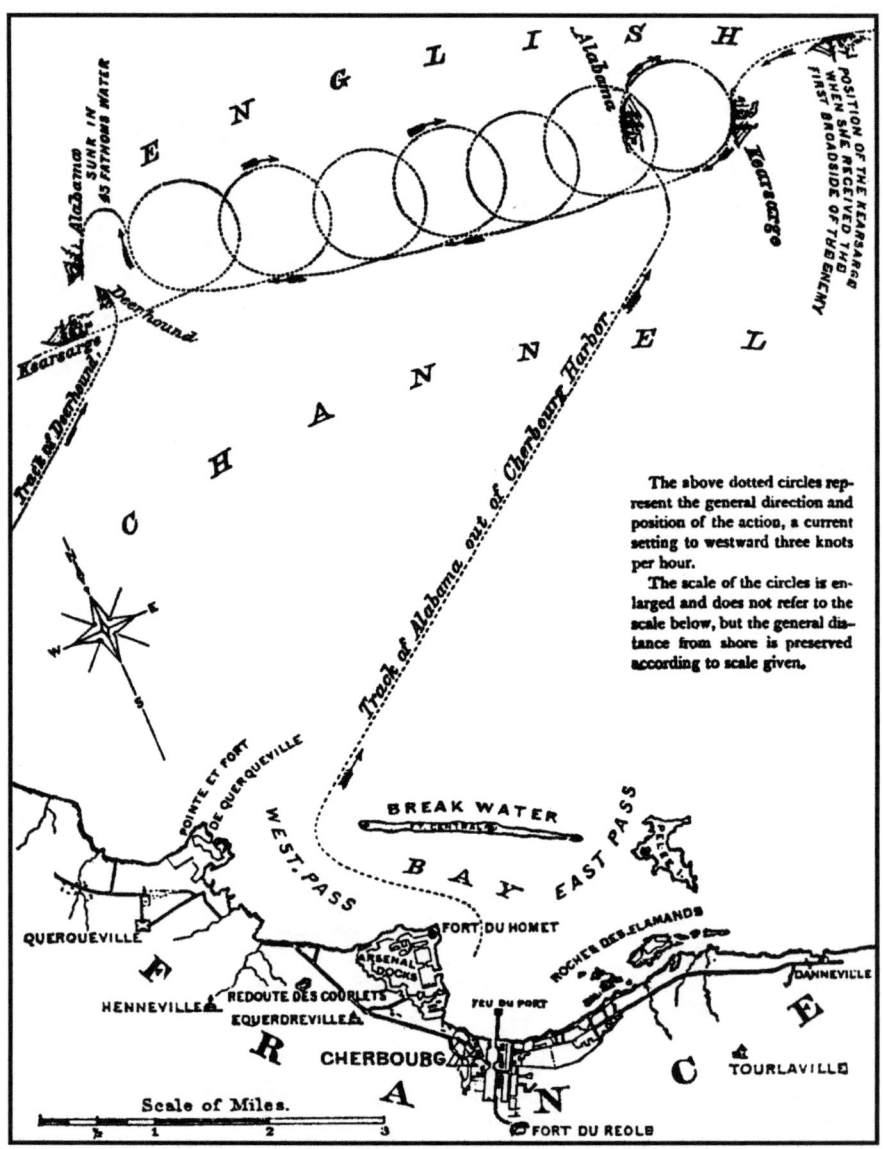

The above dotted circles represent the general direction and position of the action, a current setting to westward three knots per hour.

The scale of the circles is enlarged and does not refer to the scale below, but the general distance from shore is preserved according to scale given.

Chart of the engagement between the CSS *Alabama* and the USS *Kearsarge* off Cherbourg, France, June 19, 1864

Battles and Leaders

A boat from the *Alabama* approaches the *Kearsarge*. Master's Mate George T. Fulham was dispatched by Kell to ask for assistance in saving the *Alabama's* wounded.

Battles and Leaders

The English yacht *Deerhound* (*center*) steams to the rescue of the *Alabama's* crew.
Illustrated London News

The fatal plunge of the CSS *Alabama*

Battle and Leaders

Chapter Seventeen

I find among my old letters one written at Cherbourg on the 16th of June, that is not only a contribution to history, but an honest statement of the sentiment of the times.

C. S. Str, *Alabama*, Cherbourg, France,

June 16th, 1864.

We are on the eve of going out to engage the enemy's Gunboat *Kearsarge*, now lying off this harbor. We arrived here on the 11th inst., seventy-eight days from Cape Town. On the passage we burned two of the enemy's merchant vessels—making fifty-three that we have destroyed, released one, ransomed nine, sold one, and commissioned one, making our total captures sixty-five vessels, including the *Hatteras*. We are now much in want of repairs, and came here for that purpose, the captain immediately upon our arrival applying to have the work done. From the delay of official correspondence we have been put off from day to day, when the *Kearsarge*, happening to be at Ostend and hearing of our arrival here to undergo extensive repairs, thought she could insult us with impunity, and came steaming into the harbor a couple of days ago, and has since been laying off, communicating twice with the shore by her boats. Captain Semmes at once determined to give her battle, and applied for permission to purchase coals. This at first was refused, but afterwards granted, and we are now taking them in, and may go out to-morrow or the day following. We expect to have a hard fight, for she is fully our match, having to our knowledge two 11-inch guns, four 32-pounders, and one 30-pound rifle gun, with a crew of 160 men. She is just out of dock and in thorough order, while we are sadly wanting in repairs, with a crew of 120 men only—but they are ready for the fray, and, God willing, we hope to come out victorious!

In the year 1886 I was solicited by the *Century Magazine* to contribute to their pages an article on the fight, afterwards embodied in "Battles and Leaders of the Civil War." I did so. Some years afterward I received some letters that had been in the possession of a relative that had recently died. I copy a letter herewith, written a few hours after the sinking of the *Alabama,* which though brief is very graphic.

Kelway's Hotel, Southampton, Eng.,

June 20th, 1864.

My DEAR H— —: I have just received your telegram of J, H. A. & Co. Captain Semmes and Mr. Smith are here and much obliged, but need no funds. We shall have our money and accounts from Cherbourg in a day or two, which we landed before coming out. We left Cherbourg at half-past nine yesterday morning expressly to engage the *Kearsarge,* she laying off the port. We began the action a few minutes before 11 o'clock, about nine miles distant from the land, and had sharp work of it for an hour. We commenced the action about one mile distant, knowing the enemy had the advantage of us in his 11-inch guns, although we had the advantage of range in our 100-pound rifle (Blakely) and 8-inch solid shot. We at once discovered that the enemy had the speed of us and chose his own position, which was from three to five hundred yards. His 11-inch shell had terrific effect upon us, which, striking about the water-line, caused us to fill very rapidly. The action lasted about one hour and ten minutes, during which time we had made seven complete circles. When I found the water gaining so rapidly upon us I reported to Captain Semmes that we could not float much longer, and he ordered the course shaped for the land. We made what sail we had available to assist the engines, carrying on a running fight; but the water gained so rapidly as to put out the fires, when the engines stopped, and humanity demanded that we should haul down the colors and save the wounded. Fortunately, two of our boats were not too much injured, and we had time to lower them and get the wounded off for the *Kearsarge,* when the ship commenced to settle. Then the order was given for every man to take to an oar, or spar, and jump overboard, which was hurriedly done, and the ship went down about twenty minutes after the colors were hauled down. We were in the water about half an hour when a boat from the English Steam Yacht *Deerhound,* belonging to Mr. John Lancaster, picked us up, took us on board and kindly treated us—fifteen officers and about twenty-seven men—and steered away for this port. We left a French pilot boat and two boats from the *Kearsarge* picking up the remainder. We had nine men killed, twenty wounded, and one officer, Dr. Llewellyn and several men drowned. We learn from the officers who took the sick and wounded alongside of the *Kearsarge* that her midship section was completely protected by chain bighted from her rail to the water's edge, which was broken and indented in many places by our shot, but did not penetrate her, so that we were in fact fighting an ironclad! They also report that she is damaged in her upper works and quarter, and was pumping and plugging up shot-holes when they were alongside, so that it is likely she will he obliged to make some harbor near at hand. If so, I trust our officers and men on board will be paroled. Please return the letters sent for my wife and mother from Cherbourg, as I shall endeavor to get off to the Confederacy as soon as possible. Let me hear from you. I shall not be able to see you probably for a week or so, as I have a number of our men to look after, besides settling up our accounts before leaving.

Affectionately yours,
Jno. McIntosh Kell

I do not mean in these simple annals of my life and work to turn back and try to recall the feelings and sentiments of those "times that tried men's souls." I believe I have said that I am "writing for posterity," that those of the younger generation may know, and all that come after them may know, the part it was my privilege to act in the war that left my country desolated and myself penniless, with broken health and broken spirit in middle life, and without a profession. I feel that the generation that is passing away (my own contemporaries) are well versed in the history of that time thirty-odd years ago. That all who could read that grand book of Admiral Semmes', "Service Afloat," which dealt so largely of law and science, and our deeds, that it seems presumptuous for any one else to take up his well-handled themes that left nothing unsaid. There may be some of the present generation, however, who have not read this book, and there may be friends of mine who will take an interest in my less able narrative, so for the pleasure of these friends and my family I have told the story of the cruises once again.

The press of the world at that time teemed with the combat. The Yankee papers, of course, gloated over the victory — but what had they gained? An ironclad had sunk a wooden ship, but except the shot that remained to them unexploded in their sternpost to tell "what might have been" but for defective fuses, etc., there was no trophy! There were many beautiful notices of the loss of the *Alabama* in the papers, a few of which I here insert, as papers are perishable things and often only kept on file in their own offices.

[From the *London Times,* June 21st, 1864.]

Fathoms deep in Norman waters lies the good Ship *Alabama,* the swift sea rover, just so many tons of broken-up iron and wood, and wearing away in the huge depository of that genuine and original marine store-dealer, Father Neptune!

Should any painter conceive a fantasy of the ocean akin to that of Raffet in "Napoleon's Midnight Review," the famous Confederate cruiser would be one of the first ships that his imagination would summon from the depths of the sea, and amongst the spectral fleet of highbeaked Danish galleys, of antique Spanish caravels, of bluff and burly British three-deckers and saucy British frigates, there would be room for this quick and cunning craft that raced so swiftly and roamed the deep so long. The waves wash to and fro about her, as if in mockery of the dead mass that could once almost outstrip the hurricane, and the fish swim in and out of the port-holes and round the muzzles of the guns that will never again burn powder. For yet a day or so to come corpses of brave men killed in battle or miserably drowned will float to and fro on the summer waves—a strange and horrible sight, perchance, to French fishers busy with their nets or English yachtmen taking their pleasure in the Channel. The skipper, a wounded man, is safe on English ground, but many of his strange crew will nevermore tread a deck or answer to the boatswain's call. The *Alabama* could have found no more fitting grave, for she had lived on the waters, their child and playmate. She hailed from no Southern harbor, she was warned off from many a neutral port, and went away to her wild work amid the loneliness of the watery waste. It was well, then, that she was not destined to be laid up in ordinary, or daubed with dock-yard drab at Charleston or Savannah, while idle gossips wandered over her and talked glibly about her deeds. Beaten in fair fight, she went down in the open sea, whilst her crew, leaping from the sinking ship, swam manfully for their lives. Her career was a strange one. She was an outlaw; men called her a "corsair," and spoke of "Semmes, the pirate captain" as though he had been some ruffianly Blackbeard sailing under the black flag with skull and cross-bones for his grisly ensign. Today we do not care to quote Puffindorff, Grotius, or Wheaton; we do not concern ourselves with legal quibbles; we decline to take a lawyer's view of her. She was a good ship, well handled and well fought, and to a nation of sailors that means a great deal.

Since Philip Brooke captured the *Chesapeake* there has been no more chivalric encounter between single ships than that of Sunday last off Cherbourg, not far from the old battleground of Cape La Hague. It was a deliberate challenge. The contest did not take either crew by surprise. Semmes might have stuck to Cherbourg Dock, or trusted to speed for his escape, but he resolved to fight it out. So on a bright June morning, whilst the French folks were quietly at church, he steamed gallantly to sea and attacked his ready antagonist. The *Kearsarge* had more men, carried heavier metal and was chain-plated under her outside planking. Of this latter fact Semmes is said to have been ignorant. At any rate, he knew that a hard day's work was before him and he lost no time in grappling with his work. The story reads like a page from James's "Naval Chronicle," but with some new features about it that remind us how much the conditions of maritime warfare have changed. For instance, we see that this was at first an artillery duel at long range, the two steamers wheeling round and round as falcons might, careless of the wind. Ere long they came to closer quarters, whilst an English yacht cruising in the offing watched the fight. Twice the *Alabama* was struck heavily; the third shot carried away the blade of her fan, shattered a part of her rudder and disabled a gun. The water rushed into her engine-room and she filled rapidly. The *Kearsarge* also suffered severely, but it was plain that the battle was over, and that the *Alabama* was about to sink. Not till the very muzzles were under water would the Southern captain discontinue the action; even then he disdained to surrender, but lowering his boats and placing his wounded in them he waited till the moment before she sank, and then, bleeding as he was, jumped into the sea. His gallant and chivalric enemy sent boats to save the crew and claimed the assistance of the English yacht in the same charitable office. He inquired after Semmes' fate and was told that he was drowned, but Semmes meanwhile, although sorely suffering, was safe in the *Deerhound*, which got up steam and bore away as swiftly as possible. From thirty to forty of his comrades were killed or wounded; the rest are either in England or prisoners on board the Federal Ship.

So ends the log of the *Alabama*—a vessel of which it may be said that nothing in her whole career became her like its close! Although a legitimate and recognized form of hostilities, the capture and destruction of peaceful merchantmen is one barbarism of war which civilized society is beginning to deprecate. Yet for many reasons one can impute no moral guilt to Semmes. His enemy, the United States, specially and distinctly refused adhesion to the Paris Declaration against privateering; and his own country, "Secessia," is the weaker in the present contest. Possibly if he had been cruising with letters of marque under ordinary circumstances, with twenty ports upon a friendly seaboard eager to receive him, few would care about his fate. It was his peculiar fortune to keep the sea, almost alone, against a hostile navy, running the gauntlet of countless cruisers with no southern harbor of refuge under his lee, and carrying on the conflict without any of the usual forms of recruitment. And well did he fulfill his adventurous duties. The *Alabama* seemed ubiquitous. If suddenly on the Indian Ocean a red light was seen in the distance, and dim clouds of smoke rolled away before the wind, men knew that Semmes was at work, and was boarding and burning some Yankee trader to the water's edge. American captains homeward bound with a precious freight caught sight of the strange craft and rejoiced that they sailed under the Union Jack and not under the Stars and Stripes. The Federals tried hard to catch her, for indeed she and her sister ships threatened to paralyze their commerce, and even underwrites murmured when they heard of cargoes burned and vessels destroyed. She had many a narrow escape, had often to show a clean pair of heels and run for it, often to change her guise, to give her sides a fresh coat of paint and hoist some foreign flag. In all the sea subtlety and stratagem Semmes was as cool and crafty as even old Francis Drake himself, but also like Drake he could fight when fighting was required. Gradually men came to think that the *Alabama* bore a charmed life, that nothing could hurt her, that to all purposes she was like Vanderdecken's barque—a phantom ship coming when she listed, but never to be caught. No really mortal ship, however, can keep the sea forever, and the two-years' cruise began to tell upon the *Alabama*. She was compelled to bear up for some neutral port and sue for leave to repair. Cherbourg was the selected port, and then whilst her crew stretched their legs ashore up came the *Kearsarge* and waited obstinately. Semmes might perchance have slipped out and passed her at night, a game he has often tried successfully with other cruisers, but he may have been somewhat tired of what, after all, was hardly the pleasantest work for a gallant Southern gentleman, or, more probably, he learned that the watch on board the enemy was too good. For the last time, then, the *Alabama* got up steam and made sail. At a few minutes past eleven she was again in blue water, and by one o'clock, riddled with shot, she had sunk, never again to leave her spreading wake on the dancing waves. Beaten in fair but unequal combat by a gallant foe she has disappeared from the field of ocean to take her place in history; and destined to singular luck even at the very depth of calamity, the still formidable Semmes is spared capture and sentenced by fate to nothing worse than to be for a time the guest of England.

While the *Kearsarge* was anchored off Tybee a few years ago, Mr. Stanhope Sams interviewed me for an account of the fight. I willingly gave him the narrative, and now quote from his gifted and beautiful pen:

While single combats have not been rare in naval wars there are but few instances of a pre-arranged duel at sea, and there is not another instance of such a duel as was fought off the coast of France more than twenty-eight years ago between the wooden Confederate Cruiser *Alabama* and the Federal armored Ship *Kearsarge*. When Captain Laurence on the blood-stained deck of his gallant ship gave the famous command, "Don't give up the ship," he had gone out to meet an equal foe under like conditions. But when Admiral Semmes and his brave Executive left Cherbourg harbor for the fatal duel in the Channel, they went out naked before a steel-girt antagonist! What made the fight still more unequal was the fact that the

Alabama did not suspect that her foe was sheathed in armor. The wooden cruiser fought the *Kearsarge* as if she had been a wooden hull like herself. Had they known these things the departure from the French harbor would have been to them but a certain passage to martyrdom upon the wave they had so often glorified by their heroic deeds. They went to certain death as cheerfully as though they were sweeping onward to accustomed victory. [Then follows a full account of the fight already told.] Captain Kell remarked: "The *Kearsarge* was not quick to assist our struggling crew. Her boats did not come in time to save them. Had it not been for the help given by the *Deerhound* and French boats many would have sunk. I say this with no feeling now, but state the truth as it ought to appear in history. This cruelty sadly marred the gallantry of the fight made by our enemy." Captain Semmes took a stern view of the action of Captain Winslow of the *Kearsarge,* he regarding it almost as a meeting "under the code," certainly one to be governed by the highest sense of honor and courage. His enemy, he thought, did not act with honor in concealing the fact of her armor. Semmes would never have been guilty of such conduct himself. He did not imagine a soldier and a gentleman would willingly fight in concealed armor against an unarmored craft. But war and its animosities are past. We are concerned only with the sad but dear memories of the war, and the justice and truth of history. Whenever this story of the *Alabama* and *Kearsarge* is *falsely* told, as it is almost always told in our histories, it is the duty of a Southern man to "absent himself from felicity awhile to tell the story" of that daring ship which, for a season, alone drove from the seas the commerce of a nation furnished with fleets of war. Her record will be a proud one in the annals of American naval warfare in that she has contributed to the glories of our history and the most daring and eventful career ever run by a single ship upon the seas of the world.

I was very much pleased with an editorial that appeared in the *Macon Telegraph* some years ago, and which I gave credit without really knowing the fact to the pen of an old and valued friend, Col. H. H. Jones, of the "Independent State of Liberty."

A REFLECTION.

The *New York Sun,* after giving a fairly fair résumé of the fight between the *Kearsarge* and the *Alabama,* as gathered from recent publications in the *Century,* says: "It is one of the strange reflections on this great duel, fought in the presence of thousands of spectators who lined the heights of Cherbourg, that Winslow is perhaps less widely known to fame today than Semmes, though the Yankee vessel in an hour's fight sank her renowned antagonist."

"Truth is stranger than fiction," and there is no power that can turn or control the natural impulses of the human mind. There is no record of any service beyond the fight referred to that should fix the name and fame of

Captain Winslow in the popular mind. It even requires the pens of partial friends at this late day to accord him somewhat questionable credit. There was nothing particularly skillful or exciting in the maneuvering or fighting of the *Alabama* and the *Kearsarge,* and accident alone decided the result. The explanation of the surgeon of the *Kearsarge* as to the firing on the *Alabama* after her colors were struck, and she was sinking, cannot stand before the simple, straightforward statement of Captain Kell. If the surgeon had been at his proper post he could not have known anything of the details of the duel.

The failure of Captain Winslow to save drowning men is proof that he had been badly shaken by the fight, and that the *Alabama* did not cease to be an object of fear until she sought the bottom of the sea. Admiral Sernmes had been a naval officer of distinguished service for years. But the cruise of the *Alabama* constitutes one of the great episodes of the war, and his own graphic pen has made it for all ages to come one of the most exciting "romances of the sea." He was no more a pirate than Robert E. Lee may be called a brigand. If he had been a buccaneer outlawed by the code of nations, Captain Winslow's name would last forever in the memory of men as the destroyer of a common enemy. The world at large does not sympathize with the feelings of the Northern people towards Admiral Semmes, and in this may be read one of the reasons why his name and fame tower above those of Captain Winslow. The Confederate cause for political, commercial and social reasons failed to secure the active and practical sympathy of other nations, but the respect and admiration of good men of every civilized clime clustered about it and its leaders. Fortune does not always favor the brave, and but few niches in the Temple of Fame might be filled if they all were reserved for victors in the strifes of the world. People remember and cherish the names of brave and honorable men who have highly illustrated these qualities. We present a couple of illustrations, both in point, one homely, the other heroic. Every American is familiar with the name of George Washington. There is not one in a thousand who can recall the name of the Virginia carpenter who bested him in a fisticuffs Where's the schoolboy who cannot tell you how Leonidas held the pass of Thermopylae? Outside of a college professor or literateur, who cares to carry in his memory the name of the Persian officer who led the immediate assault upon it? The allied arms saved England at Waterloo, but the fame of Wellington has not obscured that of Napoleon.

Another tribute from the pen of the gifted and lamented poet, Dr. Frank O. Ticknor, a native Georgian, and I will to my narrative again:

THE SWORD IN THE SEA.

"The billows plunge like steeds that bear
The knights with snow-white crests:

The sea winds blare-like bugles where
    The *Alabama* rests.

"Old glories from their splendor-mists
    Salute with trump and hail
The sword that held the ocean lists
    Against the world in mail.

"And down from England's storied hills,
    From lyric slopes of France,
The old bright wine of valor fills
    The chalice of romance.

"For here was Glory's tourney-field,
    The till-yard of the Sea-
The battle-path of kingly wrath
    And kinglier courtesy.

"And down the deeps, in sumless heaps,
    The gold, the gem, the pearl,
In one broad blaze of splendor, belt
    Great England, like an earl.

"And there they rest, the princeliest
    Of earth's regalia gems,
The starlight of our Southern cross —
    The Sword of Raphael Semmes."

After landing in Southampton, Captain Semmes and I took a suite of rooms at Kelway's Hotel, Queen's Terrace. He was very much worn and jaded. Disappointment, too, had naturally broken his brave spirit, and he was greatly depressed. He had also been slightly wounded in the hand. After attending to all the business of the survivors of the lost ship, he accepted the kind invitation of the Rev. Mr. Tremlett and made him a visit at Belsize Park Parsonage. This dear "rebel home," as its inmates called it, had made very welcome many Confederates of renown. Here Commodore Maury was specially beloved, and here we all met the best of English society, and many English Navy and Army officers of note.

Captain Semmes and I parted at this dear English home of ours, I to make my way into the Confederacy to my family, and also as bearer of dispatches to the Government at Richmond. Our English friends made up a pleasant party to take Captain Semmes on the continent for his health. My dear commander, to whom I had grown greatly attached in these troublous times, was in need of rest and change, not so much of climate (for we had been in many climes), but change of scene and change of thought from the heavy responsibilities of his three years' life afloat. I believe I have told of the interest Captain Semmes took in me in my early youth—an abiding interest—for though I lost sight of him and did not meet him for many years, most of which I spent on the broad ocean, he kept me in mind, and no sooner did he gain a Confederate command than he applied for me as his first officer. Our friendship was life-long, and I trust will be eternal! In his own words of his little pleasure trip, they "landed at Ostend, passed through Belgium, visited the battlefield of Waterloo, spent a few days at Spa for the waters, passed on to the Rhine, up that historic, beautiful river to Mayence, thence to the Swiss lakes, resting at Geneva." Returning late in September, the 3d of October the captain began his journey home, determining to come by way of Mexico and Texas instead of making the effort to run the blockade, which had now become quite a dangerous experiment.

I sailed in the English mail steamer from Liverpool, bound for New York, stopping on her way at Halifax, Nova Scotia. Galt and I landed in Halifax and while we were there the Roman Catholic Vicar-General paid us the honor of a call through his chief of staff, and invited us to a handsome entertainment given us as representatives of Captain Semmes and the South, he being a Southern sympathizer and our commander a devoted adherent of his church.

The following day we sailed in the little English mail steamer for Bermuda, from which point we were to venture on the rather difficult and dangerous task of running the blockade. We found the little side-wheel Steamer *Flamingo* ready to sail, and took passage on her. The sea was smooth, and beautifully adapted to our little vessel, which only drew three or four feet of water and skimmed the surface of the ocean like a bird. We began the voyage very well, but our first experience at nearing shore was disappointing. We failed to make the lighthouse, and could not ascertain by the bearings whether we were north or south of out port of entry, and ran into the shore almost within touching distance and shaped our course along it, hoping to discover our whereabouts, but failed to find any signal. As it was nearing three o'clock in the morning we held a consultation and decided it would be more prudent to stand off to sea and get an offing by day break, for fear of being shut in by blockaders. As the day opened up a little light to us we discovered two blockaders ahead, and three on our quarters. We put on all the steam we could carry and proceeded eastward. The blockader ahead made every exertion to cut us off and fired on us, but the shot fell short, and we continued on our course—fairly flying—and soon our pursuers were out of sight and we greatly relieved to have made so narrow an escape. About eight o'clock we got out instruments to establish our longitude and at twelve o'clock we took our latitude, placed our position accurately on the chart, took our bearings on Fort Fisher, and as the evening drew on we got steam up and drew in with the land. Taking the bearings which were then open to us, we made all steam and passed in under the very guns of the blockaders, like a flash, of lightning, and as quickly as it takes to relate it we were safely anchored under the guns of the fort. A basket of champagne was at once ordered up and a toast to our successful run was heartily quaffed. The cause of our first missing our bearings was due entirely to the drunkenness of the officers of the steamer. The risks they ran seemed to inspire the desire to get up a little "Dutch courage" as occasion required, and came very near precipitating us — all our hair-breadth escapes — into the hands of the enemy!*

In Wilmington I met a friend of the Anderson family, who informed me of the report that had reached them that their brave young son had perished in the fight off Cherbourg, being "literally torn to pieces by the explosion of an 11-inch shelf." I had the great gratification of telegraphing them of his safety, he being one of the last to bid me good-bye in Liverpool. He seemed to them as one given back from the dead!

In August, 1864, Macon — my haven — was reached at last! After an absence of three years and nearly four months I found myself on her kindly soil, united to my wife and child. Death had come in my absence, while fighting the battles of my country, and bereft us of our first-born son, a manly, noble child of six years, and our one lovely daughter, a babe of three years (I left her three months old). I little feared at that time that I was never to see their fair, bright faces again! I think it due to their memories (that have influenced my whole life since their early removal) that even in this record of my public life I tell the sacrifice that was required of me on the altar of duty and patriotism!

---

* The *Flamingo*, bearing Kell, arrived at Wilmington, North Carolina, on August 1, 1864.

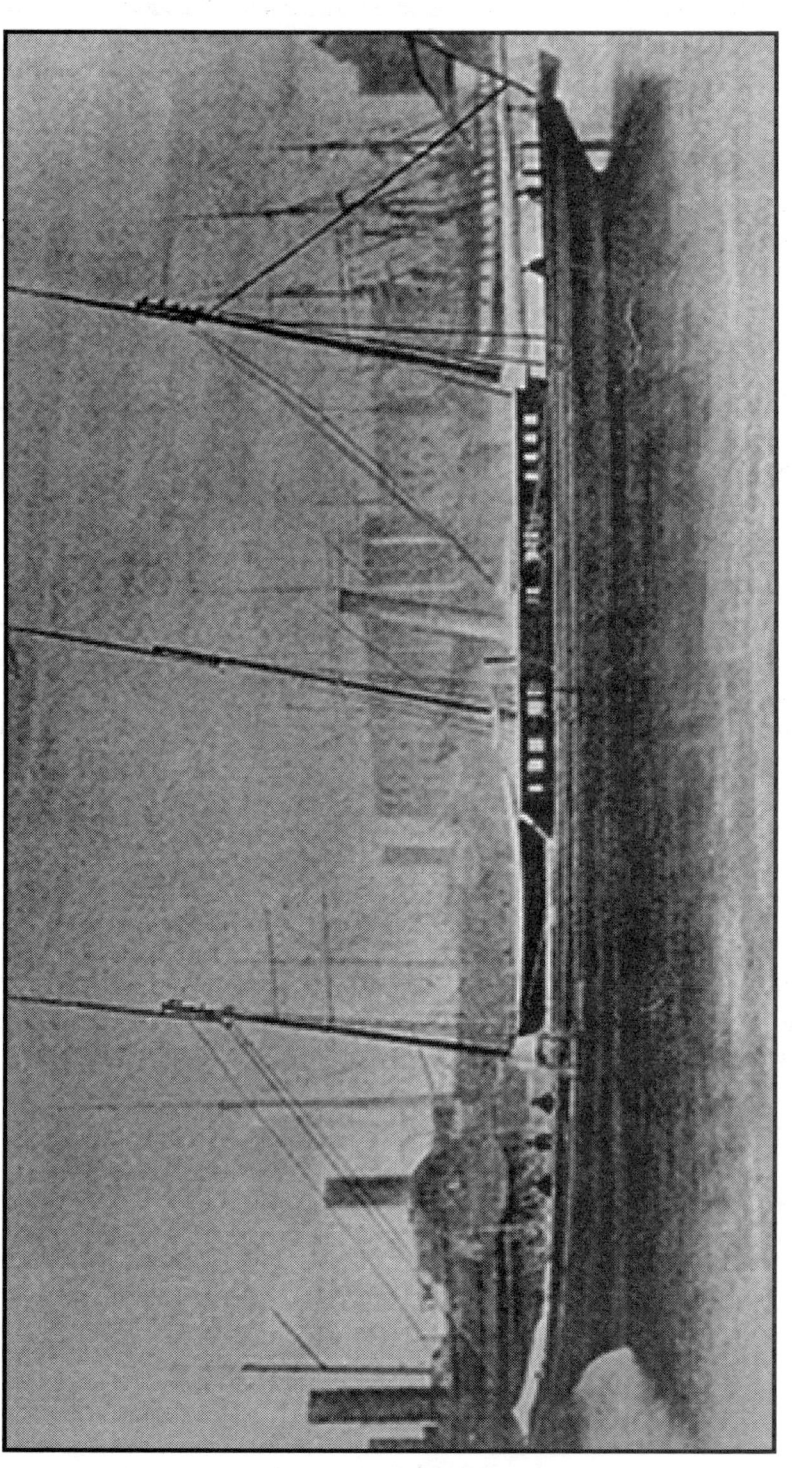

The yacht *Deerhound*, owned by Englishman John Lancaster, rescued Kell, Semmes, and several others of the *Alabama's* crew.

Sinclair: *Two Years on the Alabama*

John Kell and Raphael Semmes posed for this photograph with their English hosts after the sinking of the *Alabama*.

Chapter Eighteen

HAVING forwarded my dispatches, in ten days I left for Richmond to report and see what I could do for the failing fortunes of the Confederacy. I believe I have forgot to say that after the battle with the *Hatteras*, I had been promoted to commander, of which I was not made aware till the commission was nearly a year old, and should not willingly have left Captain Semmes and the *Alabama* even to take a command. The commission read as follows:

COMMANDER JOHN KELL, C. S. A.

SIR: You are hereby informed that the President has appointed you, by and with the advice and consent of the Senate, a commander in the Provisional Navy of the Confederate States, to rank from the 4th day of October, 1863, "for gallant and meritorious conduct as First Lieutenant and Executive Officer of the C. S. Steam Sloops *Sumter* and *Alabama*, under the command of Captain Raphael Semmes." You are requested to acknowledge the receipt of this appointment.

S. R. MALLORY,

C. S. of America, *Secretary of the Navy.* NAVY DEPARTMENT, *June 1st, 1864.*

Also this very gratifying letter:

CONFEDERATE STATES OF AMERICA, RICHMOND, VA.
COMMANDER JNO. MCINTOSH KELL, P. N. C. S., Macon, Ga.

SIR: Your letter of the 3d inst., reporting your arrival at Wilmington under orders from Captain Semmes to report to the Secretary of the Navy, was this day received. In congratulating you upon your return to your family and home, I deem it but just to you to say that the arduous duties which you have so long and ably performed as the Executive Officer of the *Sumter* and the *Alabama* are highly appreciated by your Government, and that they have achieved for you proud distinction in the naval service of your country, with whose history your name will ever be honorably associated. In recognition of your "gallant and meritorious services" I have the pleasure of handing you enclosed a commission as commander in the Provisional Navy, by direction of the President. Very respectfully,

Your obedient servant,

S. R. MALLORY, *Sec. Navy.*

August 8th, 1864.

I returned from Richmond for a little longer leave of absence with my family, and in October was ordered to the command of the new Ironclad *Richmond,* on the James River. In the meantime, with the Yankee raids through the country, and the threatened "march through Georgia," which was afterwards so effectually accomplished, I took my wife and child and left Macon as a "refugee" for awhile. I went to Commodore Tatnall, as I passed through Savannah, and told him where I would be, and asked him to call for me if need be. He said, sadly, "Well, my son, it would only be to shoulder a musket and go by my side. There seems no work for us to do; the Navy has done all it could, and you have done your share."

We went to my relatives, the McIntosh family, in Thomas County, and there spent three quiet weeks. At the end of that time I received orders to "proceed to Richmond without delay." I made three efforts to get off, without success. The creeks and rivers were swollen to danger point, and the railroads were cut or torn up in many places by Yankee raiders. Finally I had orders from Richmond to go to Thomasville, Georgia (the nearest town) and "impress a conveyance." I found a dilapidated cloth-covered wagon there, which resembled the old-time country "chicken trading" wagons. The ribs across were too low for me, and I had to push back the cloth for my head to come through; but my wife and little son, John, Jr., and the nurse managed to sit comfortably and we proceeded from Thomasville to Albany, a journey if I remember aright, of two days and two nights (camping out), to the tune (for such a conveyance!) of five hundred dollars! The camp fires at night and the very cool weather and exposure were a novel experience to the inmates of the wagon; but Southern women, even of extreme youth, bore everything heroically, and it was truly beautiful to witness the patriotism of their exalted souls, that rose so high above all discomfort or fatigue; that bore up the hearts of fathers, husbands, brothers and sons to achieve what they did. The deeds of valor on many battlefields were but the reflections of the brave hearts of women who loved home, honor and country better than life itself; and my country women, though the cause failed for which you hoped and endured so much, your deeds will live in the memory of the Confederate veteran while life lasts, and they will teach their children's children the reverence and love due to Southern womanhood!

The second night of our "refugeeing voyage," about midnight, a carriage drove up and hailed us, and called for me. It was very startling. My wife roused first, she thought the enemy were upon us, but she answered bravely. Then the voice called out, "Uncle has sent me for Cousin Blanche and the boy; he saw the orders published for Richmond, and knew you would go; he is frantic about his children, and sent me for them." We rested the horses, and before daylight started for Albany to catch the earliest train for Macon, where we arrived safely, to the relief and joy of my wife's family. I had now to face the difficulties of a trip "on to Richmond." I find in my old letters the account of it:

SPARTA, GA., December 25th, 1864.

I have just arrived in a heavy rain! I had, however, a comfortable carriage with Mr. Habersliam. He returns to Milledgeville to-morrow, having met his family in an open wagon eight miles from that town. He kindly insisted upon driving me through to this place, and in the morning I will take a seat in the regular hack to Mayfield, and hope to reach there by 10 o'clock to take the cars to Augusta, where I shall secure transportation and get on, I trust, without much delay to Richmond. Oh! what a gloomy Christmas to us, and throughout our beloved country!

RICHMOND, January 1st, 1865

I cannot wish you a happy New Year. It would be inconsistent and ironical! but I can and do thank God that you are safe in your father's house and under his loving care. Here I am with my dear Bob Minor, sharing his room for the day and night. Bob says he is just realizing, now that his eyes rest on me, that I am really in the Confederacy at last! My dear Bob, he will always be a boy, but he takes me back to the time when I was a boy, too. Yesterday I went down the river to report to Flag Officer Mitchell, who commands the ironclad *Virginia*. Captain Roots has the *Fredericksburg*, and I am ordered to the command of the *Richmond*, which is a fine vessel. These three ironclads compose the James River Squadron—so change your present address to me, and address to the ship and James River Squadron.[*] It was a terrible day on the water yesterday — heavy, driving snow storm, and I did not get back till 7 o'clock. Shall be very busy to-morrow, as I take command the next day. I think we will be quiet for a while. The obstructions in the river and the great severity of the weather prevent the enemy moving by land or water, though we are in sight of the Yankee lines, and have picket boats out every night. I think Richmond is about the securest spot in the Confederacy at present. The ships lay about nine miles from the city. I called on Mrs. Mallory on New Year's day. She sent her love to you. I also met your friend Mrs. Clay. Eaneas Armstrong is attached to the *Fredericksburg.* I sent his mother's letter to him. Richard is in Charleston at his own request, on torpedo service.

C. S. Ironclad *Richmond,* January 6th, 1865.

I cannot give you a very glowing account of my new quarters. I had two staterooms knocked into one to give me room. The bed allows me to turn over on the mattress of sweetened hay with a few sticks in it; this is no disadvantage, however, as I should not sleep too sound these "war times." I borrowed six yards of Macon factory cloth to make the mattress from Colonel C., and it must be returned on his first visit South. I have a little pine table and an attempt at a set of drawers or bureau. I bought a tin basin and pitcher, and as they cost me eighteen dollars, I grew economical! I have also drawn from the ship seven yards of double-width gray cloth, and gave sixteen dollars a yard to the government for that; would have paid double or treble that price if bought on the market, and now that I have got the cloth it seems too expensive to have it made up, though I should like by doing so to keep in nice order the handsome uniforms made up in London — but enough of myself, and now of my ship. Her shield is covered with five inches of iron and she mounts four-inch rifle guns, all in fine condition; with a crew of one hundred and twenty men, exclusive of officers. This morning I heard the Federal drums beating quite lively over the hills, but they do not seem disposed to make an attack on our works at present. I believe I would prefer good weather for a fight.

C. S. Ironclad *Richmond,*

JAMES RIVER SQUADRON, January 26th, 1865.

It is a month since I left home, and I have had no reply to my first letter. This may be the first news you have to relieve your anxiety in regard to the

---

[*] The James River Squadron at this time was commanded by Captain John K. Mitchell. The ironclad *Fredericksburg* was captained by Commander Thomas R. Rootes, however, he was absent most of the time because of illness and Lieutenant Francis E. Shepperd was temporary in command. Kell lists Mitchell as commander of the *Virginia II,* however, Lieutenant John W. Dunnington commanded the vessel while Mitchell commanded the entire squadron from on board the *Virginia II.* Other vessel of the squadron included the gunboats *Beaufort, Drewry, Hampton, Nansemond, Patrick Henry* (the Naval Academy's school ship), *Raleigh, Torpedo,* and several small torpedo boats.

movements of our fleet down the river, which move no doubt reached you through the papers. The object of our expedition, I regret to say, was not accomplished, resulting from a series of misfortunes. The greatest of all was getting on shore the two most formidable ironclads, the *Virginia* and this ship, just above the enemy's obstructions and under the fire of their batteries. They pelted us for over six hours, doing little or no damage to this ship, but succeeded in cutting up the *Virginia* considerably. We were absent a little over twenty-four hours, leaving here the evening of the 23d and returning here the morning of the 25th, during which time I was on my feet day and night, so you can imagine my extreme fatigue. God's mercy and your constant prayers call for my gratitude in largest measure! The weather is intensely cold, ice forming in the river in great quantities. How must our poor soldiers suffer in the trenches! I have sad news to give you, which has just reached me officially. Eaneas Armstrong was drowned to-night at 8 o'clock while on picket duty down the river, being run over by the flag of truce boat. I saw him two hours before in the commodore's office, and looking so well. He went to ask a permit to go to Richmond to see Richard, but the Commodore told him "the Squadron was under sailing orders;" so of course he could not get the permit; and his brave young life went out a sacrifice upon the altar of his country! The bleeding hearts of wife and mother, brothers and sisters, will surely find pity and love from Him who does not leave us comfortless, for the death of one who dies nobly, in the path of duty and of right.

This is my birthday. Need I say it has been a sad birthday to me? But one has no right to think of birthdays in such times!

The report read as follows:

C. S. Ironclad *Fredericksburg*,

JAMES RIVER SQUADRON, January 27th, 1865.

COMMANDER KELL

SIR:　　It becomes my painful duty to report, that while the steam Torpedo Boat *Hornet* was proceeding down the river last night upon her first tour of picket duty, she was run into and sunk by the flag of truce Steamer *William Allison*, and First Lieutenant Eaneas Armstrong, P. N. C. S., was drowned.

Lieut. E. T. Eggleston, C. S. M. C., who was in the *Hornet* at the time, reports the following facts in connection with this sad affair: About 7 p. m., and just after getting through the passage at the obstructions in Kingsland Reach, discovered the *Allison* coming up the river. Lieutenant Armstrong, to avoid a collision, ordered the *Hornet* to be steered to the south bank, and made every effort to attract the attention of the approaching steamer, but failed to do so in time and her bow struck the *Hornet* just abaft the smokestack, causing the latter to sink immediately. All hands were precipitated into the river, but all, with the exception of Lieutenant Armstrong succeeded through the exertions of the crew of the *Allison* in reaching the steamer in safety, she having stopped her engine just before striking. Lieutenant Armstrong was, unfortunately, drifted by the current so far below the Steamer that no trace of him could be found after a vigilant search was made for him by Lieutenant Eggleston in one of the boats of the *Allison*. Owing to the excessive cold he doubtless soon became cramped, and in consequence sunk before aid could reach him. A search was made of the south bank of the river this morning with a view to the recovery of his body, but such was unsuccessful.

The service has thus been robbed of an officer whose merits gained for him an enviable reputation; and during his service under my command in the recent trying operations of our squadron, it gratifies me to say as a slight token of my regard for his worth and an humble tribute to his memory, that he behaved with marked coolness and bravery.

Very respectfully, your obedient servant,
T. E. SHEPPERD
Lieut. Commanding

TO COMMANDER KELL
C. S. Ironclad *Richmond,* James River Squadron.

C. S. IRONCLAD *Richmond,*
JAMES RIVER SQUADRON, *February 1st, 1865.*

I am truly distressed that the mails fail to be carried through. I have written regularly three times each week. On our return from our most unfortunate trip down the river I made a visit of twenty-four hours to the city. I found Colonel S. and the baby all well and spent a long evening with Captain Semmes. I found him looking remarkably well. He delivered your package and told me of his visit to you. The Colonel and T. were very anxious for me to remain and have the captain to dinner with us, but I felt obliged to return on board ship, for I have a very severe cold, and I am sorry to say that drinking the James River water is affecting my health very much. I went to bed and took some medicine the surgeon gave me, and hope to feel better in a day or two.

February 3d.

Just received two letters from you fifteen days on the journey. Had just sent a letter to You by private hand, the mails seem so unreliable. Though I am only nine miles from the city I have only been up once, and then on a special visit to see Captain Semmes. I am glad to see him looking so improved in health since we parted in England.

February 16th.

Glad to hear you received four letters from me at once. You must be very anxious at the news we have of the road being cut by Sherman. I send this by private hand. I rejoice with you at the mention of "gallant conduct" of your one dear brother. There is a rumor to-day of Hampton defeating Kirkpatrick, and I hope the next news will be that Johnson has defeated Sherman, upon which so much depends. If Sherman marches victoriously into Virginia, Richmond must be evacuated. Every precaution has been used for the immediate removal of all papers of the different departments of the government, but it is understood that General Lee will hold the city to the very last moment that prudence will admit. It will be impossible for you to get a package or small trunk through to me from Macon while Sherman holds Branchville. The weather is so cold and the river so frozen over, the steamboats cannot run. The river water and the intense cold together are making me ill, so being utterly disabled and unfit for duty I came up to spend a few days with the Colonel and your sister, to see if I can get better without going into the hospital. I met our old friend and groomsman Gailliard. He has just gotten twenty days' leave of absence to go home and get married (he tells me) to the daughter of the Member of Congress from South Carolina, Mr. Ker. Boyce. I told him these were very troublous times for getting married in, but he was too radiantly happy even to regard an allusion to the present times. I suppose you have seen through the press that Captain Semmes has been made admiral (an honor richly deserved) and is to take command of the James River Squadron.[*]

RICHMOND, VA., *March 17th, 1865.*

I am still here with your dear sister and the Colonel. They are very kind to me. The doctor forbids my return to the ironclad till I have quite recovered. I suppose you hear all sorts of rumors about the evacuation of Richmond. Orders have been given for the removal of the different departments; the work-shops, too, all of which is precautionary. Should Sherman be successful in his march through North Carolina it may become necessary to give up Richmond, and our ironclads will share the same fate as those off Charleston, while we fall back with the Army. Bob puts his horse at my disposal, so I get a nice ride on horseback every day, and think I am getting a little stronger. To-morrow I will go to Greensboro, N. C., with your sister and the baby. It is best for them to be out of Richmond till matters are more settled. I do hope the little change will do me good and that I may return in a week or ten days quite restored to my post of duty.

March 18th.

Yours of the 15th of last month, which you gave to Mr. and Mrs. Clement Clay, reached me to-day, relieving me of much anxiety. They did not come further than Augusta owing to the bad condition of the road. I have written by every opportunity going south. So much depends upon

---

[*] Raphael Semmes assumed command of the James River Squadron on February 18, 1865. Because of Kell's illness, Lieutenant Hamilton H. Dalton was ordered to take command of the *Richmond*.

our holding Richmond, — if that is given up gunboats and ironclads must all be destroyed. The naval forces will fall in with the Army. Our Navy has been destroyed by piece meal by the evacuation of first one and then another of our seaports. However, confidence is being restored in our holding this city within the last few days. I send you in a little package twenty-four dollars in gold. It is now worth seventy for one, and is a balance paid me upon rendering my account of traveling expenses home from the *Alabama*. I send package and letter by one of the Colonel's clerks going direct to Macon.

DANVILLE, VA., *March 20th.*

I am getting very much discouraged! I gain no strength at all, even with the change and the very desirable good weather. The news is very cheering — General Johnson's army victorious several times with severe loss on the enemy's side. Mrs. General Hardee and her daughter are our next-door neighbors, so we get the latest news by telegraph direct from the General. Affairs around Richmond in *statu quo*, much depending on Johnson's success. (Which hoped-for success, alas, never came!)[*]

No improvement in health coming to me, of necessity I gave up my command, and on sick leave came home to Macon, and was in Macon, broken completely in health and spirit, when news reached us that General Lee had surrendered. The dreaded blow had fallen! The South had fought the world and might had overcome! When news of the armistice was carried out to meet the incoming army of General Wilson to Macon they at first refused to credit it. Knowing that the army was approaching, through the advice of my physician, with high fever upon me, I left Macon, taking a favorite servant with me, whose parents and grandparents had served my family for generations. I found friends and a warm welcome with Colonel P. M. Nightengale, near Hawkinsville, he having moved his family there from the coast for safety. They cared for me as though I were a younger brother. The evening of the day after our arrival the temptation was too great for my servant Henry, and he took "French leave," carrying off my pistol, a fine navy revolver, with him. I forgave the departure more readily than I did the theft. I have never seen him since, but his old grandfather served me fondly and faithfully till death set him free a few years ago, his last hours made happy and peaceful by the love and care of my family for him in old age, and he died giving us all his blessing and farewell.

In due time I was paroled as a common soldier, and passed through Macon to Spalding County, Georgia, to sojourn with the uncle and aunt of my wife, where (though I did not dream of it then) I was to

---

[*] Kell consistently misspelled Joseph E. Johnston's name as "Johnson."

make a home and spend the rest of my life. In three weeks my wife and little son joined me in this quiet country home for a short visit. After this, for a long while, with broken health and penniless, for, as Admiral Semmes said of himself, like him "I had the honor to come out of the war without a dollar, life seemed to me full of chaos and destruction." I had not the health at the time to seek to take up my profession or work in another country. Many of my friends and brother officers went out of the South — some to South America, some to Egypt to serve the Khedive, quite a colony took refuge in Nova Scotia, and some remained in Europe where the collapse of the Confederacy found them. We passed a quiet summer. In July a son was born to us, whom I named for the admiral, his dear name being associated with my last dream of glory. In the fall of 1865 I made up my mind to start a little farm, to "turn my sword into a ploughshare" and "sit in peace under my own vine and fig tree." The Confederate banner having been furled to live in the faithful hearts of the Southland, the banner over me should henceforth be that of love and home.

Next door to our uncle and aunt, they having given us a double log cabin, and my wife's father adding to it and making us very comfortable, we began life anew as Spalding County farmers, and no palace ever held such joy and content as ours. We made a fine vegetable garden, on which I took several prizes the following spring at the "Middle Georgia Fair." Our flowers were the admiration of all beholders. For a year or two I refrained from reading the newspapers, unless something special was brought to my notice, but I took a number of agricultural journals, the *Southern Cultivator* and *Maryland Farmer* specially. I tried to be practical, but having no experience, my neighbors often laughed at my theories and book-learning, though I sometimes astonished them in a race for success. I only knew by hearsay who was President or governor, and my wife and the two happy little boys forgot all city ways and fashions. As I look back upon those days they seem to have been very happy, except that my restoration to health was very slow; and the loss of health will mar the happiest surroundings.

In the winter of 1865 Captain Semmes was arrested — I think it was on the 15th of December; Mr. Davis was in prison; General Lee had an indictment of treason against him, and but for the interference of General Grant would no doubt have been tried; Wirtz, the commandant of the Southern prison, though a paroled prisoner, had met death by execution; Madame Surratt, an innocent woman charged with being an accomplice in the assassination of Mr. Lincoln, had been hung; Mr. Clement Clay suffered imprisonment, though guilty of nothing more than being a Confederate Cabinet officer, so the arrest and imprisonment of Captain Semmes assumed a very serious aspect. A squad of soldiers took him from his home in Mobile to Washington, where he was kept a close prisoner for four months. Out of this dilemma he helped himself in his able and powerful defense, which was of course the theme of the daily press at the time. His appeal to the Chief Executive closes with these words:

> I have thus laid before you tediously, I fear, yet as concisely as is consistent with clearness, the grounds upon which I claim at your hands, who are the custodian of the honor of a great nation, my discharge from arrest and imprisonment. I have spoken freely and frankly as it became an American citizen to speak to the Chief Magistrate of the American Republic. We live in times of high party excitement when men, unfortunately, are too prone to take counsel of their passions; but passions die and men die with them, but after death comes history! In the future, Mr. President, when America shall have a history, my record and that of the gallant Southern people will be engrafted upon, and become part of your history, the pages of which you are now acting, and the prayer of this petition is that you will not allow the honor of the American name to be tarnished by a perfidy on those pages. In this paper I have stood strictly on legal defenses, but should those barriers be beaten down, conscious of the rectitude of my conduct throughout a checkered and eventful career, when the commerce of half a world was at my mercy and when the passions of men North and South were tossed into a whirlwind by the current events of the most bloody and terrific war that the human race has ever seen, I shall hope to justify and defend myself against any and all charges affecting the honor and reputation of a man and a soldier. Whatever else may be said of me, I have at least brought no discredit upon the American name and character.
>
> I am, respectfully, etc.,

RAPHAEL SEMMES.

WASHINGTON CITY, *January 15th, 1866.*

I believe the alleged object of the arrest of the admiral was "his illegal escape off Cherbourg harbor," with added charges of "cruelty to prisoners," etc. As soon as he got to Washington (or very soon after) he wrote to ask me to hold myself in readiness to come to him at any day, which I did not need to be asked to do; but his case never came to trial—his able self-defense proved sufficient.

It was the cause, however, of my losing a very valuable correspondence—many of the admiral's letters, several from Commodore Tatnall, and very many from my brother Navy officers. Thinking it safest in those troublous times, I made a large package of them and let them down by a cord between the wooden walls of the farmhouse in which I was then living, waiting for our log castle to be finished. The following spring or summer, when I went to liberate my valued correspondence from its concealment, the enemies of man—mice or rats—had cut the cord, and upon removing the plank where they had fallen I found my letters in mincemeat! A ruin of great and beautiful thoughts and sentiments, a noting of deeds grand and heroic, so much that would have been a precious heirloom to my children.

A few years after the war my dear senior officer honored my humble domicile by a visit of some days. Meeting my wife at the door he took both her hands in his and said: "How safely you have anchored my friend Kell; I am glad to have a welcome in his port." She smilingly presented the children, saying, "These are the anchors, Admiral." Our manly boy John, Jr., came to him; then his little namesake, who from that time during his visit took a seat as of right on his knees, and then our baby girl Marjory had her full share of his caresses. He took a deep interest in all around me, and said, "Kell, you must plaster this house," which I afterward did, at least a part of it. My wife told him she "would give him leave to lecture me on my sectional pride and prejudice; that she thought him an example to me of conservatism," etc. He replied, very gently, "He has fifteen years (or more) longer to live to feel as I do; I am at least fifteen years his senior. Give him that long to grow reconciled to things as they are." During the visit we discussed the past a great deal, and on one occasion the old Confederate scrap-book was brought out, containing many pictures from the English papers of the *Alabama's* cruise, officers and career. My picture being first, my wife said, apologetically, "Admiral, you will easily see who is the hero of the ship to me." He smiled and said, "And so he is to me my right hand, and I knew he would be ready when I called him." That he should have been satisfied that I had done my duty was very dear praise to me, and I here record it, not from vainglorious pride, but the desire that my posterity may know that I did my duty. Though Captain Semmes lived several years after this I never saw him again; but his pleasant, cheerful letters came sometimes to brighten us, specially to his little namesake and godson, in whom he showed an abiding interest as long as he lived.

Of the many fine tributes to the bravery of Captain Semmes and his ship I have seen none finer than the following, sent to me by Armstrong, our second officer and, as he remarks, it is the tribute of an enemy!

[From the *Toronto Leader,* July 8th, 1864.]

BRAVERY OF CAPTAIN SEMMES.

(From the *New York News.*)

The *Alabama* cannot be captured. No beam or plan or spar or rope or sail of the far-famed sea-rover will ever be a trophy in the hands of her enemies. The ocean that has been the scene of her career protects her now forever! She seemed fated to battle and defy in disaster as well as in success. There is sometimes glory in misfortune and triumph in defeat. The words of the dying Laurence urging resistance against hope are more memorable than the records of his victories. The fate of the *Alabama* will be a theme for admiration with friend and foe, and we venture to prophesy that many a pen that has been active in denouncing her career will acknowledge a certain sublimity in its close. The commercial welfare and the naval reputation of the North are certainly most beholden to the commander of the *Kearsarge* and his subordinates for their successful efforts to destroy this formidable enemy, but they have "scotched the snake, not killed it." All accounts state that the *Alabama* had suffered severely by the wear and tear of her active existence. She had lost much of her capacity for mischief and her speed was reduced, and she was in fact worn out with hard service and in absolute need of such repairs as no neutral port would furnish. It was the indomitable spirit, the untiring zeal, and the splendid management of Captain Semmes that still rendered her formidable. That spirit, that zeal, and that capacity for management are yet in the service of the Confederacy. The happy star of Semmes watched over him after the last plank sank beneath him. He, too, escaped capture. The romantic attributes of the fight off Cherbourg harbor, and its thrilling denouement, will but serve to add to his renown and popularity with friends of the South. There is more éclat attached to his name by the circumstances of his defeat than by the long list of his successes. A public dinner was tendered him immediately upon his arrival at Southhampton after the engagement. Captain Semmes will be lionized, feted and encouraged. We doubt not that before long a second *Alabama* will be at his command. Meanwhile her commander has lost no prestige. He has sacrificed perhaps a little of his reputation for sagacity in risking an encounter with an opponent far his superior in speed, armament and strength of build, but human nature is more apt to sympathize with reckless daring than to condemn it. He has saved a handful of his men, who will serve as a nucleus for another crew, and there will be no lack of adventurous characters ready to serve the man who fought his ship till her guns were under water and then committed her to old Neptune's eternal embrace, leaving no vestige behind but the record of her deeds.

[From the *South Atlantic Magazine*, November, 1877.]

CAPTAIN JOHN N. MAFFITT,
ON LIFE AND SERVICES OF RAPHAEL SEMMES.

On the 29th day of August last the startling intelligence was announced by telegraph that Admiral Semmes, the Bayard of the late Confederate Navy, had calmly "welcomed the Peaceful night of long repose" and ceased to be numbered among the living. This sad annunciation affected every Southern heart with melancholy and grief, intensified as memory's panoramic review of past events pictured to the mind's eye the battle and the storm, the daring seaman and incomparable Viking of the ocean. Raphael Semmes was born in Charles County, Maryland, on the 27th day of September, 1809. At the age of sixteen was appointed midshipman by President John Quincy Adams. In October, 1826, on the Sloop of War *Lexington,* sailed from New York for Port Spain, Island of Trinidad, to convey to the United States the remains of the lamented Commodore Oliver H. Perry, the hero of Lake Erie, who, while attending to important diplomatic duties, died of yellow fever in the town of Angostura, on the Orinoco River, August, 1819.

The young midshipman from the time of entering the Navy was remarkable for studiousness. The board of examiners awarded him the first honors of his class. His active mind was never "off duty." While a passed midshipman on leave of absence he entered the office of his brother, a distinguished lawyer, and began with avidity the study of law. At the conclusion of the Mexican War (in which he took an active part) he was ordered to command the Ordnance Transport *Electra.* He occasionally practiced at the bar. In 1858 he was ordered to Washington city to assume the position of Secretary to the Lighthouse Board, upon which duty he remained until February, 1861, when, following the fortunes of his adopted State, Alabama, he severed his connection with the United States Government. Raphael Semmes for thirty-five years in the United States Navy had enjoyed an unblemished reputation as an officer and high-toned gentleman. His attainments were of the highest order, not only professionally, but also from a scientific and literary point of view. Later, he developed his master genius in the great arena of national strife, and displayed a chivalry that crowned him in the estimation of the unprejudiced world, Viking of the Seas.

He had ever

> "The keen spirit-seizes the prompt occasion—
> Makes the thought start into instant action
> And at once plans and performs, resolves and executes!"

Captain Semmes fitted out the little *Sumter* and unfurled the first Confederate flag upon the ocean. [The story of his many captures and grand successes has already been told.] * * * In the history of the world there is no record of the existence of so terrible a cruiser as the *Alabama,* the proud ship that met her doom in the historic British Channel. Over the taffrail rolled the waves, as deeper and deeper the noble craft settled. Raising his sword with affectionate solicitude, he gently placed it on the binnacle, sorrowfully exclaiming, "Rest thee, excalibar, thy grave is with the *Alabama!*" Giving one last sad look from the stem to the stern of his lost ship, a thousand glorious memories flashed proudly through his mind as accompanied by his first lieutenant he sprang into the sea. * * * England received him kindly, a beautiful sword replaced the lost one, and a lady of high rank made for him with her own hands out of richest silk, a mammoth Confederate flag. Returning home his government commissioned him admiral, his being the second promotion to that position that had occurred in the Confederate Navy. After the defeat of the cause he served so nobly he edited a daily paper in Mobile, and subsequently a daily journal in Memphis. Later, he returned to his first love and resumed the practice of law in Mobile, where he achieved a high reputation as a constitutional lawyer and an earnest practitioner at the bar. Modest and unassuming, his dignified deportment won for him the respect and confidence of the community in which he lived. * * *

On the 17th of August, 1877, Admiral Semmes complained of feeling ill and the resident physician at Point Clear, Alabama, was summoned. After repeated visits he became anxious, and expressed a desire for a consulting physician. The admiral objected, saying to him, "I know my race is run; there is not sufficient vitality in my old and worn-out frame to battle successfully with the disease that grapples me unto death." Four days before he expired he received the last sacrament of the Romish Church, of which he was a devoted member.

Gently, calmly, this chivalric king of the sea surrendered to the great conqueror — King Death. His body was carried by steamer from Point Clear to Mobile, attended by his family, the clergy and a large number of citizens. The pallbearers, consisting of members of the First Regiment of Alabama State Troops and many of Mobile's most distinguished citizens, under the escort of the Mobile Rifles and the members of the bar, conveyed the remains to the cathedral, where Father Ryan, after the celebration of mass, delivered an eloquent oration on the character of the deceased. Bishop Quinlan concluded the services at the cathedral and the hearse, drawn by four white horses, was escorted by the various civil and military associations and a general gathering of the people through the solemn streets of the city to the Catholic Cemetery, where, in the language of the *Mobile Register*, "all that was mortal of one of earth's greatest heroes was left to that sleep that knows no earthly waking."

During the day all official places, stores and business offices were closed and draped in mourning. From sunrise to sunset, at intervals of half an hour, funeral guns were fired, and every mark of honor, esteem, and sympathy was exhibited that seemed appropriate to the melancholy occasion. "Yesterday he was ours: to-day he belongs to fame and to history." A fame that is not the exclusive endowment of the South. It enriches the world, the pages of whose history confess no truer gentleman, no more stainless hero in all the illustrious catalogue of the dead. Without fear and without reproach he may appeal to history. We can say with the poet —

> "Nor wreck, nor change, nor winter's blight,
> Nor Time's remorseless doom
> Shall dim one ray of holy light
> That gilds thy glorious tomb."

The CSS *Richmond* of the James River Squadron
Kell commanded this vessel from December 30, 1864 until February 1865.

Navy Official Records

Captain John K. Mitchell, commander of the James River Squadron during the time that Kell commanded the CSS *Richmond*

Scharf's *History of the Confederate States Navy*

Two grounded Confederate ironclads, including Kell and the CSS *Richmond*, come under heavy enemy fire at the Battle of Trent's Reach, January 24, 1865.

Naval Historical Center

Chapter Nineteen

THE solitude of our country home was often broken in upon by friends, who sought us out with unforgetting love. My dear Robert Minor walked in upon us unexpectedly one day, and oh! the joy of that meeting! that reunion! Our eldest son, John, Jr., was having a birthday party with his little friends and schoolmates. Bob was the happiest of the lot. He entered into all the youngsters' games and mirth, nearly hugged the breath out of little Semmes, and held the baby girl Marjory with patience unrivaled, telling us all the time about his own loved ones and home. Bob was an embodiment of bravery and tenderness— all children loved him. That my posterity may value this friend of my youth and my life, I here insert some extracts of letters, and his graphic account of the battle between the *Monitor* and the *Virginia*, or *Merrimac*, in which he took an active part, and volunteering to fire the *Cumberland* was wounded. The following letter was written to my wife soon after the battle:[*]

NAVAL HOSPITAL

NORFOLK, VA., March 8th, 1862.

MY DEAR FRIEND: The Yankees have shut me up for a while with a ball through my side, but with the blessing of God and the aid of a strong

---

[*] First Lieutenant Robert D. Minor served on the *Virginia* and later served as head of the Bureau of Ordnance and Hydrography in Richmond.

constitution I hope to be up and at work again before very long. The papers have no doubt told you all about our terrible conflict and subsequent victory, and I can add but little to that you already know, save to tell you that we went into battle to do our best, trusting in Almighty God to guard and protect us, and most signally has His Merciful Providence been extended over us, for which in my heart I try to be thankful; but I fear that I am not sufficiently so, nor can I ever be for sparing me to meet again those so inestimably dear to me. Kell's old friend, Captain Franklin Buchanan, of the *Susquehanna*, of East India celebrity, was our flag officer, and most bravely, most nobly did he take us into action, right up to the enemy, and exposing himself entirely too much for his own safety and the ultimate good of our country. He did me the honor to appoint me flag lieutenant of his squadron, consisting of all the vessels in the waters of Virginia, and as you would no doubt like to know who the other officers were, I annex a list of them, among whom you will find some of your old acquaintances:

Flag officer, Franklin Buchanan; 1st lieutenant, Catesby ap R. Jones; 2d lieutenant, Chas. C. Simms; flag lieutenant, Robert D. Minor; 3d lieutenant, Hunter Davidson; 4th lieutenant, John Taylor Wood; 5th lieutenant, John R. Eggleston; 6th lieutenant, Walter R. Butt; paymaster, James Semple; surgeon, R. B. Phillips; assistant surgeon, Algernon S. Garrett; captain of marines, Reuben Thorn; chief engineer, Ramsey; sailing master, Parish; midshipmen, Littlepage, Foute, Marmaduke, Rootes, Long, Craig; commodore's clerk, Arthur Sinclair Jr.; secretary, D. A. Forrest.

Among our several engineers I found one originally from the vicinity of Macon, a young Mr. White, who told me that he knew your father very well. He did his duty well, and stood fire like a true Georgian. The crash into the *Cumberland* was terrific in its results, for in thirty minutes after the action commenced the ship was at the bottom with, I fear, hundreds carried down in her. Radford was her captain, but was absent. George Morris and Stribling are said to be her lieutenants, and have probably perished. Our cleaver fairly opened her side, and down she went, though fighting as long as she could. Her masts, inclined at an angle of forty-five degrees, now mark the remains of this once gallant ship. She will never burn another navy-yard on Southern soil!

The *Congress* engaged us a while, but soon knocked under, and Billy Parker, commanding the C. S. Gunboat *Beaufort*, was sent with orders to "let her crew go ashore, her officers to be brought on board, and to burn the frigate," then hard aground near the Point. While endeavoring to execute the directions of the flag officer the enemy opened on him from the shore so hotly that he was forced to retire, but the commodore and myself, not knowing this, and seeing that the *Congress* was not in flames, the old gentleman became very anxious to destroy her, which he could not do while she had the white flag flying, and though he had once declined my volunteered offer to burn her, he accepted it when I made a second offer. For this purpose I took some eight or ten men in our only remaining boat and pulled towards her, while the fight was going on between the James River Squadron and the *Minnesota*. The flag officer ordered Lieutenant Webb in the *Teaser* to protect me in my little boat, for as I drew near the *Congress* the soldiers on shore opened on me with artillery and musketry, and very soon two of my men and myself were knocked down. I was only down a second or two, and, steering my crippled boat for the *Teaser*, Webb took us to the *Virginia*, where it had already been reported that they were firing upon me, and the flag officer, seeing it, deliberately backed our dear old craft up close astern of the *Congress* and poured gun after gun, hot shot and incendiary shells into her, when the smoke began to arise from her. The fierce flames exploded her magazines a little after midnight with a shock so terrible that it shook the windows of houses miles away from the Point. The flag officer was severely wounded while this cannonading was going on, being struck in the left thigh by a minnie or musket-ball, which so disabled him that he was taken below, and Catesby Jones, our brave and determined 1st lieutenant, fought the action out, which on Saturday resulted in the sinking of the *Cumberland*, the burning of the *Congress*, the serious injury of the *Minnesota*, the defeat of the *St. Laurence*, the retreat of the *Roanoke* (all first-class, heavy ships), and the destruction of a tug and some schooners—a good day's work for the *Virginia*, ably assisted as she was by the *Patrick Henry*, Commander Tucker; *Thomas Jefferson*, Lieutenant Commanding Barney; *Teaser*, Lieutenant Commanding Webb; *Beaufort*, Lieutenant Commanding Parker, and *Raleigh*, Lieutenant Commanding Alexander. Saturday night the battle ceased, the wounded among the crews being sent to this place, while the flag officer and I remained on board till Sunday morning, the action recommencing soon after we left between the *Virginia* and the *Minnesota*, hard aground in such shoal water that our ship could not approach her closely, and the *Monitor* (your old acquaintance, John L. Worden, commanding) coming to her assistance, a hard fight took place between these two ironclad batteries, which resulted in nothing but some little damage on both sides, and so the *Monitor*, clearing out towards Old Point, our squadron came up to Norfolk. As soon as the *Virginia* is ready (by Saturday, I hope) she will drive ahead at them again. Thus ended our first big naval fight, and I thank our Merciful Father for giving us the victory over our enemies. Our total loss among all the ships was nine killed, among them Lieutenant James Taylor, of Virginia, and Midshipman Hutter, also of Virginia; about fifteen or eighteen wounded, one of whom has since died. The flag officer is here and is doing quite well, though his wound is quite a severe one. The ball struck me in the side, glanced around, and came out near the heart, and though not serious, is a severe wound, one which the doctors say will keep me off duty for about two months. D. heard of it Sunday and came at once to me Monday. God bless the women! What would the world be without them? Our children are in Richmond with my brother, where we hope to rejoin them. And now I have done with self, except to ask you to pardon this ill-looking scrawl, as I write in bed and by "fits and starts," as I get a chance.[*]

Julian Myers (brother of Purser Myers of the *Sumter*) told Parker and myself a few weeks ago that the *Sumter* had destroyed 109 vessels, and Lieutenant McCorkle told me that she had $1,400,000, most of which he supposed had been sent to England; but I am inclined to think from later and more direct news that this latter item is all a mistake, for Captain Pegram of the *Nashville* sent Captain Semmes some money at Captain Semmes's request to Gibraltar. The Yankee vessels taken by the little *Sumter* have not generally had much money on board, hence Semmes's request for funds. I do not believe the printed report that Semmes was arrested at Tangier; but even if it is true the Confederate Government would have in his successor as brave and gallant a captain for the *Sumter* (now far-famed) as ever trod a deck or struck a blow for his country's cause. I hope most earnestly, my friend, that you have had letters from him by the *Nashville* or the *Economist* at Charleston, Chas. Fauntleroy on board. D. and I think and talk often and often of both of you, and deep would be our joy to see you united once more in safety, which we pray God may soon be granted. Yes, my friend, I pray for him, for you, and your little children, and when this war is at an end, oh, how glad we will be to see you all in Virginia! Now our beautiful country is given up. "Linden," "Eastern View," and the "Grove" are between our lines and the enemy, and we know not what will be the result! I think the President was right in withdrawing our army from Manassas. How are the two little boys and the dear little girl, my godchild? Give my warm regards to your father, write me at Richmond, and tell me all you know about Kell, also of his mother and sisters. D. sends her best love to you, and I am affectionately and sincerely your friend,

ROBERT D. MINOR.

This devoted friend of my boyhood watched my movements abroad with loving interest, and always tried to cheer my family if unfavorable news of the *Sumter,* and later of the *Alabama,* was reported, and no brother could have been more faithful. Once he writes:

Of course it would be no use for me to write on any other topic till I tell you all about the little *Sumter* and her brave fellows. She is not "wrecked!" She has not "gone to the Pacific." She was heard from in September at the Island of Trinidad. The Navy Department wishes that she was now in some port of the Confederacy, in which I know you piously join! But to details.

---

[*] Total Confederate losses were approximately 27 killed or wounded while the Federals suffered around 325 casualties.

Early in September there was a report in circulation, originating somewhere in the fertile region of lies, that the little craft had been lost by running ashore at night and for a while it was believed to be so, but seventeen days later than the date of her loss she was at the Island of Trinidad. She did not remain long, but continued her cruise in accordance with instructions giving her a "roving commission to go where she could inflict most injury on the commerce of the enemy." The latest news of her at the Navy Department is to the 16th of September. My impression is that after cruising two months or more off the coast of Brazil she returned to the West Indies to operate there, or else (as is barely possible) she may have relied on her sails to take her across to the British Channel; but the steamer is small and her capacity for storage of supplies so limited I hardly think they could have favored this step. I hope and believe she has "doubled" on her pursuers, the *Powhatan* and the *Keystone State,* and is once more on her "native heath" among the West India Islands. Although Kell is doing our country good and noble service, for your sake I do wish he was at home, for there is duty enough to be done here, and we want clear heads and strong wills to work out the problem of our independence, of which I have never had a doubt, so great is my reliance on the righteousness of our cause and the high protection afforded by Almighty God.

Of course I cannot conjecture when the *Sumter* will return to the Confederacy, but I think it cannot be long. She may from several causes have to discontinue her cruise. It would not surprise me if she were sold in a foreign port, and her officers and crew find their way home as best they may! So you need not be surprised to see him, and next to you and his mother there is no one who would hail his safe and speedy return more gladly than myself, for not only were we friends as boys, but our friendship has "grown with our growth and strengthened with our strength!" God bless the old fellow is my daily prayer. May He watch over and bring him back in safety to those who love him so well! I hope to pass many merry, happy days with him yet, and when he brings you all to see us one of these days I'll show the little boys "specimens of natural history," the like of which the broomsedge hills of Georgia never saw! Very, very happy days were those at the Pensacola Navy Yard, when Kell's was a charming home for us, on the little *Preble.* I felt very sorry for the ship when I read her fate, but not a whit of sorrow for those on board of her, handling *my* guns, sleeping in *my* room, and working the little ship I loved so well. I have lately been in a very perilous expedition planned by Commodore Mathew F. Maury. Some time since I had several shots at the U. S. Steamer *Pocahontas,* and two days after the Battle of Manassas I found the body of Lieutenant Douglas Ramsey, of the U. S. A., on the field and had it decently interred as he was an old acquaintance of mine, and the son of Captain Ramsey of the Navy. Sometimes I have two or three men's work to do in Ordnance Department. D. is with me. Do you get

Richmond papers daily? They will be full of interest for the next three months. Always let me know if I can do anything for you; it gives me such sincere pleasure to do it. Always write me when you have news of John. Give love to his mother and sisters. Kiss my little goddaughter and hug the little boys. Don't let them forget me, the devoted friend of their father and mother. Does "Mundy" still pray for "Bob?" I hope so! God bless you and yours.

Affectionately, your friend,

R. D. MINOR.

The loving brotherhood that existed in the friends of the old Navy is something dear and sacred beyond words to look back upon. He, my boyhood's friend, has long since preceded us to the "better land," and it is sweet to remember him as one who loved God and his family and friends with faithful heart, and served his country, doing his full duty with noble, patriotic fervor. God grant us a happy reunion beyond the Sea of Time!*

---

* Lieutenant Minor died of a stroke in Richmond, Virginia, on November 25, 1871. He was only 44.

Lieutenant Robert D. Minor, devoted friend of Blanche and John Kell
Editor's Collection

Chapter Twenty

AMONG the pleasant things that came into my life about this time I will mention this little incident. I had occasion to go to the coast, and in crossing over in the little steamer from Brunswick to Darien the captain came to me and said, "Is this Captain Kell?" I replied, "Yes." "Well," he said, "Captain Kell, I am glad to see you, and you are expected. I promised to give a signal to the shore when you were on my boat when we pass Barratt's Island. You have an old comrade there, one of your men on the *Alabama*." "What is his name?" I inquired. "Rawse, sir." I tried to think, but the name was not familiar to me. However, I knew that seamen seldom use their own names. In a short time we came in sight of the island, and soon quite near it, and the signal was given. Out came a man, whom I recognized even at that distance as our master-at-arms. I raised my hat, and he uncovered his head and proceeded to give me from a pile of muskets at his side, that he had arranged for the purpose, a commodore's salute of thirteen guns, deliberately one by one! I waved my thanks and the little steamer passed on. Loyal Rawse, he knew what should have been my rank, but for ill fortune and defeat, and determined that he at least would recognize it! The next day he came up to see me, and was very happy at the meeting. I said, "Well, Master-at-arms, I am glad to see you once more; tell me all about yourself." I found he was a sort of sentinel guard, or watchman to the convicts, that island being worked by convict labor. While in the city of Darien, Dr. Duncan, one of the owners of the island and lessees of the convicts, came to me and said: "Your friend Rawse gave us a terrible scare yesterday. We thought at the repeated firing of the muskets kept for our protection that the convicts had risen in mutiny and our island was in a state of insurrection. We were rejoiced to find it was a salute to our Georgia commodore instead."

It has been a great pleasure to meet at times the loyal, brave fellows that served with us, and Savannah held quite a number — Brooks, one of our efficient engineers; Marmelstein, our young signal officer, who had the honor of unfurling the first Confederate flag to the breeze on the ocean; the brave seaman, Michael Mars, who picked up an unexploded shell during the action with the *Kearsarge* and threw it overboard, perhaps saving lives thereby, and who only a few short years ago passed away from earth. I love to meet the brave and gallant fellows who made the glory of our little ship and were so loyal hearted.

Three years after the Civil War closed a great sorrow befell my family in the death of my wife's father. Thinking it best to make a change for them, and hoping the change would benefit my still weak health, I took my family out to Nova Scotia for some months. Armstrong, who resided there, had long ago suggested it to me as a motive for renewing health.[*] We sailed from New York for Halifax in one of the fine English steamers, and I had four days of pleasure on Old Ocean again. We had a very pleasant season in that unrivaled summer climate, spending some weeks in the city of Halifax. Commodore Tatnall's family, Captain John Taylor Wood, the Wilkersons, the Sinclairs, ex-Governor Charles J. Jenkins and family, Lieutenant Hoge, my friend and comrade Armstrong, his young wife and child, and many other Southerners formed a delightful society for us. We went into the country for a couple of months, to Petpeswick Bay, Musquidoboit Harbor, where the fishing was fine — mackerel, cod, herring and salmon, fresh from the water, making a wholesome diet, and all so great a change to us from our sunny Southern home. I do not think there can be in the whole world anything more beautiful than this Arcadian country, where I have somewhere heard or read that Longfellow went to write his "Evangeline" or others of his poems, where one can readily imagine the task could be made easy in the sight of the limpid streams and little miniature lakes, a chain of which we passed in our thirty mile drive from Halifax to the bay. Our beautiful evening walk was usually to a small church, beside which was the manse embowered in vines and flowers, all so suggestive of the "Lights and Shadows of Scottish Life," the stories so enchanting to youths in days gone by. It is the land of

---

[*]   Richard F. Armstrong, a former lieutenant on the *Alabama*.

mosses and lichens, where one scarcely sees the face of the earth for its beautiful adornment of green, and the deep blue sky above is heavenly in its color (like October skies at home); and gazing into its depths of either one must be drawn away in thought and made for a time, at least, to forget earth's desolate unrest. The summer was blessed to us in the re-establishment of health, and we returned in the fall to the dear old "red clay hills" of middle Georgia, quite invigorated. I had no complaint of invalidism thereafter, and with my active outdoor life and constant exercise soon did credit in health and strength to the blood of my Highland ancestors.

In the fall of 1873 a message came over the wires to me from Selma, Alabama: "The doctor has been very ill; is convalescing; will come to you for a change." Back flew the answer: "Rejoice to hear it; come at once." One of the beloved friends of my life, Dr. Charles Frederick Fahs, of the United States Navy, with whom I spent the cruises to China and Japan in our youth, and whom I had not seen for seventeen long years, came to my home to die. With his wife and brother they left Selma, and he seemed to improve each mile of the way, till nearing Atlanta a chill of congestive nature set in, and his condition became alarming. Upon arriving in Atlanta Dr. Westmoreland and other physicians were summoned, who urged delay, and that he should remain there; but he steadily refused, saying, "If I must die, I would rather die with Kell." The cars brought him to my door at nine o'clock in the morning. On a bed he was brought into my house, but growing weaker each moment. Before the sun set, nine hours after he came, his noble spirit departed unto God who gave it, as he leaned upon my breast to die. His triumph, in departing (though he had so much to leave in lovely wife and children) was beautiful to see, and something never to be forgotten, increasing our faith, enlarging our hope, telling us, "It is not all of life to live, nor all of death to die!"

Dr. Charles Frederick Fahs was a man of science and learning, who adorned his profession, and who, like the great Maury, was a man of noble simplicity of character and childlike faith in God. He wrote the flora and fauna for the Japan Expedition, which added much to Commodore Perry's published volumes for the United States Government of that very interesting period. Peace to the ashes of one so noble, and beloved.

> "Friend of my early days,
> None knew thee but to love thee,
> None named thee, but to praise."

In the year 1886 I was invited by the *Century Magazine* to write an article on the historical fight between the *Alabama* and the *Kearsarge*. The use of the pen has always been a burden to me, and my life has been one of deeds, not words. I at first declined. I thought Admiral Semmes' book was enough for history and the world. I had been solicited by many leading journals, and the press of the country often, to write, but my farming life left me little time, and I had always declined. After a second invitation, yielding to the earnest entreaties of my home circle, who considered it a duty I owed to the "Lost Cause," I wrote the historical article embodied in their "Battles and Leaders of the Civil War." It was really amusing and interesting to see my mail for some time after. I felt offended that the lying sailor yarn preceded my article, and that the "hearsay," though able, article of Dr. Browne followed it, but I made up my mind to take no notice of it, when to my great pleasure I found Galt could not stand it, and emerged from the solitude of his country home to defend the truth of history.

CIVIL WAR HISTORY.

To the Editor of the Sun:

SIR: In the April number of the *Century Magazine* appeared long-looked-for articles on the *Alabama,* which attracted notice rather from the expectation of their containing new developments of an already well understood story of the war than from any hope that what was already known would be correctly stated by Northern writers. As one of the *Alabama's* officers, who served on board her whole cruise, it is not out of place for me to correct some of the gross errors which the sailor's story willfully, and the doctor's through hearsay, are more or less full of, and between which Captain Kell's direct and truthful narrative was sandwiched and shrouded by some curious stories and pictures which have amused those who were present on the scene. The story of the sailor is such a vulgar misrepresentation of the history of the ship that it has excited surprise that a reputable journal like the *Century* should permit such a tissue of statements worse than errors to have a place in what is supposed to be history, even though pictorial, of the Civil War. The man's name is unfamiliar to me, but if it be a *nom de plume* he has done the most decent thing he could to hide his identity when telling such stories about his ship. If he was a sailor on the ship his account at once convicts him of a treacherous record, and if he has been writing from hearsay he has simply been paid for an elaborate series of forecastle inventions utterly without truth. Nor can my memory refer me to any one on board whose career was so bad (except the man Forrest) as to have tried to traduce the record of the ship. The article would not have been considered worth notice had not the *Pall Mall Gazette* judged from that account harshly of the discipline on the *Alabama,* and thus tried to injure the reputation of as fine a crew as ever served, whether English or other. The stories of mutiny and want of subordination are such absurd exaggerations that one hardly knows how to deny them, and the well-known record of the *Alabama's* work in every phase of her career is the best commentary on such trash as the sailor has put forth. It is difficult to understand why such accounts were published, except on the ground of enduring malice an the part of some writers and readers owing to the great damage done on the high seas by the *Alabama,* and when it is known that the editor of the magazine desired Captain Kell in his article not to let the bitterness of the past be introduced, it is somewhat singular that this narrative should have been flanked by a series of statements which the merest tyro in criticism must have seen to be gross exaggerations. The loyalty of the crew of the *Alabama* to the flag they served under, the cheerfulness with which they stood up to the varied emergencies of her career, and the gallant fight they made at the last against their invulnerable enemy could not have been surpassed! The greater part of the crew were English, and they behaved with the customary bravery and fortitude of their race. If Haywood was of that race he has certainly managed to distinguish himself, nor has the *Century* added much to the character which it has striven for as a pictorial recorder of the late Civil War. Among the items in the sailor's account as especially absurd is the idea of Captain Semmes being thought by the crew to have been a parson! While that would have been no discredit, it is however the case that he was a consistent member of the Roman Catholic Church, and there was nothing in his bearing to indicate that he was anything but what he looked and acted—an officer of great determination, with intelligent direction of resources in peace and war; an admirable judge in managing his crew with a high appreciation of the great responsibility of his position, which he worthily maintained under all circumstances.

Other misrepresentations are the stories of the conduct of the boarding crews on prizes. Notwithstanding the very great temptations to pillage, I cannot recall any complaints made by the boarding officers. Nor do I remember complaints on the part of masters of prizes about the undisciplined conduct of our men. The account of the conduct of the crew at Martinique is a pure fabrication, especially the story of the "connivance of French Naval officers and shore authorities" to assist us in getting clear of a supposed United States man-of-war. There are scattered through the whole of this sailor's story these repeated accounts of the crew which are totally unworthy of credit, such as the smuggling of liquor from prizes, wholesale desertion at the Cape of Good Hope, and in fact almost his entire narrative shows a hopeless want of regard for the truthfulness which is just as becoming in the forecastle as elsewhere. Dr. Browne's article is a very much more creditable contribution to the Northern side of the question, as was to be expected. The doctor very naturally, from his position on board the *Kearsarge,* must have written most of his piece from hearsay. As both his commander and executive officer were dead, he probably thought himself, as an old Navy man, better qualified by observation and experience to give a correct account of the fight with the *Alabama,* as the other line officers, he says were mostly from the merchant marine. His only error of any consequence is in reference to the *Alabama's* firing after her surrender. This is simply not correct! The fire of the *Alabama* was suspended for awhile, as Captain Kell says, "owing to the shifting of her battery," but after the flag was hauled down there was no shot fired from that ship. The story the doctor tells as heard from the "prisoners" about the junior officers of the *Alabama* firing after the surrender is entirely without foundation, as was also the report that additional men were taken on board the *Alabama* at Cherbourg. It is very probable that the firing from the *Kearsarge* after the *Alabama's* hauling down her flag was the result of flurry and doubt on the part of Captain Winslow, who perhaps felt himself surprised into a victory over a vessel which had been so conspicuous during the war and had hitherto eluded the best efforts of capture.

The doctor would have shown better taste if he had omitted his opinion of a rather murderous kind about the *Alabama's* deserving to be sunk with all on board for her supposed firing after surrender! The hesitancy of the *Kearsarge* to send boats after the fight, was no doubt owing to that same doubt as to whether the *Alabama* was really sinking or not, though it seems that it might have been noticed, or the captain might have imagined that the *Alabama* was about to take a dive under to reappear as a submarine torpedo to effect against her enemy what her shot could not against the enemy's well-cabled sides. This delay to send boats to the sinking ship very naturally determined the officers and crew of the *Alabama* to look out for themselves, and thus deprived the enemy of the great satisfaction of getting Captain Semmes and others. The results of the fight of the *Alabama* were adverse for very simple reasons, as stated by Captain Kell, the damaged condition of the powder, the efficient plating of the *Kearsarge* and the foul bottom which injured the *Alabama's* speed. In fact, like all other important disasters to the Confederacy, it was the result of want of resources in material which the greatest skill and heroism could not cope with.

There is nothing but favorable report to make of the condition of the *Kearsarge* after the fight, and the treatment of prisoners and wounded men taken on board was all that medical attention and courtesy could have desired.

Francis L. Galt,
Surgeon of C. S. Steamer *Alabama*.

Upperville P. O., Fauquier Co. Va.

May, 1886, the *Century's* editor wrote me:

DEAR SIR: By an oversight this copy of a letter received by us from Mr. Walt Whitman goes to you rather late, for which we apologize:

Camden, New Jersey, April 3d, 1886.

MY reading for the last two or three days (limited) of the articles in *Century* about *Kearsarge*, and *Alabama*, which I have just finished. They form by far the best contribution I know to the literature of the Secession era, and are full of realism and thrill. The pictures are masterly. I only, wish we could have accounts of all the swell episodes of the war in the same way, or approximately to it. I want personally to thank you all, writers and picture-makers.

WALT WHITMAN.

I had scores of letters from personal friends, whose approbation and appreciation of my contribution to history gave me much pleasure.

Left to right, John Kell, Dr. Weblin, and Raphael Semmes in England after the sinking of the *Alabama.* Semmes is concealing his injured hand.

Library of Congress

Chapter Twenty-one

MANY years ago, when Mr. Davis was invited to make his tour of triumph through the South and be present at the unveiling of the monument to the gifted son of Georgia, the Hon. Benjamin H. Hill, I received a letter from Mr. Henry W. Grady—generous, noble Grady!—always on the alert to honor and give pleasure to an old Confederate, asking me to accompany the escort of veterans that were to meet Mr. Davis at Montgomery, Alabama. His letter read as follows (I accepted the invitation of veterans):

> MY DEAR SIR: I enclose you a ticket to the platform next Saturday to witness the unveiling of the Hill statue. It is an appropriate compliment that you should be here to meet Mr. Davis, and it is my personal request that you come. Mr. Davis will be glad to see you, the people will be glad to see you, and I will be glad to see you, for I have always admired you and loved you for your gallantry in the cause for which my father gave his life, more than you have ever suspected! I shall look for you on that day.
>
> Yours very truly,
HENRY W. GRADY.

I gladly accepted these kind invitations, and it was the first time in many years that I had left the seclusion of my country home (I enjoyed every moment of the time) to take part in any public occasion. The glad exaltations of the Southern people to greet the patriot who to

199

them embodied the dear "Lost Cause," to say nothing of the magnetism of his own personality, was beautiful beyond words to express. I hope and believe the shouts of welcome and words of love of that time and tour lived and re-echoed in his heart and memory until the unseen angels came to carry his great soul beyond the shores of time, where loyalty and patriotism (though but human virtues) may count for their true value before the Judgment Seat of Him who made our human hearts, and who has promised after death's long sleep that those who love and serve Him shall "awake and be satisfied!"

I have been asked many times in my life how I bore the quiet of a farmer's life after such activity as I had always known, or how I existed without a sniff of salt air and sea breezes? Man is the creature of habit. My habit of life chanced and gave place to new tastes and experiences. This being a history of my public life and services, I will not intrude upon my readers, friends and posterity much of the home and farming life, combining so much of "the joy and sorrow with which the stranger may not intermeddle." While I made a support for my family, I never found anything remunerative in farming. I suppose I was too much of a sailor to farm well, except in enthusiasm. It has often been an amusement to myself to see how far away my thoughts sometimes were from my work. I was obliged once to let the family enjoy with me a joke upon myself. I was seated in my two-horse wagon and had a new darkey alongside of me driving, my thoughts of Spain and a famous fox hunt I once enjoyed there, when looking up I saw the boy was going in the wrong direction. Quick as lightning I called out, "Port your helm!" The darkey evidently thought my nautical language a majestic swear, and called out in a startled tone "Sah?" I laughed in spite of myself—and he never understood why—and I said quietly, "Drive to the right, boy," and we continued our journey.

Among the happy summers of our life I recall the one of 187—, when we had as next door neighbors the family of the lamented, gifted Lanier. His wife and mine had been loving friends from the cradle of Mrs. Lanier, my wife being her senior several years—their mothers loving friends before them. Mr. Lanier was just then going on to Baltimore to join the orchestra with his magic flute. Such music I believe the world will never hear again, when the very soul of the master seemed to breathe out in its heavenly cadences, and the rapt listeners scarcely realized their mortality, so strong were the spiritual affinities at work within them. The very air of home seemed blessed in the happy evenings in which he made music for us. One morning he walked into our little sitting-room, and with a wearied look on his face threw himself on the sofa and exclaimed, "Such a delightful walk as I have had in and out of the beautiful corn rows in the field next to us. I never saw such corn before. I luxuriated in the rustle of its leaves!" This walk was the inspiration of the poem, "Corn," among his finest — if one can discriminate among his soulful lyrics. Even the heathen said, "Whom the gods love, die young," and this true, pure, manly soul was early called to heavenly blessedness; but the world is better for his life lived here, his music, and his songs.

A correspondence (our only communication with the outside world) is a great pleasure in country life, and yet when letters come with such clippings as these, how stirred up I feel to give battle to the falsehoods that are supposed to make history. In a recent letter Armstrong writes me:

> In my last letter I referred to the enclosed and promised to send you a copy when I came across it. It so happened that an old classmate of mine, owner of the Steam Yacht *Intrepid*, came into port and behold! my old antagonist (and friend) J. Schuyler Crosby, a guest on board. This brought to mind the incident of my letter to the *New York Sun* in reply to Colonel Crosby's speech, revealing this precious bit of history, and a search among my papers brought it to light. Crosby was a colonel on Sheridan's staff after the war.

UNITED STATES CONSULATE
Florence Italy, September 4th, 1879.

Hon. WILLIAM HUNTER,
Second Assistant Secretary of State,
Washington, D. C.

SIR: Within the last few days the following circumstances came to my knowledge, and I deem them of sufficient historical interest for the subject of this dispatch. An acquaintance of mine, Sir John Burgoyne, in the course of conversation told me that a few hours before the engagement between the *Kearsarge* and *Alabama* he took the lieutenant of the latter on board the *Kearsarge*. He was dining at the Crown Hotel, Dover, and his neighbor at table, who turned out to be an officer of the *Kearsarge*, invited him to visit her. The next day at dinner at the same hotel, another stranger, who got into conversation with Burgoyne, asked him what was the war vessel lying off Dover, if she was ironclad, what her armament was, and to what country she belonged? Sir John found him an agreeable and intelligent companion, and on his saying he was going aboard the *Kearsarge* acceded to his request to permit him to accompany him. On going aboard the next day the officer who had invited Burgoyne was not on board, but the officer of the deck, on seeing Burgoyne's card, invited him and his friend on board and showed them every part of the vessel, in which inspection the stranger showed a marked and intelligent interest.

When Sir John and his companion returned ashore his unknown acquaintance said, "Thank you so much; you little know what a service you have rendered me, Sir John, for I am the first lieutenant of the *Alabama*." The subsequent meeting of these two vessels took place with the result all the world knows.

I have the honor to be, etc.,

[Signed]   H. E. HUNTINGTON,
Vice-Consul.

Copy of dispatch to State Department, Washington, furnished me at St. Augustine, Fla., by Colonel J. Schuyler Crosby.

R. F. ARMSTRONG.

"Oh, how this world is given to lying," and never since Ananias was so suddenly silenced was a more absurd lie given to history! I never was at Dover in my life, I never made the acquaintance of a Sir John Burgoyne, and I never set foot on the deck of the *Kearsarge!*

Armstrong's able and caustic pen saved me the trouble of refuting, and the *New York Sun* soon published the following:

THE SECOND MATE OF THE "ALABAMA"
REPLIES TO COLONEL CROSBY.

To the Editor of the Sun.

SIR: In Your Washington correspondence of December 6th there appears an article headed "Lord Burgoyne's Remarkable Story Concerning the *Alabama's* Last Fight," in which Mr. J. Schuyler Crosby, recently appointed First Assistant Postmaster General, relates some very interesting incidents for the edification of the Loyal League. The only single fact in the whole story is that off Cherbourg on a certain day in June a fight did take place. The English yacht which rendered such efficient service in saving life on June 19th, 1864, was the *Deerhound* whose owner was Mr. Lancaster—not *Greyhound*—and if Lord Burgeyne was on board the *Deerhound* it is the first time that any one has ever heard of the fact. The *Kearsarge* did not come to an anchor before the fight, and the, only communication had with her from the shore was by the United States Consul in carrying to Captain Winslow the challenge of the *Alabama*. The only other craft, besides the *Kearsarge,* which shared the honors of saving life on that occasion was a French pilot-boat, and the writer asserts most positively that Lord Burgoyne was not on board of her. Our first lieutenant, Kell, was saved by the *Deerhound,* and I think I can trust my memory so far as to state that. Lieutenant Kell did not leave the side of the *Alabama* from the day she entered Cherbourg until she steamed out of the port—in fact, was not on shore at all—and therefore could not have met "Lord Burgoyne" at a hotel, or elsewhere.

But, Mr. Editor, the necessity given for such a visit is the unkindest cut of all, and the reflection cast upon the officers of the *Alabama*—of not being able to locate the boilers of the steamship without a personal inspection—is such a slander upon our *Alma Mater,* the United States Naval Academy, that I feel called upon to resent it. But where is the use of further proving the romance of Lord Burgoyne's remarkable statements? But, then, Colonel

Crosby has had but little experience of the sea, and of those who navigate thereon, and it is but charitable to presume that this "slip-over" effort of the gallant colonel was in the nature of one of those yarns we always tell to the "horse marines."

[Signed] ,   THE SECOND LIEUTENANT OF THE "ALABAMA."
ST. AUGUSTINE, FLA., *December 26th.*

Armstrong in his youth found home and happiness in another country; he never lived in reconstruction times, and I am afraid I shall have to give him thrice the fifteen years of additional age the admiral allowed me in which to become conservative. I am in receipt of an amusing article of his, as yet unpublished —

THE "ALABAMA'S" CROCKERYWARE AND FLIGHTS OF
FANCY IN CONNECTION THEREWITH.

Editor Art Interchange.

In your September number appears an article entitled "Ceramic Relics of the Confederate States of America," One would judge from viewing the cut of the only article which properly can be classed under so pretentious a title, the hospital and antebellum hospitable jug, that these people could hardly claim distinction in ceramic art. Perhaps in their semi-barbarous and unæsthetic condition they laid more store by their military prowess than their manufacture of pottery. *Ars est celare artem,* and in the little brown jug the maxim is fully accomplished—in fact in simplicity of design and finish this example of fine art makes towards pure æstheticism, and distinctly makes an evolutionary period in the history of a hitherto rude and uncultured people.

Mr. Edwin At Lee Barber, who, from his præcognomen, I should judge to be of the Flowery Kingdom, and consequently an expert in pottery affairs, shows a commendable spirit in delving into the hitherto unexplored field of Dixie, and it is to be regretted that his search for objects *d'art et virtu* of the Confederate period has been so barren of results. In fact, his search for these ceramic art treasures has apparently, been so disappointing as to force him to draw upon the crockery establishment of Messrs. Badley & Co., of Staffordshire, and bring into the service of his article the crockeryware supplied by that house for the alimentary comfort of the officers and crew of the *Alabama. Mirabile dictul* the plates, cups and saucers, and perhaps other pottery vessels, have been invested with miraculous flotative power, and with the factor of avoirdupois eliminated, like the wonderful borrowed axe of Elisha, have been made to rise from full fathom five to supply relics of "the famous sea-rover." I have heard of this putative *Alabama* crockeryware before, and in point of fact have in my possession a rather hefty specimen of it, no doubt obtained from the same source as those in the treasured keeping of the "daughter of the Confederate officer in Georgia" and the "lady in Florida." Hitherto I have attached but little value to my soup-plate, and as a specimen of fine art it is considered hardly up to some of the productions of Sevrès or even those of Mr. At Lee's own country; but now the case is entirely different, and in so well authenticated a relic "recovered from the vessel after she had been sunk" and *ipso facto* necessarily invested with miraculous power, I consider that I have a treasure which it is my duty to transmit as a valued heirloom!

Several years ago in St. Augustine, I was asked by the Rev. Dr. Prime, of Holy Land memory, to authenticate one of these plates as a genuine relic of the *Alabama*. I asked the reverend gentleman if he had ever read of the little *affaire à deux* off Cherbourg? He replied that he had. "Then, Doctor, would you not think that at that time we were otherwise engaged than in saving crockery?" I must confess that the miracle theory had not occurred to me at that time, and I have probably prevented this particular plate from appearing in the lists of the genuine relics no doubt obtained by the gentleman in Palestine and other Eastern countries. Perhaps there is no more cause to doubt that the crockeryware of the *Alabama* bobbed up serenely from the bottom of the English Channel, and ergo, that the "plate, cup and saucer, said to have been recovered from the vessel after she had been sunk" are as genuine as half the Christian relics that we swear by, and far better authenticated! As time passes we shall, no doubt, hear more of these *Alabama* relics, so for the nonce I shall assume the rôle of "the bull in the china shop" and put a quietus upon the crockery part. Therefore, relic hunters, give ear to my story and attention to my relation.

The contract with Messrs. Laird Bros. was for a ship of certain dimensions and power, furnished complete with everything for the voyage. This, of course, included crockeryware, and accordingly four sets of this ware (with designs as shown in the illustrations) were put on board of the ship before she left Birkenhead. The designs in all were the same, only the colors were different—that for the captain being gold; for the wardroom, blue; for the steerage, green, and for the crew, brown. This latter set had short shift on board, and as its disappearance from the present investigation of Confederate ceramic art treasures constitutes the first crockery smash-up of a series. I will adorn my tale and perhaps point a moral by relating the circumstances. In those days—1862—of square-rigged ships and sail power it was essential that the crew of a man-o'-war should be sailors—it is not so necessary now, when artisans, mechanics and soldiers compose the personnel of a modern fighting machine, and the old-time shell-back has been educated out of existence—and the crew, according to immemorial custom, was divided into convenient messes, each in charge of one of its numbers, designated mess cook. The deck served for a table, a tarpaulin for a cloth, and the table furniture consisted of tinware—in not too excessive quantity. Each sailor was entitled to a pot, pan and spoon, and these, with his sheath-knife, comprised his whole mess outfit. The swinging-table and crockeryware abominations are of later introduction into the Navy, and it remains to be seen if such enervating luxuries have improved the morale of man-o'-war Jack.

Well, the *Alabama's* crew started on a crockeryware basis, and these emblematic plates, cups and saucers were a source of constant trouble. Shortly after going into commission, and while we were gradually but surely bringing our Liverpool packet material up to the standard of man-o'-war discipline, the complaints against these mess cooks were loud and frequent. This one did not wash the plates, that one failed to polish the cups, and they were altogether a bad lot! Finally, the patience of our executive officer, being wholly exhausted, and perhaps thinking it about time to give the disciplinary screw another turn, he ordered the whole of the men's crockery to be brought up from below. Jack was jubilant at the prospect of punishment being meted out to the delinquent cooks, but his joy was short lived, for as soon as the master-at-arms reported "all up, sir," overboard went about half a ton of Confederate States ceramic art, and perhaps it is now under the aesthetic arrangement of sea naiads' hands embellishing the abysmal caverns of sunken Atlantis. Jack's service thereafter was of bright tinware, and as *this* was what he had been accustomed to, he soon forgot his prized crockeryware and borrowed no further trouble about his mess arrangements.

There is a moral in this plain tale of the sea, but I shall leave it to the perspicacity of the reader to pick it out. I remember on one occasion chasing a vessel throughout the midwatch and turning the chase over to my successor of the deck. About daylight the chase, having been brought to and proving ripe for destruction, i. e., of the proper nationality, with no neutral cargo aboard, she was accordingly despoiled and fired. The captain and mate of the prize were assigned as guests of the midshipmen's mess. At breakfast, when coffee was served, the captain, examining the cup with far too critical an eye for a guest, blurted out, "Wall, look-y-here, Mate, I'll be goldarned if this here ain't one of our own cups and sassers." And no doubt the captain was right, for in those halcyon days such was the easy transfer of property on the high seas, that it was quite possible for this captain to have sipped his tea *from his* own cup on his own ship in the evening, and taken his coffee *from* the same cup on board "the pirate" at eight bells on the following morning.

It would appear from this anecdote that wear, tear and breakage had so diminished the midshipmen's stock of "this famous crockery" as to render it necessary for them to "draw upon the enemy for a further supply." Having thus disposed of the brown and the green, an indignant posterity must hold the *Kearsarge* responsible for having played the devil with the rest of it!

John McIntosh Kell after the loss of the *Alabama*. Several photographs of Semmes and Kell were taken after their rescue and arrival in England.

Miller's Photographic History

Chapter *Twenty-two*

ONE day in the summer of 1886, coming in tired from my work, my wife, at her sewing on the porch "behind the morning glory vines" that shut out the world, called out to me, "Here's a letter for you from the *Constitution* office," but none can imagine my surprise at its contents! It seems that my friends had been thinking of me, and resolved to do something for me. The kindly thought originated in the mind of Col. L. N. Whittle, but it only needed to be suggested to others. Judge Richard H. Clark, Col. L. Q. C. Lamar, Hon. David J. Bailey, Sr., his sons, and my friend Frank Flint and my kind neighbors at Sunnyside, and Griffin, the county seat of Spalding, where I came to abide, and where my children were born, all lent a helping hand. Colonel Whittle wrote my wife and said: "Your husband must have position under the incoming administration. General Gordon will be Governor. Captain Kell, I know, will solicit nothing, but his friends will do it for him." Fearing some disappointment to me, knowing I had never taken part or interest in politics, my home circle kept very quiet and waited events. The suggestion reached the ears of Mr. Grady in connection with the place of Commissioner of Agriculture, and his letter to me read as follows:

Atlanta, Ga., July 27th, 1886.

My DEAR CAPTAIN: I write you at the suggestion of my partner, Evan P. Howell. He and I were talking things over to-day and I suggested that you had been mentioned as a possible candidate for Commissioner of Agriculture, and that you ought to have something from the State. There are certain difficulties in the way of that office, but Evan then suggested that you apply to General Gordon for the position of Adjutant-General. I think the place pays about $2000 and is a good place. It is in the Capital, near the governor, and is a place of dignity and such work as would come to your inclination. In making such application you will have the earnest support of both Mr. Howell and myself and Mr. Hemphill, and indeed all of the *Constitution.* This I am sure will give you the place. Your application would be kept quiet, and if anything should go wrong would never be known. I am *sure,* however, it will be right.

Yours with high regard,

H. W. GRADY.

In August he wrote me again:

My Dear Captain Kell: I feel sure that the matter I wrote you about will be settled satisfactorily. I have spoken to General Gordon, and his views coincide with mine entirely, and there is no reasonable doubt that the appointment will be made. In giving you this news, I congratulate the State and General Gordon very much more than yourself. It is but small returns for the great debt that Georgia owes you; but I am grateful at being the humble instrument by which even so small a part of the obligation may be rendered. It will be well to say nothing at present. With high regard,

Yours very truly,

H. W. GRADY.

To this I replied:

Sunnyside, Spalding Co., Ga., August 22d, 1886.

H. W. GRADY, Esq., Atlanta, Ga.

My Dear Sir: Yours of the 20th is received. Need I assure you of my sincere thanks for your interest and service in my behalf. I am pleased that General Gordon has been so kind as to consider my claim with the same generous feeling that prompted you. The complimentary manner in which you have been pleased to convey to me this news is appreciated with that warmth of feeling which can be experienced only by one who has served his country and tried to do his duty. Permit me again to assure you of my gratitude, and with sincere regard remain,

Yours very truly,

JNO. MCINTOSH KELL.

The Atlanta correspondent of the *Macon Telegraph* gives the following information of a movement in this line:

The *News* (Griffin) has long advocated giving some appropriate recognition by the State of the past distinguished services of one of the most noted citizens in its borders. As modest as he is brave, Captain Kell has refused to seek any office, and it is all the more reason one should be given him, and we heartily endorse the present move of our distinguished Representative, Hon. D. J. Bailey, toward such an end.

Again the *News* says:

There is a movement on foot in connection with this office which will meet with warm endorsement throughout the State. The movement is to urge Governor Gordon to tender the appointment of Adjutant-General to Captain John McIntosh Kell, of Sunnyside. I do not know that he is in any way an aspirant for this office, but there is a strong feeling among his friends that he should get it. The head and front of the movement is Hon. David J. Bailey, the Representative from Spalding, the "grand old Roman" of the House.

He prepared the petition to-day, asking Governor Gordon to make this appointment. It was one petition that all seemed to sign with sincere pleasure. Such appointment will give a higher honor to the office and be a happy tribute to a gallant gentleman.

In November I received this letter from Governor Gordon:

STATE OF GEORGIA, EXECUTIVE DEPARTMENT,
ATLANTA, November 16th, 1886.

CAPT. J. MCINTOSH KELL:

My DEAR SIR: Your friends throughout the State have urged your appointment to the position of Adjutant-General. The office is not at this time vacant, but the present able and efficient incumbent, Colonel John A. Stephens, informs me that failing eyesight will make it necessary for him to surrender his post at the end of the present year. It affords me great pleasure to tender that position to you, and to express the hope that it may suit your views to enter upon the discharge of its duties on the 1st of January next. I would be pleased to receive notice of your acceptance at an early day.

Very truly yours,
J. B. GORDON.

To this I replied:

Sunnyside, Ga., November 17th, 1886.

To His Excellency J. B. Gordon,
Atlanta, Ga.

My DEAR SIR: Your esteemed favor of yesterday is received. I am extremely gratified for the compliment paid me by my friends throughout the State in requesting of you the appointment of Adjutant-General in my behalf. I regret sincerely the affliction "of the present able and efficient incumbent," Colonel John A. Stephens, and in accepting the appointment to fill the position he will be necessitated to surrender at the end of the present year, I can assure you that my earnest desire will be to sustain and advance the interest of the military under your command, and all other duties pertaining to the office. Thanking you for your kindness in so pleasantly tendering me this office, I am, with high regard,

Very truly yours,

JNO. MCINTOSH KELL.

The outcome of these letters and the deep and abiding interest of my friends has brought about the congenial work of the later years of my life. I trust I have not disappointed them in the fulfillment of my duty in the high position they tendered me, for their approbation and kindly feeling is very dear to my heart. Among my greatest treasures are the many kind and loving letters of congratulation received upon my appointment to office. The first to reach me was the following:

U. S. POST OFFICE,

Macon, Ga., November 19th, 1886.

Capt. J. McIntosh Kell,

DEAR Sir: You will pardon an humble individual like myself for expressing his great gratification at your appointment to the position of Adjutant-General of Georgia.

I care not how many worthy and graceful acts Governor Gordon may do, he can perform no one that will strike the heart of all Georgians with more real joy than the one of your appointment. Accept the congratulations of one who professes to be your friend and admirer.

THOMAS HARDEMAN.

Augusta, Ga., November 19th, 1886.

My Dear Captain: Permit me to congratulate you and the Commonwealth upon your selection for, and acceptance of, the office of Adjutant-General of the State of Georgia.

Very truly yours,

CHARLES C. JONES, JR.

There is little more for me to tell in these annals of my life. Since this appointment, for more than eight years past, through the love and respect of my fellow Georgians and the courtesy of succeeding Chief Executives, I still hold my honorable position. I have reached three-score years and ten (the allotted life of man). My life has been long, happy and eventful. Of course it has been checkered with the griefs and sorrows that fall to the lot of all, but nearing the sunset of my days, beyond which are the "hills of light," I can look backward into the past of holy memories without regret, and hopefully into the future, my lifeboat gliding on, no anchor dragging, Christ's love at helm, and God aloft!*

---

* John McIntosh Kell became one of Georgia's most beloved sons. He retained his position as adjutant general until his death, although from 1895 onward, it was mostly honorary. At 7:30 p.m., on October 5, 1900, with Blanche and his son Semmes gathered around his bedside, John Kell heeded his captain's call and began his final voyage—homeward bound.

Major General John B. Gordon, CSA
As governor of Georgia, Gordon appointed Kell adjutant general of the state in 1887.

National Archives

John McIntosh Kell, adjutant general of the state of Georgia, 1887–1900

Editor's Collection

Appendix

"290"

STORY OF THE SINKING OF THE *ALABAMA*

THE FAMOUS CONFEDERATE STATES CRUISER

An Interview With Captain John McIntosh Kell,
Executive officer of the *Alabama*,
Given to Alfred Iverson Branham,

June, 1883.

(This Interview was given to Alfred I. Branham, and was Published in the Eatonton, Georgia, *Messenger*, and the Atlanta *Constitution*, and in a London, England, periodical.)

Half mile south of Sunny Side, within forty feet of the track of the Atlanta division of the Central railroad is a plain, one-story white house. This is the home of Captain John McIntosh Kell, First Lieutenant and Executive officer of the famous Confederate States steamer, *Alabama*. The high wooden fence that encloses the grounds around Captain Kell's house offers no indication of the paradise that is within. More than flowers, of which there is an abundance, more than the rare and beautiful curiosities with which the house is filled, there is within those grounds a family whose father is a hero, whose mother is a sweet and gentle lady, whose children are bright with health and happiness, and whose every-day life is an exemplification of all that is best among human beings.

The Family

Captain Kell's family consists of himself, his wife and six children, two of them boys and four girls. Captain Kell is of tall and commanding appearance; his face is deeply bronzed; his eyes twinkle with good humor; his hair is dark and curly; his mustache is heavy, and his beard is long and pointed. In manner he is somewhat nervous. His voice, clear and ringing, indicating that he was born to command, can express in his very tones the utmost kindness and the most genial hospitality. Although most of his life has been spent upon the sea, where self-assertion is absolutely a necessary qualification to success, Captain Kell is a very modest man, and shrinks from the public gaze. He is about sixty years of age, and yet he is as strong and as energetic as if he were but forty. A native of Georgia, hailing from "The State of Liberty," he is the peer of any other man ever produced by the Commonwealth.

Mrs. Kell is a daughter of the late N. C. Monroe, himself one of the great Georgians. It may be very safely said that the match between Captain Kell and his wife was made in heaven. They are exactly fitted for each other, and I imagine that no other husband and wife are more tenderly considerate of each other than they. The quiet, easy, unaffected hospitality of Mrs. Kell is a heritage, a priceless heritage, from her ancestors. After conversing with her for an hour, I was not surprised when her children were presented to find them possessed of the gentle and lovely characteristics of their mother. Captain Kell, the hero, has for a wife, Mrs. Kell, the heroine. While he was cruising in the *Alabama*, she did not hear from him for a year and four days. During that time, newspaper reports from northern sources had Captain Kell captured, drowned, hung as a "pirate," suffering, in a few words, all the evils that it is possible for a human being to bear. Sadder still, she lost two of her children. Through it all she bore herself proudly and well, supported, I am sure, by the thought that if her husband should lose his life, it would be in doing his duty to a cause as glorious as that for which Paoli, Washington, or any other unselfish patriot, ever fought. Captain Kell had no knowledge of the death of his two children until just at the time the *Alabama* was preparing for her last fight. His feelings may be imagined, they cannot be described. Mrs. Kell had no definite information concerning her husband's fate until she received a telegram from one of Captain Kell's classmates at the Naval Academy. The telegram was as follows: "John is safe. *Alabama* sunk off Cherbourg."

How Captain Kell Became Associated with Admiral Semmes

After I had persuaded Captain Kell into talking about the *Alabama*—he is much averse to being interviewed—I asked him how he became acquainted with Admiral Semmes.

"In this way," he replied. "I entered the United States Naval Academy in 1841, the year it was established. After my graduation, and while I was serving as passed midshipman on the *Albany*, I got into trouble. On a cruise in the *Albany* to the West Indies, I was ordered to call a Lieutenant, light his candle, and inform him that it was time for his watch. I was willing enough, of course, to obey the order to call the Lieutenant, but I flatly refused to light his candle. Some of the other passed midshipmen also refused to light candles for officers. I was ordered to report to the captain, Victor M. Randolph, of Virginia. When I went into the captain's cabin he said to me, 'What is this I hear, sir? Do you refuse to obey an order?' I told him that I did not refuse to obey an order, but that I was not employed by the government to do menial duty and that I would not do it. 'I will break you, sir!' exclaimed the irate captain. 'I will dismiss you from the navy!' 'Very well,' said I, 'you can do as you please.' I was ordered below hatches, where I remained until we reached Pensacola. Semmes, who happened to be there at the time, volunteered to defend me against the charges preferred by Captain Randolph. Notwithstanding Semmes' able defense, I was dismissed from the navy. The government, however, soon reinstated me. When the War Between the States began and Semmes was put in command of the *Sumter*, he made me his First Lieutenant. After the *Sumter* was laid up at Gibraltar, I went by Semmes' request to the *Alabama* as First Lieutenant and Executive Officer."

Naval Services Previous to the War

"How long, Captain, did you serve in the United States Navy before the war?" I asked.

"About twenty years," he replied. "During that time, I was in many cruises, and became acquainted with nearly every port of the world. Perhaps, my most important cruise was that with Commodore Perry's squadron to Japan. The Japanese were decidedly unwilling to permit us to land, but Commodore Perry informed the authorities that we must be permitted to land or they must fight. We landed. This expedition was the preliminary step to the first advantageous treaty of the United States with Japan."

Old Naval Officers

"Whom do you consider," I inquired, "the best among the officers of the old United States Navy?"

"Joshiah Tatnall was the most perfect gentleman and sailor I ever knew," was the prompt response. "None save those who were associated with him could fully appreciate his magnificent abilities as an officer and his unblemished character as a gentleman. Raphael Semmes was one of the purest and best men I ever knew, let be said what may as to his 'piracy' and similar nonsense. He was a man of the quickest insight, the greatest firmness and the most reckless daring.

"He was never imprudent, but he was absolutely without fear. His love for the South was unbounded. As an illustration of his daring, I may mention his intention of destroying Banks' expedition against Galveston. He proposed to destroy a whole army with a single armed vessel. He would have succeeded had Banks transported his forces to Galveston. The recapture of Galveston by the Confederates prevented the success of the scheme. As it was, the destruction of the *Hatteras* was the sole result, but was a brilliant result.

"Tatnall was a greater sailor than Nelson—Semmes was Tatnall's equal."

The Sinking of the *Alabama*

After a bountiful and elegant dinner, such a one as used to grace the boards of Southern homes before the war, I cornered Captain Kell on the front porch of his house and said to him:

"Now, Captain, tell me about the *Alabama*'s last fight."

"After a cruise of two years," the captain said, "during which the *Alabama* had driven the commerce of the United States from the seas, our ship was sadly in need of repairs. Such being the case, Admiral Semmes determined to run into a French port, dock ship, and repair her. We anchored in the port of Cherbourg a few minutes past noon, on the 11th day of June, 1864. The next day, the Admiral went on shore to obtain permission of the port Admiral to dock the *Alabama* and repair her. The port Admiral said that as all the docks at Cherbourg were government property, he could not grant the request until he could gain the Emperor's consent. The Emperor was then at Biarritz and would not be back in Paris for several days. While we were waiting the Emperor's return to Paris, the *Kearsarge*, which had been lying at Flushing, steamed into Cherbourg and took her station at breakwater, just outside the harbor. Immediately after the *Kearsarge* arrived, Admiral Semmes sent for me. I went to his cabin."

"'Take a seat, Mr. Kell,' he said. 'I have sent for you to discuss the advisability of fighting the *Kearsarge*. As you know, the arrival of the *Alabama* at this port has been telegraphed to all parts of Europe. Within a few days, Cherbourg will be effectually blockaded by Yankee cruisers. It is uncertain whether or not we shall be permitted to repair the *Alabama* here, and in the meantime, the delay is not to our advantage.

I think we may whip the *Kearsarge*, the two vessels being of wood and carrying about the same number of men and guns. Besides, Mr. Kell, although the Confederate States government has ordered me to avoid engagements with the enemy's cruisers, I am tired of running from that flaunting rag!' He referred to the United States flag flying at the peak of the *Kearsarge*."

"I fully agreed with Admiral Semmes. There are those who have censured him for engaging the *Kearsarge*, but there was nothing else that could be done. The two vessels were both of wood. The *Alabama* had a crew of 149 men, all told, and the *Kearsarge* had 162. The *Alabama* mounted eight guns — one 8-inch, one rifled 100 pounder, and six 32 pounders. The *Kearsarge* mounted seven guns — two 11-inch Dahlgrens, four 32 pounders, and a rifled 28 pounder. The bore of the shell guns of the *Kearsarge* gave her an advantage of three inches in size of shells. The crew of the *Alabama* were in splendid condition, and were anxious to fight. There were but two things that prevented our whipping the *Kearsarge*; our powder, which had been exposed to all kinds of weather for two years, was bad, and the Commander of the *Kearsarge*, a Southern man, by the way, resorted to a miserable trick to prevent injury to his vessel. He iron-plated her with heavy cable chains and covered the armor with a thin sheeting of plank to hide the deception."

"As soon as it was determined that we should fight the *Kearsarge*, Admiral Semmes sent Captain Winslow, the Commander of that vessel, a message to the effect that if he would wait outside until the *Alabama* could take on board a supply of coal, we would go out and fight him."

"On Sunday, the 19th of June, we weighed anchor and steamed out to meet the *Kearsarge*. The hills above Cherbourg were crowded with people from Paris — some came from distant parts of Europe — to witness the fight. A number of French pilot boats went out with us, as also did a French ironclad frigate, the *Couronne*, which went out to see that the neutrality of French waters was not violated. Another vessel, the English steam yacht, *Deerhound*, belonging to Mr. Lancaster, also went out with us. It was charged by the Yankees that the *Deerhound* went out to assist us. This was untrue. Mr. Lancaster, himself, told me that on the day we steamed out to engage the *Kearsarge*, he wanted to go to church, but when the question as to whether his party should go out to witness the fight or go to church was put to a vote, his wife and children outvoted him in favor of witnessing the fight. This vessel afterwards rescued Admiral Semmes, myself, and a number of the *Alabama*'s crew. The first intimation I had that the *Deerhound* was anywhere near was after I had jumped into the water. After I had jumped into the water I heard somebody exclaim, 'There is our First Lieutenant,' and soon after I was pulled into one of the *Deerhound* boats. Considering the innumerable lies told about the *Alabama*, it is fortunate that Admiral Semmes lived to write his 'Service Afloat.'"

"When we discovered the *Kearsarge*, as we steamed out, Admiral Semmes ordered me to send the crew aft. Mounting a gun-carriage, he addressed the men for the second and last time since the *Alabama* was put in commission. I quote his words literally:"

"'Officers and seamen of the *Alabama*! You have at length another opportunity of meeting the enemy—the first that has been presented to you since you sank the Hatteras! In the meantime, you have been all over the world, and it is not too much to say that you have destroyed and driven for protection under neutral flags one-half of the enemy's commerce, which, at the beginning of the war, covered every sea. This is an achievement of which you may well be proud, and a grateful country will not be unmindful of it. The name of your ship has become a household word wherever civilization extends. Shall the name be tarnished by defeat? The thing is impossible! Remember that you are in the English Channel, the theater of so much of the Naval glory of our race, and that the eyes of all Europe are at this moment upon you. The flag that floats over you is that of a young republic who bids defiance to her enemies whenever and wherever found. Show the world that you know how to uphold it! Go to your quarters!'"

"The action between the *Alabama* and the *Kearsarge*, which was in progress one hour and ten minutes, may be described in ten minutes. We began to fight when within about a mile of the *Kearsarge* by opening with solid shot. The two vessels rapidly approached each other, and the remainder of the fight occurred at a distance of not more than 500 yards. The vessels circled around each other as the fight progressed, in order to keep their broadsides towards each other. A few minutes after the fight began, Admiral Semmes, who was standing on the horse block, said to me, 'Mr. Kell, our shells strike the side of the enemy's ship but they fall into the water. Try solid shot.' This I did, but with no better effect. The hidden armor of the *Kearsarge* prevented the *Alabama*'s shot from doing serious damage. One shell from our eight-inch gun was buried in the stem of the *Kearsarge*, but poor powder and a defective fuse prevented the shell's exploding. If that shell had exploded, the *Kearsarge*, instead of the *Alabama*, would have gone to the bottom of the deep blue sea. Without boasting, I may say that no other crew ever fought as bravely as did that of the *Alabama*. My position was near the eight-inch gun. An eleven-inch shell from the *Kearsarge* entered a port hole and killed eight of the sixteen men serving that gun. The men were cut all to pieces, and the deck was strewn with arms, legs, heads and shattered trunks. One of the mates nodded to me as if to say, 'Shall I clear the deck?' I bowed my head and he picked up the mangled remains of the bodies and threw them into the sea. The places of the dead were instantly filled, and not a single survivor exhibited the slightest fear. At the expiration of the time I have mentioned, one hour and ten minutes, the engineer came on deck and reported that the water let in by the wounds in the ship caused by the enemy's shells, had put out the furnace fires. Admiral Semmes ordered me to go below and see how long the vessel would float. I went below and examined the damage. The holes in the side of the poor old *Alabama* were large enough to admit a wheelbarrow. I returned to the deck and reported to the Admiral that the vessel could not float ten minutes longer. 'Strike the colors, Mr. Kell,' he said; 'it will not do in the nineteenth century to sacrifice every man we have on board.' The colors were struck, but the *Kearsarge* fired five shots into us after they were hauled down. Captain Winslow tried to explain this infamous action by declaring that he could not see that the colors had been struck. Considering that we were within four hundred yards of him at the time, it is very singular that he did not see that our colors were down. We must, however, be charitable and try to believe him. When the *Kearsarge* fired those last five shots into us, I said to the crew: 'Stand to your quarters, men. If we must be sunk after our colors are down, we will go to the bottom with every man at his post.' Upon hearing this order every man stood silently at his post. As soon as the *Kearsarge* ceased firing, I went over the decks and ordered every man to secure what he could cling to and then jump overboard. This order was issued to prevent any of the crew being carried down in the vortex made by the sinking ship. But two men went down with her. One was a man who had deserted from a Yankee vessel, and the other was a carpenter, who, poor fellow, could not swim. He jumped overboard, but afterwards climbed back into the ship. In all the last sad and dangerous moments before the *Alabama* sank, there was no fear nor hurry-up on the part of the men. Everything was done quietly, as if the crew were preparing for an ordinary ship inspection. The *Alabama*'s total loss in the action was nine killed and twenty-one wounded. Ten others were drowned after the ship sank."

"Admiral Semmes and I were among the last to leave the ship. I stripped myself to my underclothes and was about to pull off my boots, when a sailor stepped up to me and said, 'Lieutenant, let me pull off your boots.' I yielded to his request, and while examining the man, discovered that he was one whom I had been compelled to punish a number of times. Notwithstanding, he was anxious to do me a favor."

"A number of incidents similar to this, occurring both to me and to Admiral Semmes, serve to show how devoted the sailors of the *Alabama* were to their officers. When Admiral Semmes and I jumped into the water the ship was rapidly sinking. After swimming off a few yards, I turned to see her go down. As the gallant vessel, the most beautiful I ever beheld, plunged down to her grave, I had it on my tongue to call to the men who were struggling in the water to give three cheers for her, but the dead that were floating around me and the deep sadness I felt at parting with the noble ship that had been my home so long deterred me. In all the two years of the *Alabama*'s career, I was off the ship but twenty-two hours. Down she went—she had never had a home within the country she so gallantly served. She had been christened on the broad seas, and now she met her death and burial upon the same bosom that had quivered at the sound of the cheers uttered when she was named. A fitting end. No foe men ever trod her deck as victor."

After Incidents

There was a perceptible quiver in the Captain's voice as he concluded the account of the *Alabama*'s last fight. There was a silence of a few moments, broken only by the exclamation of an enthusiastic friend sitting near me: "If that eight-inch shell had but exploded—what a different tale Captain Kell could tell!" As far as I was concerned, I believe I uttered but a single sentence: "More, if you please."

"More?" said the Captain. "There is but little more to tell. Some things occurred while I was in the water that I can never forget. Eugene Maffitt, one of the *Alabama*'s gallant young officers, could not swim. He was supported by a life-preserver. The brave and unselfish boy, observing that I was much exhausted, cried to me to take his life-preserver and actually tried to take it off in order that he might give it to me. Of course, I would not permit him thus to sacrifice his life. Another incident, which occurred while the fight was in progress, was another example of the love of the men for their officers. A sailor had been terribly wounded and had been carried below to the surgeon's quarters. As in the case of the sailor who pulled off my boots, this wounded man had been several times punished by my order. After he had been carried below, he sent several times, urgently requesting me to come and see him. Finally, I left the deck and went down to see the poor fellow. He could not speak, but, with his eyes full of affection, he grasped my hand, kissed it, and died. The *Deerhound* and the French pilot boats picked up the greater part of the *Alabama*'s crew. The *Kearsarge* sent out two boats after the *Alabama* had sunk. These boats saved a few of our men. The course pursued by the *Kearsarge* seems to have been suggested by W. H. Seward's implied instructions to let the *Alabama*'s crew perish. When the *Hatteras* was sunk every man of her crew was saved. The *Hatteras* was sunk at night. When the *Alabama* was sunk, in broad daylight, the enemy made no vigorous effort to save life. The contrast, to say the least, is suggestive. The only thing I saved from the *Alabama* was my wife's watch. I attached it by its chain—my wife's hair—to my underclothes, and when I was rescued, I found it entirely uninjured. Everything else I had on the ship went down with her. After those of us who were rescued by the *Deerhound*'s boats had been transferred to that vessel, Mr. Lancaster and his wife treated us with the most distinguished kindness. At the suggestion of Admiral Semmes, Mr. Lancaster carried us to Southampton. When we reached that place, I borrowed a pair of trousers and a pair of carpet slippers from Mr. Lancaster and walked from the landing to the hotel in my shirt sleeves. The proprietor of the hotel treated the Admiral and me as if we were princes. In fact, he was at some pains to tell us that the room he had prepared for us had been but recently occupied by a prince. The next day the Admiral and I went to a tailor to buy some clothes. The tailor invited us back to his private apartments and insisted on our partaking of cake and wine. While we were enjoying the feast, the tailor, who had left the rooms, returned and said: 'Gentlemen, I shall have to request you to return to your hotel. Your presence here has completely blocked business on this street.' When we went out we found that the street was packed with thousands of people who had come to catch a glimpse of us. Policemen had to clear a way back to the hotel for us. The English, at heart, were undoubtedly with the South. During our stay in England, they showed us distinguished attention in a thousand ways. Many young men from the very best families were anxious to join us in our new ship."

Return to the Confederate States

"How did you get back to the Confederacy, Captain?" I inquired.

"I had some trouble in doing that," he replied, "but the same kind Providence that had cared for me all my life brought me safely home. I embarked at Liverpool in an English mail steamer which ran to Canada and New York. On the steamer was an officer of the *Kearsarge* who was on his way to Washington with dispatches announcing the sinking of the *Alabama*. I am not sure that he relished my presence on board the ship. When I arrived in Canada, I embarked in a little mail steamer for the Bermudas. Arrived there, I embarked in a little flat-bottomed steamer; a blockade-runner, for Wilmington, N.C. After a perfectly smooth voyage, we sighted the coast one evening about dusk. The officers of the blockade-runner, called the *Flamingo*, had made themselves altogether too well acquainted with grog, and in consequence, missed the reckonings and ran almost into the jaws of some United States War Vessels. We put about and ran out to sea."

"I, together with some Confederate Naval officers, who were on board, took charge of matters, found our bearings, and at night again made for Wilmington. This time we made the run safely, though we passed right under the guns of a United States man o' war. Arrived at home, I reported to the Naval Department, and was ordered to duty on the James River. After the war, I returned to Georgia, where I have remained in the peaceful pursuit of whatever her old red hills may produce."

Last Words

Captain Kell's splendid abilities as a Naval officer, and his quiet, unassuming, unimpeachable character as a gentleman, are too well known to render it necessary for me to say anything in his defense against the absurd and low flung charges of Yankee authors as to his "piracy." I may, however, be permitted to quote some words of Admiral Semmes' concerning him. On page 123 of "Service Afloat" Admiral Semmes thus speaks of Captain Kell: "See how scrupulously neat he is dressed, and how suave and affable he is with his associates. His eye is now beaming gentleness and kindness. You will scarcely recognize him as the same man when you see him again on deck, arraigning some culprit 'at the mast' for a breach of discipline. When Georgia seceded, Lieutenant Kell was well on his way to the Commander's list, in the old Navy, but he would have scorned the Commission of an Admiral, if it had been tendered him as a price of treason to his State.... When it was decided at Montgomery that I was to have the *Sumter*, I at once thought of Kell, and at my request, he was ordered to the ship, Commodore Tatnall, with whom he had been serving on the Georgia coast, giving him up very reluctantly." In his official report of the sinking of the *Alabama*, Admiral Semmes thus spoke of Captain Kell: "Where all behaved so well, it would be invidious for me to particularize, but I cannot deny myself the pleasure of saying that Mr. Kell, my First Lieutenant, deserves great credit for the fine condition in which the ship went into action, with regard to her battery, magazine and shell rooms, and that he rendered me great assistance by his judgment as the fight proceeded." Captain Kell was promoted to a Captaincy by reason of his gallantry in the action with the *Hatteras*, but his absence from the Confederacy and the close of the war prevented his receiving his Commission.

Since the stirring days of the *Alabama*, times are changed, but men still are men, and memory continues to hold her sway. So long as these two things remain as facts, the heroes of the *Alabama* will live.

It is related that in one of the far Northern States there is a lake of surpassing beauty. Upon the shores of that lake once lived a tribe of Indians. When the white man took possession of the country and forced the red man to follow the setting sun, this tribe refused to quit their home beside the placid lake. But the white man multiplied and coveted the beautiful dwelling place of the unfortunate children of the forest. Unable to drive the invader off, and still determined not to leave the home which had been theirs through countless ages, the tribe assembled late one calm lovely day in June, and singing a sad, sweet dirge, marched down into the smiling waters and forever disappeared. From that day to this, at nightfall of the quiet days of summer, plaintive music seems to issue from the waves of the lake as they gently lave the shore, thus serving as an eternal reminder of the fate of that Indian tribe. So there is a plaintive music which seems to issue from the heroic deeds of Southern soldiers and Southern sailors, and that music forever heard by every true man of the South will serve as an eternal reminder of the gloriously unselfish patriotism of those who wore the gray.

Notes

PART ONE—THE FORMATIVE YEARS

1. Eileen A. Ielmini, Archivist, Georgia Historical Society Library, Savannah, Georgia: letter to the editor.

2. John McIntosh Kell, *Recollections of Naval Life* (Washington: The Neale Company, Publishers, 1900), p. 708.

3. Norman C. Delaney, *John McIntosh Kell of the Raider Alabama* (Birmingham: The University of Alabama Press, 1973), pp. 7–8.

4. Delaney, pp. 13–14.

5. Ibid., pp. 15–16.

6. Kell, letter to Margery Kell, July 30, 1842.

7. Delaney, p. 17.

8. Kell, p. 15.

9. Ibid., pp. 17–18.

10. Delaney, pp. 30–32.

11. Kell, p. 32–34.

12. Delaney, pp. 36–37.

13. Kell, pp. 36–39.

14. John R. Eggleston, letter to Blanche Kell, *Confederate Veteran*, Nashville, December 28, 1909, vol. 18, no. 2, p. 61.

15. Kell, pp. 39–40.

16. Kell, letter to Mary Kell, June 4, 1849.

17. Delaney, pp. 54–55.

18. Ibid., pp. 56–59.
19. Raphael Semmes, *Service Afloat During the War Between the States* (Baltimore: Kelly, Piet, 1869), p. 123.
20. Delaney, pp. 61–63.
21. Kell, pp. 58–60.
22. Kell, letter to Margery Kell, September 23, 1852.
23. Kell, pp. 85–87.
24. Delaney, pp. 71–75.
25. Ibid., p. 77.
26. Kell, p. 96
27. Delaney, p. 83.
28. Ibid., p. 87.
29. Ibid., p. 91.
30. Ibid., pp. 94–95.
31. Ibid., pp. 99–101.

Index

225

Mid   9·Sept 41
Lieut 15·Sept 55
res.   23·Jan 61
Lieut 26·3·61
Cdr   Oct 4, 63

Profile

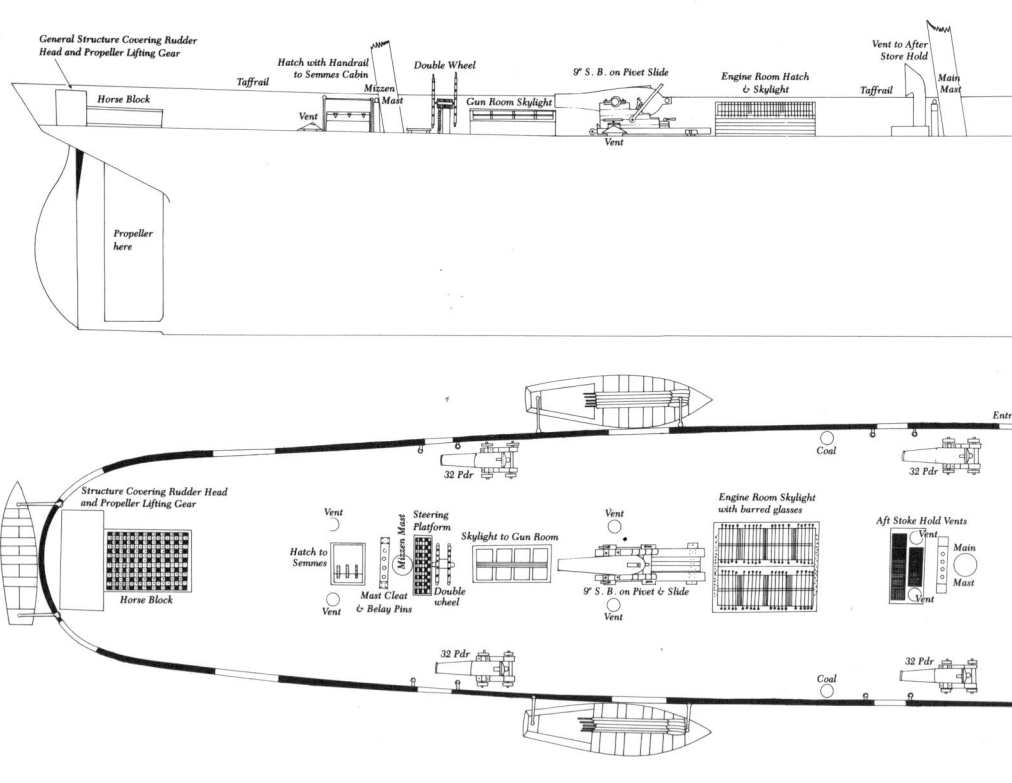

General Structure Covering Rudder
Head and Propeller Lifting Gear

Taffrail

Horse Block

Propeller
here

Hatch with Handrail
to Semmes Cabin

Vent

Mizzen
Mast

Double Wheel

Gun Room Skylight

9" S. B. on Pivot Slide

Vent

Engine Room Hatch
& Skylight

Taffrail

Vent to After
Store Hold

Main
Mast

Structure Covering Rudder Head
and Propeller Lifting Gear

Horse Block

Hatch to
Semmes

Vent

Vent

Mast Cleat
& Belay Pins

Mizzen Mast

Steering
Platform

Double
wheel

Skylight to Gun Room

Vent

9" S. B. on Pivot & Slide

Vent

Engine Room Skylight
with barred glasses

Aft Stoke Hold Vents

Vent

Vent

Main
Mast

32 Pdr

32 Pdr

Coal

32 Pdr

Entr

32 Pdr

Coal